IMAGES
of America

COLUMBIA COUNTY

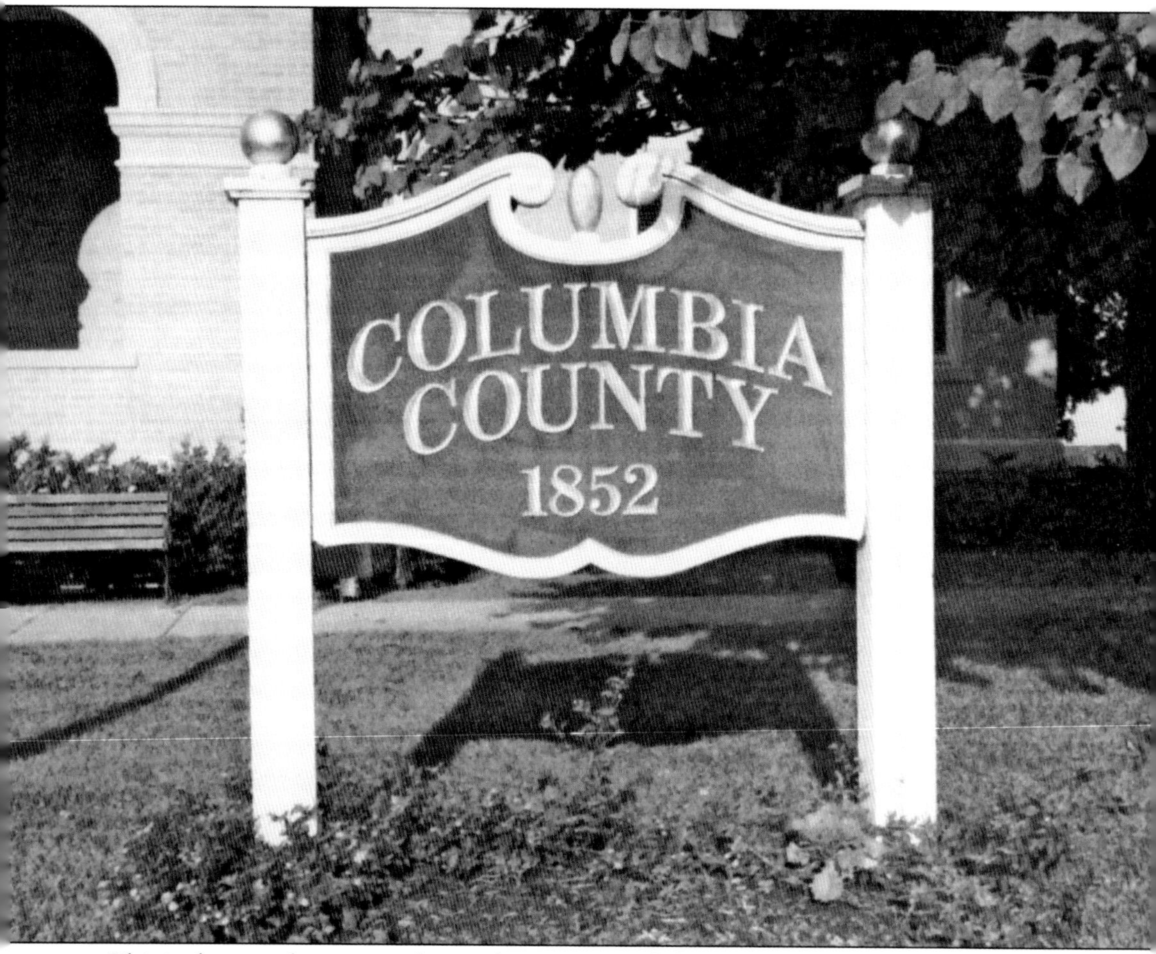

This is the sign that sits on the northeast corner of the Columbia County Courthouse lawn. (Authors' collection.)

On the Cover: Pictured around 1910 in Sharman community are, from left to right, Earl Owen, Searcy Garrard, Keith Hines (who married Fred Tubb), Grady Ragsdale, and Duo Keith (who married Solon Keith). Not shown are Signor Hines, George Keith, and Myrt Hines (married Roy Martin). (From the collection of Keith Hines Tubb, courtesy of Neil Tubb.)

IMAGES
of America

COLUMBIA COUNTY

Laura J. Cleveland, MLIS, and Dana Thornton
on behalf of the Columbia County Library

ARCADIA
PUBLISHING

ISBN 978-0-7385-9870-3

Published by Arcadia Publishing
Charleston, South Carolina

Printed in the United States of America

Library of Congress Control Number: 2012954029

For all general information, please contact Arcadia Publishing:
Telephone 843-853-2070
Fax 843-853-0044
E-mail sales@arcadiapublishing.com
For customer service and orders:
Toll-Free 1-888-313-2665

Visit us on the Internet at www.arcadiapublishing.com

In honor of Thomas Archimedes "Archie" Monroe, perhaps this county's greatest natural resource, and in memory of Harold Herbert Fincher, an honorable humanitarian

Contents

Acknowledgments 6

Introduction 7

1. Early Families and Settlers 9
2. Churches and Congregations 29
3. Schools and Activities 39
4. Businesses and Occupations 57
5. County Seat and Court Square 77
6. Early Transportation 85
7. Public Service and Military Service 97
8. Outdoor Columbia County and Disasters 109
9. Magnolia 119

Bibliography 127

ACKNOWLEDGMENTS

This book would not be possible without the legacy left by the lifetimes' works of two dedicated public servants: Dr. Robert Bradshaw Walz and Glenn Gardner Martel.

Dr. Robert Walz (1918–1988) spent 29 years as a history professor at what is today Southern Arkansas University (SAU) in Magnolia. His students still say that his love of history and storytelling abilities made his classroom lectures "magnetic." His own education included an associate's of arts from Magnolia A&M College (later SAU), a bachelor's of arts from Henderson State College, and a master's and doctorate from the University of Texas at Austin. Dr. Walz traveled extensively over southwest Arkansas copying and preserving more than 3,000 historical photographs depicting the region's history. He took training from the Kodak company in Rochester, New York, to turn the photographs he had compiled into negatives, thus enabling him to expand and print 8 by 10s of all the pictures without distortion. Dr. Walz left his entire photographic collection housed in three separate facilities: Southern Arkansas University's Magale Library, the Southwest Regional Archives in Old Washington, Arkansas, and the Columbia County Library in Magnolia. Many of the photographs in this book are from his collection.

Glenn Martel (1896–1967) was president of the Arkansas Historical Association from 1948–1949 and postmaster in Magnolia for nearly 40 years. He taught history and social science courses for 14 years at Southern Arkansas University when it was the Agricultural & Mechanical College, Third District. Before becoming an educator, he toured the American West as a member of the Redpath Horner Chautauqua Troup and was later pivotal in bringing the Chautauqua experience, replete with teachers, speakers, musicians, preachers, entertainers, and experts of the day, to Magnolia. His own education included a bachelor's of philosophy degree and a bachelor's of voice from Henderson-Brown College and a master's of arts from the University of Arkansas. His master's thesis was titled *Early Days in Columbia County, Arkansas*. It is available for checkout at the Columbia County Library and is essential reading for any local history enthusiast.

The authors are also extremely grateful to members of the community who participated in this work by the loan of their family photographs.

INTRODUCTION

The native peoples were here first. According to Dr. Frank Schambach, the Caddo/Kadohadacho people were in this area starting about 900–1000 AD and their ancestors or other tribes for several thousand years prior to that time. Arrow points recovered in Columbia County date back to this Paleo-Indian period. Following the decline of the Caddo tribes, the Choctaw (and others) moved into the area. Bands were known to exist north of what would later become Village and near Brister. In some cases, early settlers cultivated fields that had actually been cleared by Indian tribes. Pres. Andrew Jackson's passage of the Indian Removal Act of 1830 hastened the movement of Native Americans both into and through this area. The Choctaw and Chickasaw would be relocated through here, which bears the progeny of those who escaped from the path, the scars of those who left tears on the trail, and but a few place names as testament of their time here.

In the early 1840s, the first settlements centered around Glenville in the north (today southern Nevada County), Calhoun in the southeastern area, Lamartine in the north central region, and Brister in the south central vicinity. Atlanta, in the extreme southeastern part of the county, was settled about the same time as was College Hill, formerly called Godbolt. The Sharman/Dorcheat area was settled early due to its coveted place on the "Bayou Dorcheaux." An 1855 map of the county shows five communities, Falcon, Lamartine, Godbolt, Calhoun, and Atlanta; however, much study by scholars points to either Calhoun or Lamartine vying for title of "the first village" to be settled by families, due primarily to the military roads that ran through these areas. White settlement was hastened by Indian removal, the Irish potato famine flight (1841–1845), and farm families seeking increased opportunity. Most of these immigrants haled from Alabama and Georgia. There were no stores, no mills, and few neighbors.

First, a new settler sought out all the timber possible that could be converted into rails. Then, undergrowth was cut and piled into brush heaps; small saplings were cleared and taken home for fuel and kindling. Large trees were "circled," its entire circumference cut and the bark removed to stop sap from rising. These wounded trees would die off and fall in a matter of time. Later, when all was dry, a pen was made of the logs and the undergrowth placed in the center. This was the time to call in neighbors for the "great burning." His field now cleared, a rail fence would be built around it to keep animals out. On average, a man and a mule can plow up to five acres a day, dependent upon three things: the man and the mule are fit, the ground has been plowed before, and that it has rained recently. With a first crop, the yield might pay for the first year's cultivation. The second year's production will outdo the first, and the third year is generally of maximum productivity.

As Glenn Martel stated so splendidly, "From the beginning of the purely agricultural economy that came with permanent home makers, cotton was the great commercial cash crop; but because of the great difficulty in reaching the source of supplies, every planter had to be as self-sufficing as his circumstances demanded and his ingenuity made possible. This often approximated one hundred percent."

By an act of the Arkansas Legislature in 1852, Columbia County was created from portions of the counties of Lafayette, Union, Ouachita, and Hempstead. Hempstead County had at one time been the parent county for all of these divisions. The bill provided that an election be held in February 1853 to elect the commissioners who would decide the county seat. An important provision required that it lie within three miles of the geographic center of the new county. Ferguson and Morgan's Store, near the Frazier plantation home, later dubbed "Frog Level," was the temporary seat of power. It is related that the site chosen for the county courthouse in Magnolia was some of the best hunting ground in the county, and there was some objection to the decided location; nevertheless, Magnolia, and indeed the entire county, would prosper through the sweat of the brow and the hard work of committed men and women.

According to James Harris Atkinson, an early University of Arkansas student from Columbia County's College Hill community, "When the term was over, I returned to my home, and at once began helping my father with the crop. It was long days 'laying-by-corn,' 'chopping cotton,' 'plowing out middles,' 'running around the cotton,' 'plowing the watermelon patch,' etc. The sun was hot and the work was tiring, but it was probably good for me physically."

Columbia County, Arkansas, would be a part of the United States of America for less than a decade when the gathering clouds of war would bring on immense changes. Following the shots fired at Fort Sumter, Charleston Harbor, South Carolina, representatives of seven Southern states met in February 1861 at Montgomery, Alabama, and organized the Confederate States of America. On May 6, 1861, Arkansas would elect to join that group by a vote of 69-1 and secede from the Union. Over 1,000 men answered the call to arms, but sadly, only about 300 returned. Though Columbia County escaped being involved in actual battles, a great deal of troop movement took place here. Researchers continue to seek information, archeologists continue to unearth relics, and in 2012 the grave of Gen. John Porter McKown, the highest-ranking officer in the Confederate States Army to be buried in Arkansas, was marked here in Magnolia by the United Daughters of the Confederacy and the Arkansas Civil War Sesquicentennial Commission.

Columbia County has always been an interesting admixture of culture both refined and primitive. From cut-crystal to coonhounds, we have got it all. We think these pictures bear that out. But if you visit our area today, you will find that many local families retain a liking for both.

Finally, if you have elders, seek them out. Spend time with them and listen to them. Write down or record their stories to share with others. Gather generations of family and take photographs, then carefully record the names (and dates) for future reference. Place boxed photographs close to exits and back up digital files. Spend time tending and cultivating your roots—they will nurture your tallest and strongest self.

One

Early Families and Settlers

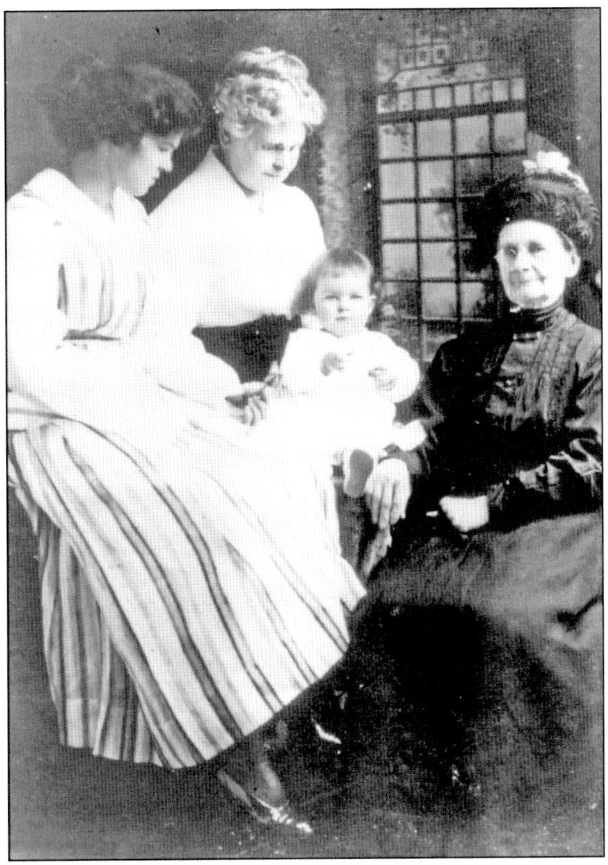

A pioneer of Calhoun, Columbia County, Arkansas, and three generations of her descendants are, from left to right, Grace (Bird) Dodson, Martha Alice (McGowan) Bird, little Alice Dodson (Harrell), and Martha (McDonald) McGowan. At age 92, Martha was the homecoming queen at the dedication of the Harvey Couch School in Calhoun on August 10, 1928. (Selma Bird.)

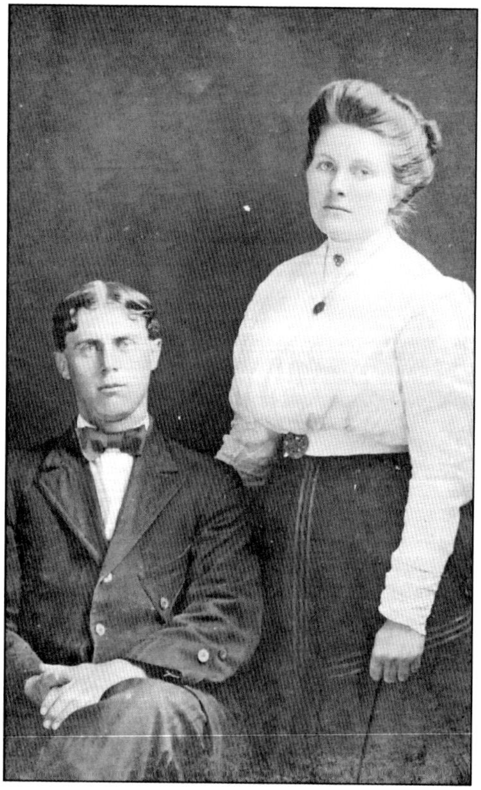

Pictured are Sam and Gussie Whaley Keith. They ran the general store at the intersection of Columbia County Road 1 and Columbia County Road 15 from the late 1890s into the 1950s. The store, while not operational, still stands into the 21st century. (Dana Thornton.)

Sam and Elizabeth Grayson, pictured, had two daughters, Nina and Helen. Sam Grayson owned and operated one of the largest sawmills in Columbia County during the early 1900s. He was also a pioneer in the local banking industry and led the way into many commercial endeavors for the county. (Molly Harsh Burns.)

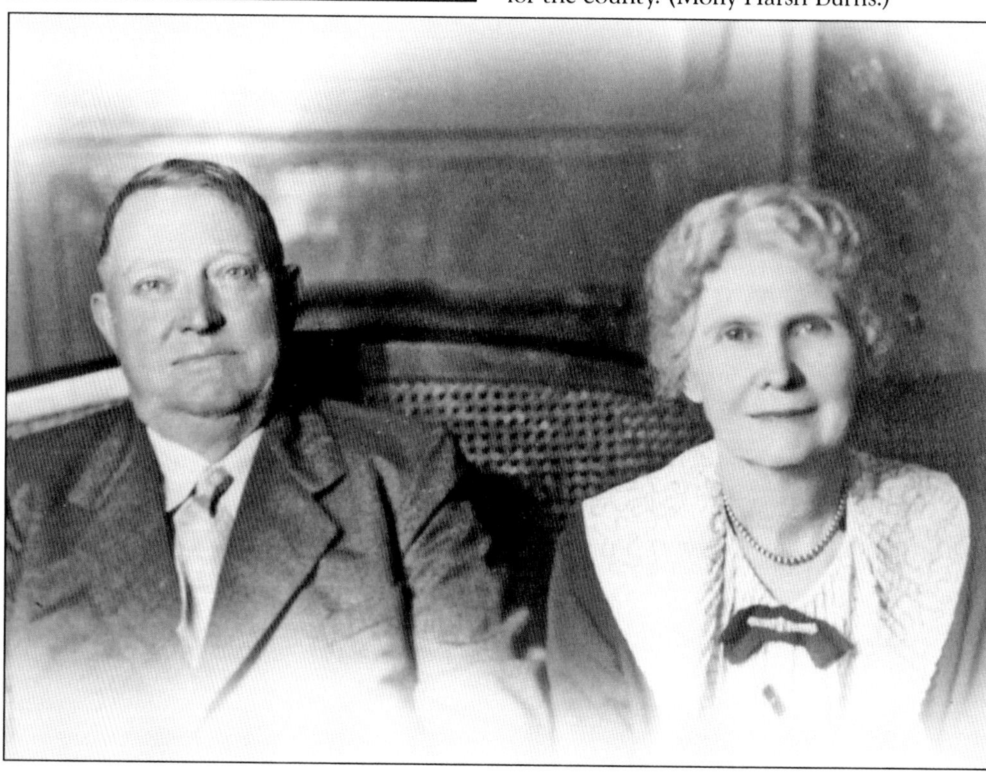

Norborn (or Norbourne) and Sarah Elizabeth Harper Young are pictured around 1870. Norborn helped to survey Magnolia in 1853, and tradition has it that Sarah Elizabeth (they were engaged at the time) suggested the name "Magnolia" for the town. (Ann Machen Callison.)

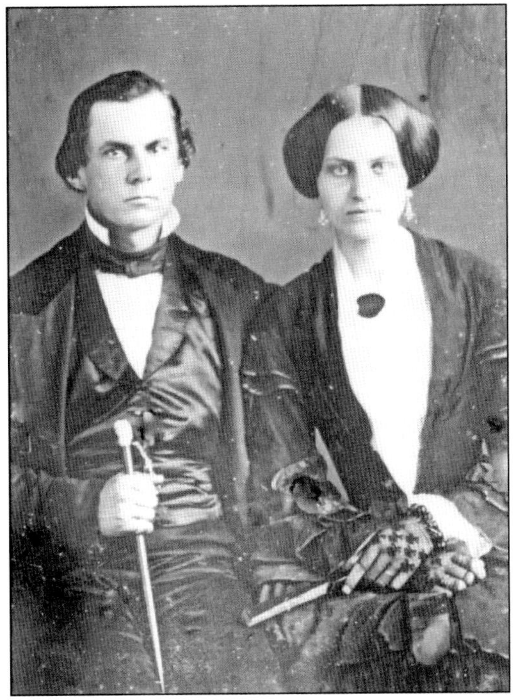

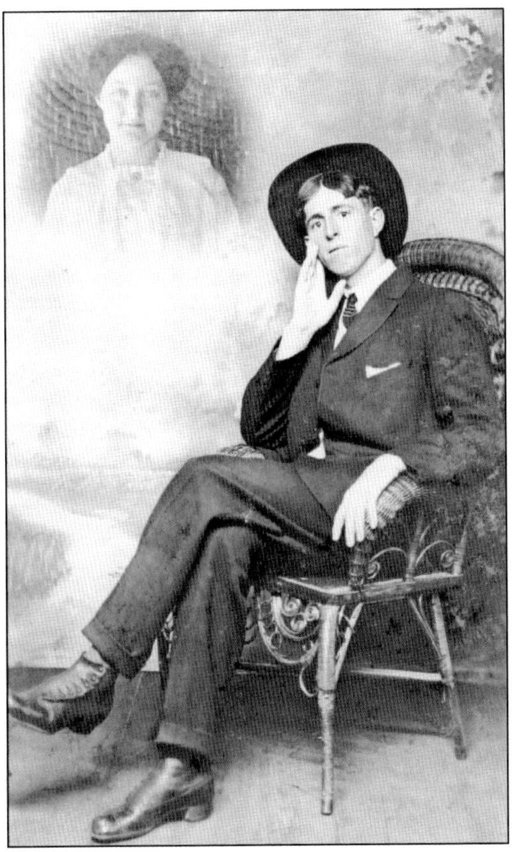

While visiting Columbia County, Walter B. Williams of Duncan, Oklahoma, met Ida Ester Booth and a courtship began. Ida's brother Rowland S. Booth was against the relationship and forbid her to see him. After a physical altercation between Rowland and Walter, Ida eloped, and the couple was married in Columbia County on December 30, 1915. Ida died a short five years later on February 28, 1920. This image shows a lonely Walter pining for his lost love. (Betty Faye Lewis.)

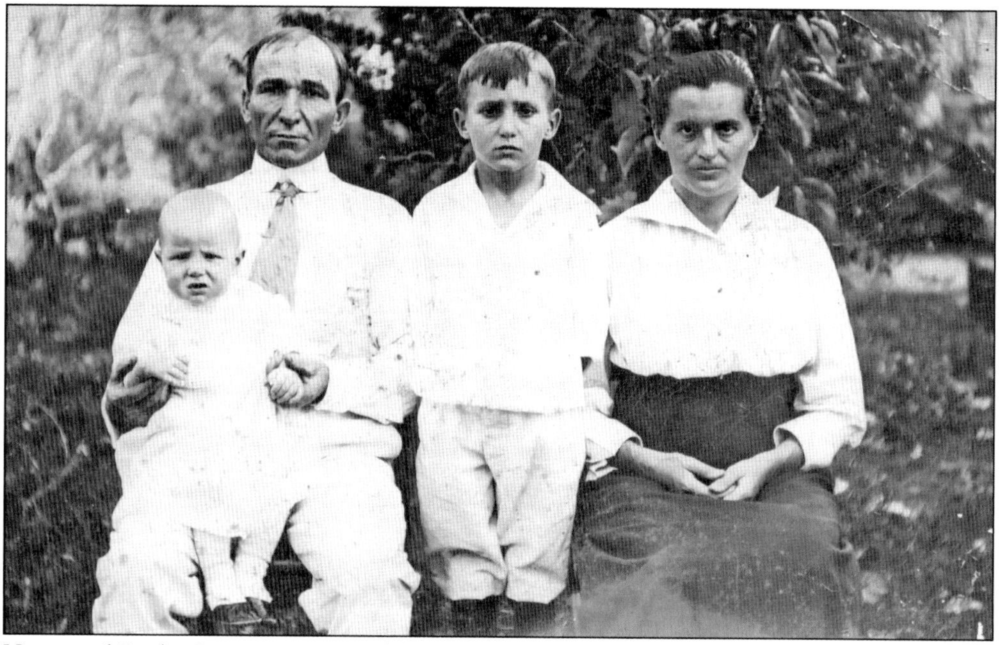

Henry and Emilie Genestet emigrated from France in 1904 and later settled in Waldo, Arkansas. From left to right are Henry (holding Robert), Raymond, and Emilie Grandet Genestet around 1919. Robert was the father of Bob Genestet, and Raymond was the father of Rochelle Genestet McMahen. (Bob Genestet.)

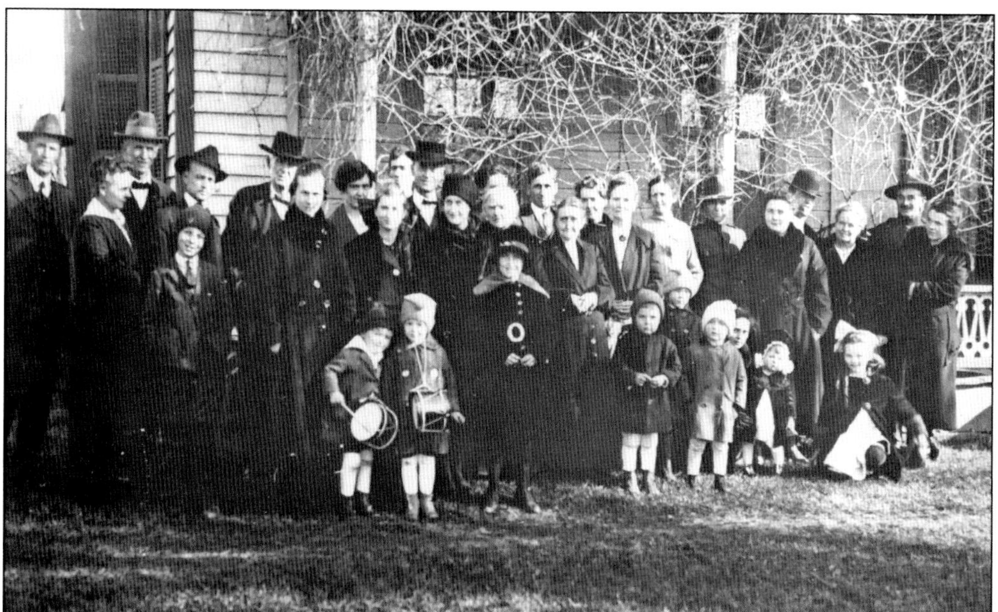

The Goode family is shown at home on South Washington Street in Magnolia, Arkansas, around 1918. From the attire of the family, it appears that they have gathered for a Thanksgiving feast. (Mary Woodward Lewis.)

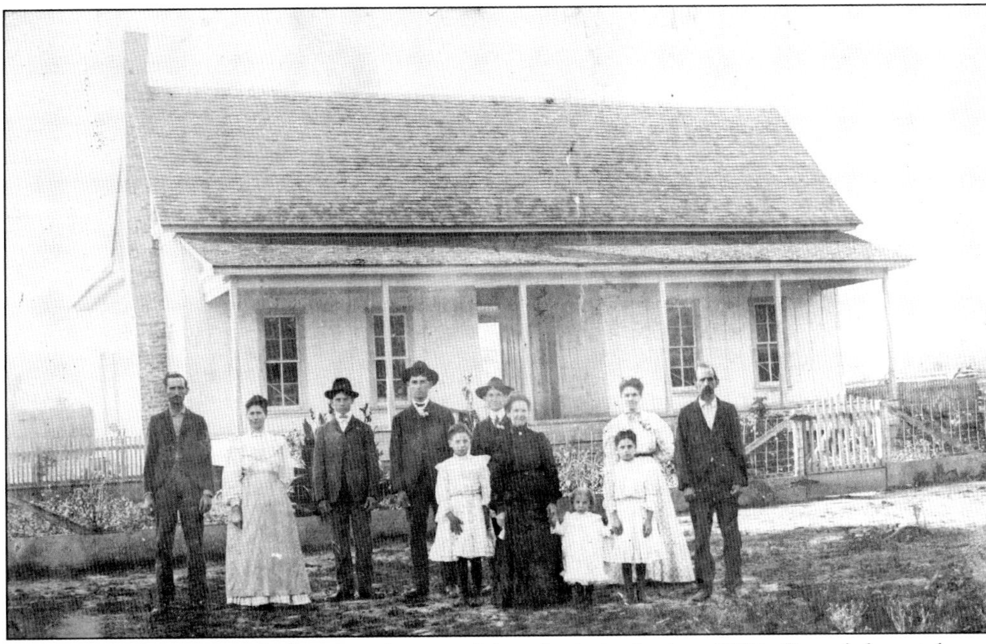

This is the Clayton Franks family at home in Macedonia in the late 1800s. From left to right are Clayton Franks, Lizzie Franks, Hildred Souter, Wesley Souter, Essie Souter, Lester Souter, Emma B. Souter, Alverta Souter, Ola Souter, Pricilla Souter, and Jake Souter. (Christine Butler Snider.)

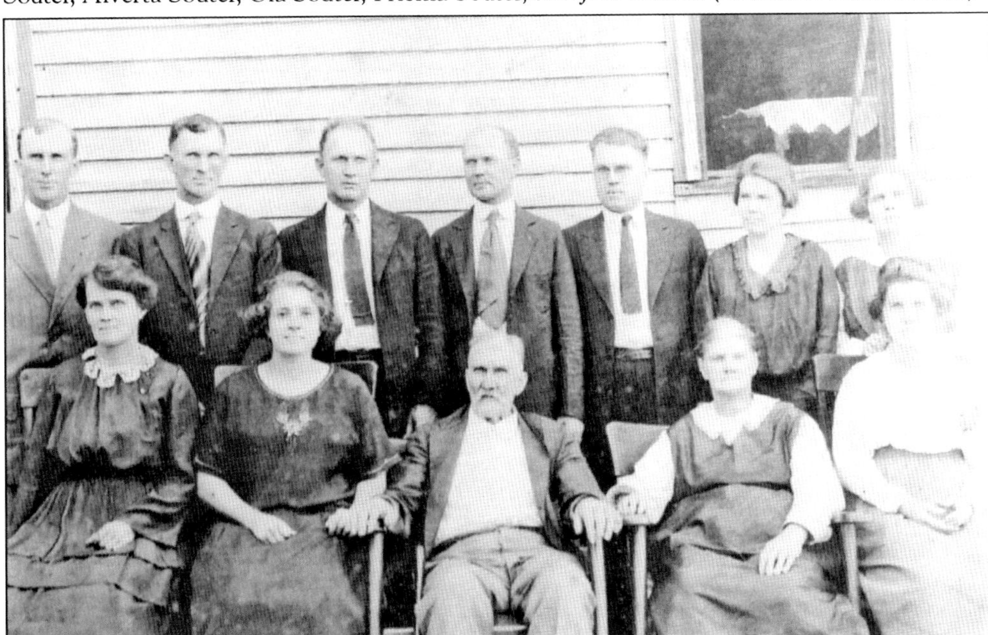

Pictured are members of the Cooper family. They are, from left to right, (sitting) Cora, Annie, Isaac Lee, Percilla Dudney Cooper, and Mary; (standing) Ben, Jim, Felix, Luther, Ike, Nancy Eunice, and Etta. The Cooper plantation land was sold to Gresham Shinn for the development of a growing town. A family story indicates that the streets in the subdivision were to be named after Isaac Cooper's descendants. Thus, the streets are Felix, Raye, Joy, Lee, and Cooper in Magnolia. Dudney Road was given its name in honor of Percilla's family, the Dudneys. (Eileen Nall.)

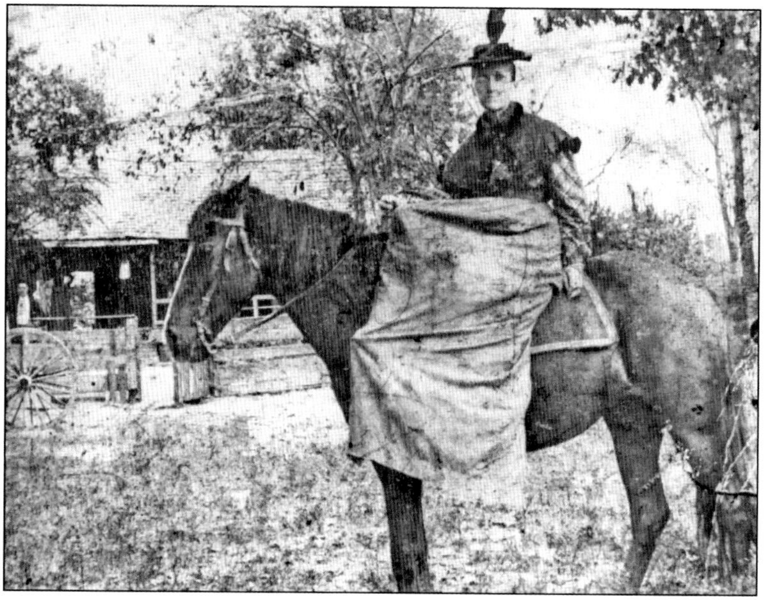

This photograph was thought for many years to depict "Aunt" Fannie McGowan; however, the March 2011 issue of *The Arkansas Family Historian* identifies the lady on this horse as Mary Ella Medlock Wilson (1846–1925). A second image in the article features Mary holding her Bible. (Rebecca Wilson.)

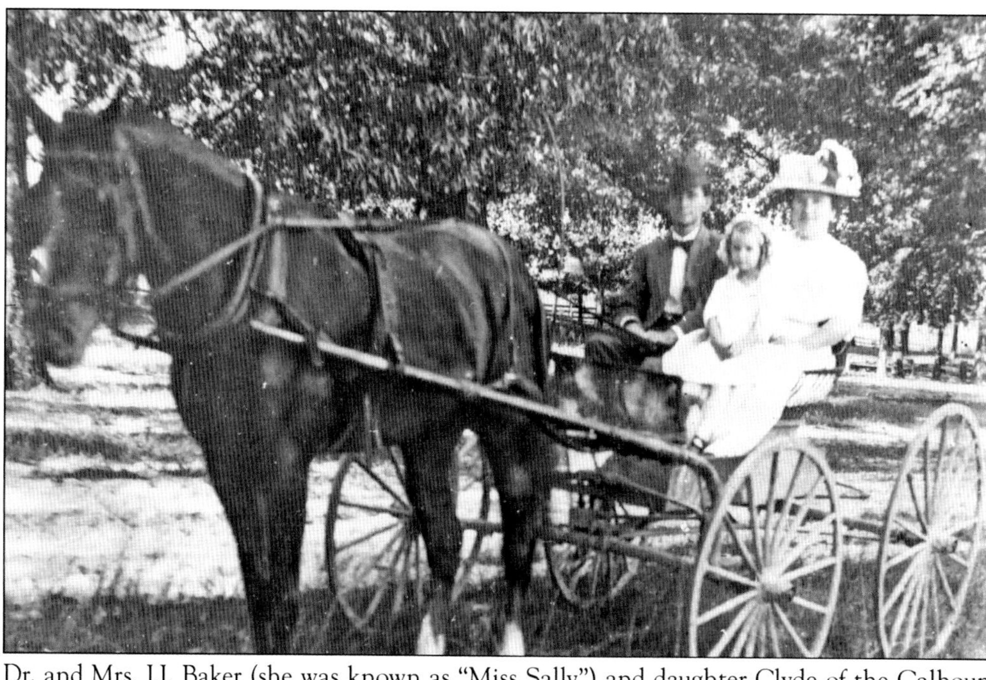

Dr. and Mrs. J.J. Baker (she was known as "Miss Sally") and daughter Clyde of the Calhoun community are pictured around 1910. Dr. Baker practiced medicine for 50 years in Columbia County: the first 10 years he worked as a physician in Calhoun, and the last 40 years he practiced in Magnolia. (Clyde Baker.)

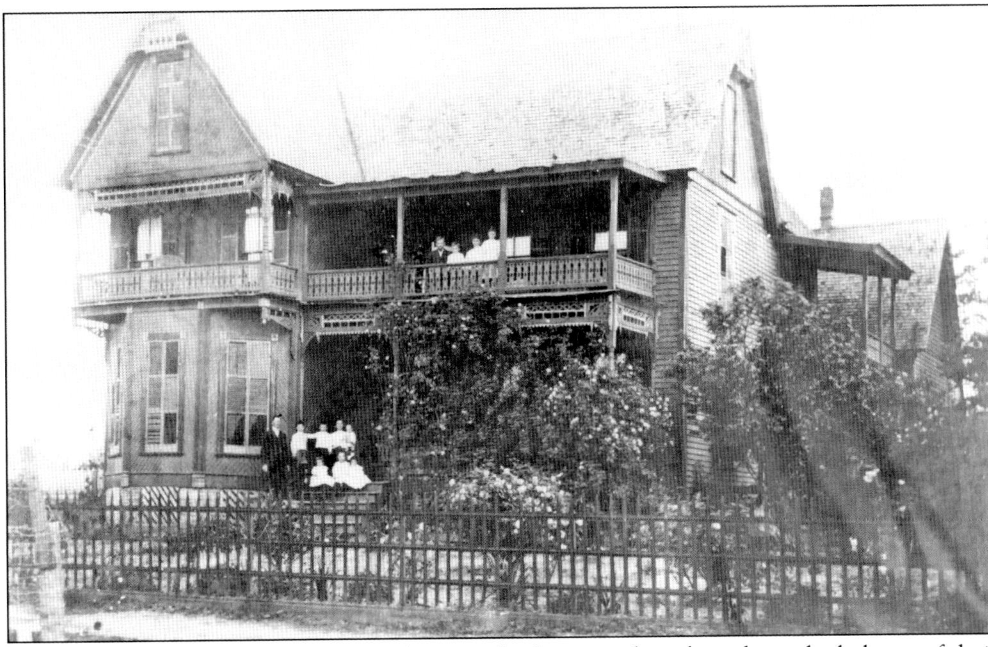

Members of the Dr. C.D. Stevens family sit on the front porch and perch on the balcony of their home on East Main Street in Magnolia around 1900. The Stevens home was a two-story mansion at 414 East Main that was razed in the early 1960s to clear the site for the Columbia Shopping Center. (Alice Couch Monroe.)

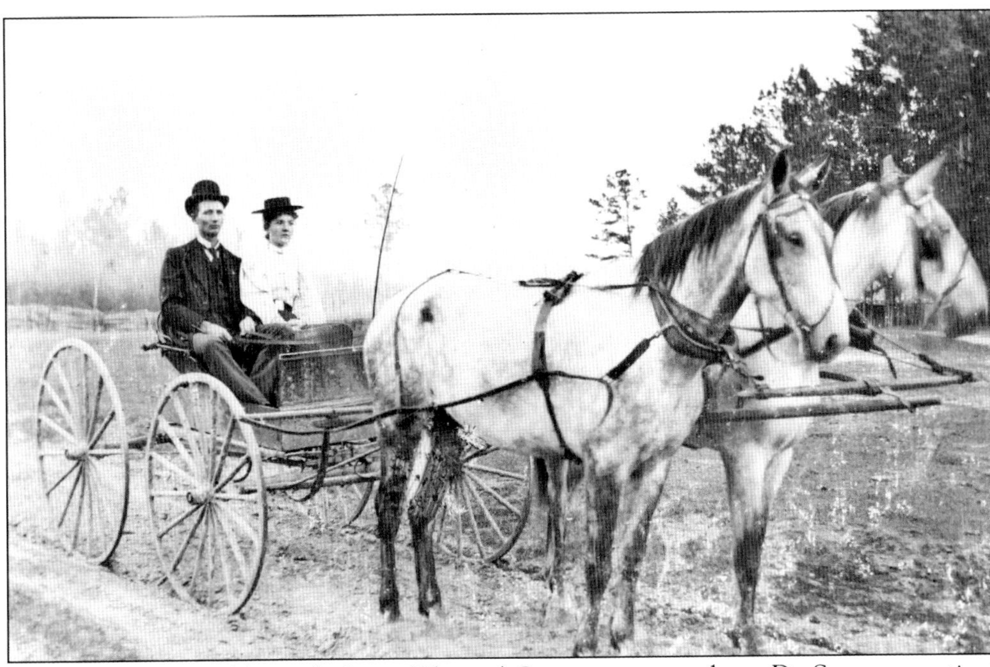

Dr. C.D. Stevens and his wife, Lena (Clayton) Stevens, are seen here. Dr. Stevens practiced medicine in Magnolia from 1904 until his death in 1927. He was a partner of Dr. Alvan Longino until their office burned, after which they remained friends but practiced from different locations. (Beulah Stevens Godley.)

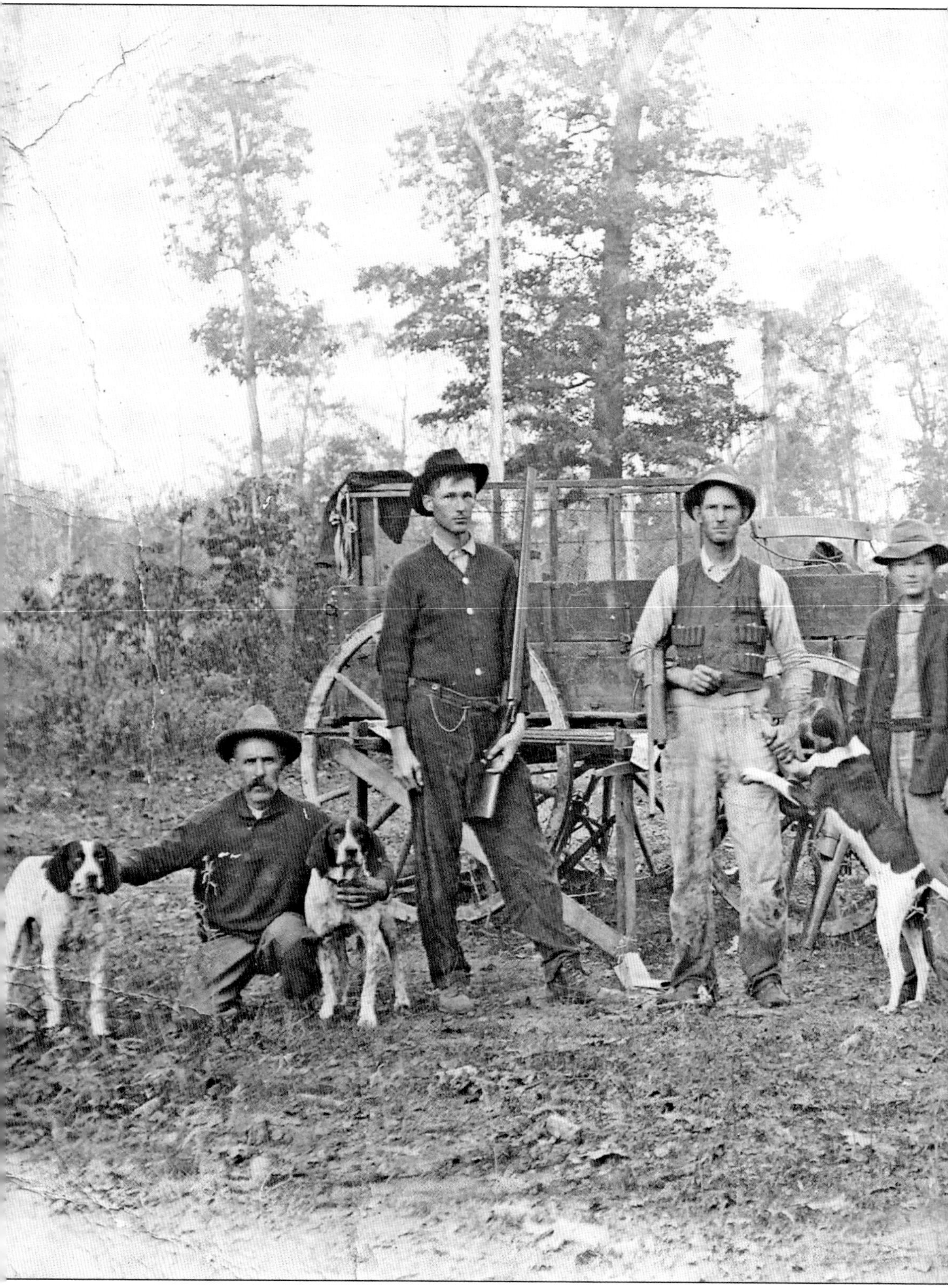

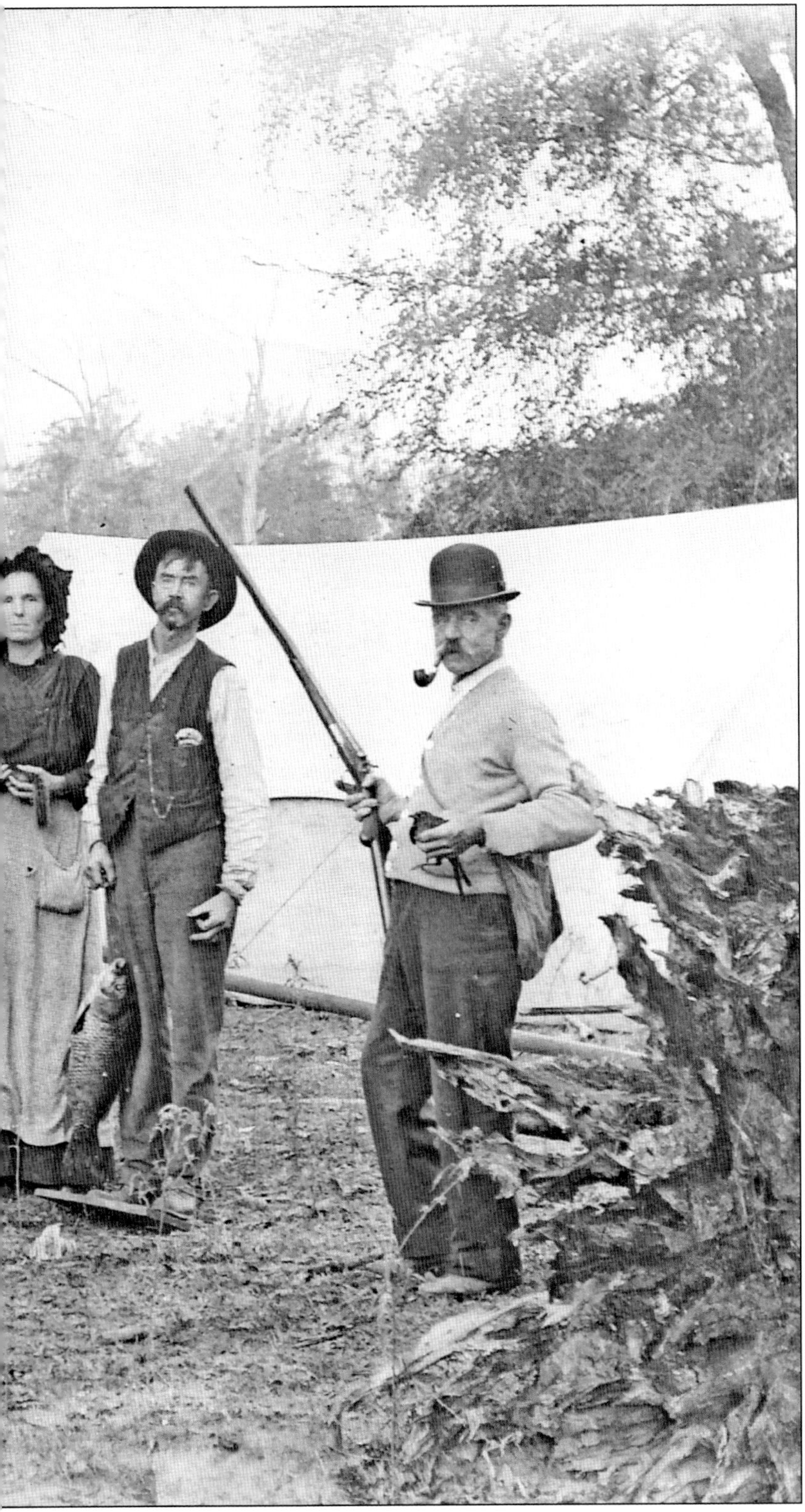

This photograph, taken after 1903 near Taylor, Arkansas, shows the diverse bounty of Columbia County. The hunting trip has been successful, as is evidenced by the game held by three of the campers: the woman is holding a squirrel, the man to the right of her a fish, and the gentleman in the bowler hat a bird. Note the strength in the upper bodies of the working dogs. The dogs on the left are spaniels, and the one in the center is a coonhound. Good dogs often made the difference between a successful hunt and hunger. (Ronald Orrick.)

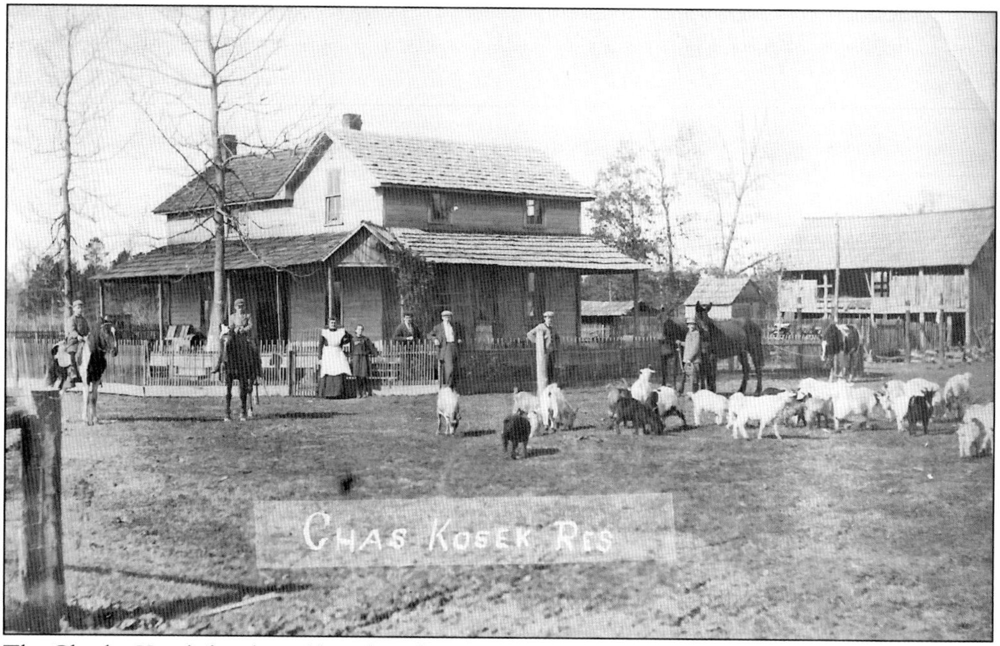

The Charles Kosek family and hired workers gather outside their appealing two-story farmhouse in Taylor. This photograph shows the various types of stock raised in the area in the early 1900s. The Koseks' stock included goats, horses, mules, and pigs. Note the immense size of the barn in the background. (Ronald Orrick.)

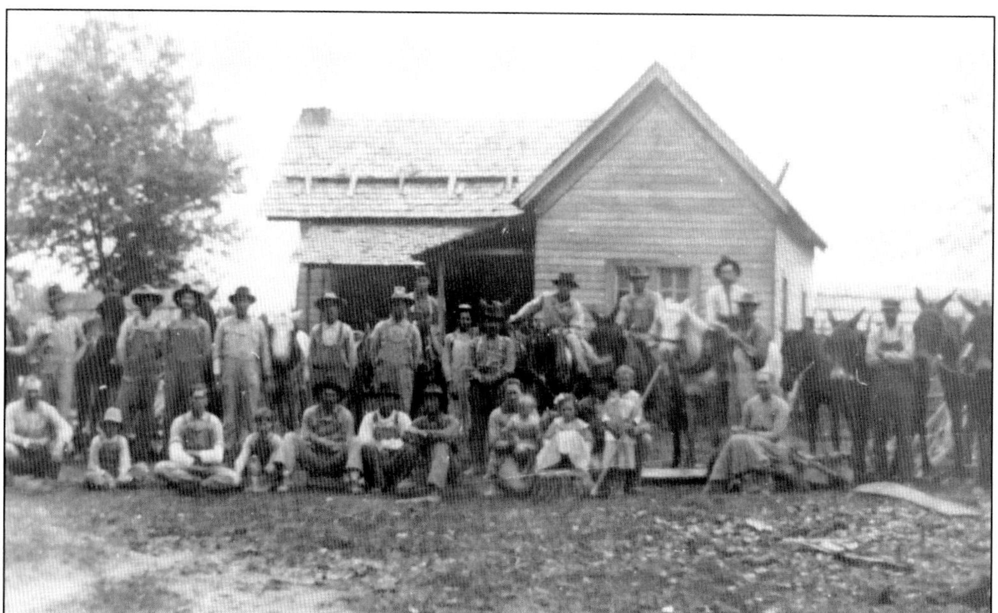

This photograph is of neighbors at a "corn-planting" at Rufus Wilson's place near Village in 1914. There had been a house fire earlier, injuring Audrey Wilson (at age 8), who can be seen sitting in the chair, front and center. (Hudson Phillips.)

Columbia County's oldest home, "Frog Level," was rented to the Wise family in the 1930s. From left to right are (first row) Guy Wise and Desteen Wise Smith; (second row) Dock Lewis and Seabie Smith; (third row) G.G. Wise, Eula Wise, James Wise, and Selene Wise Lewis. (Betty Faye Lewis.)

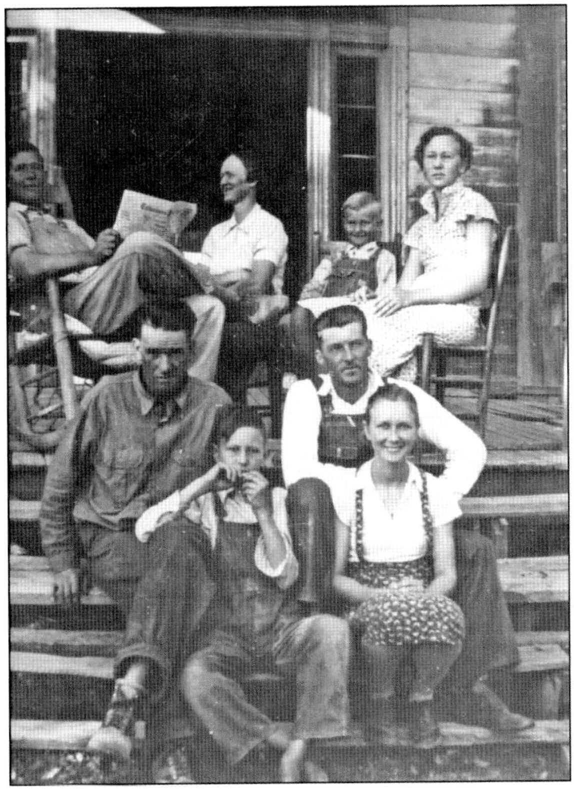

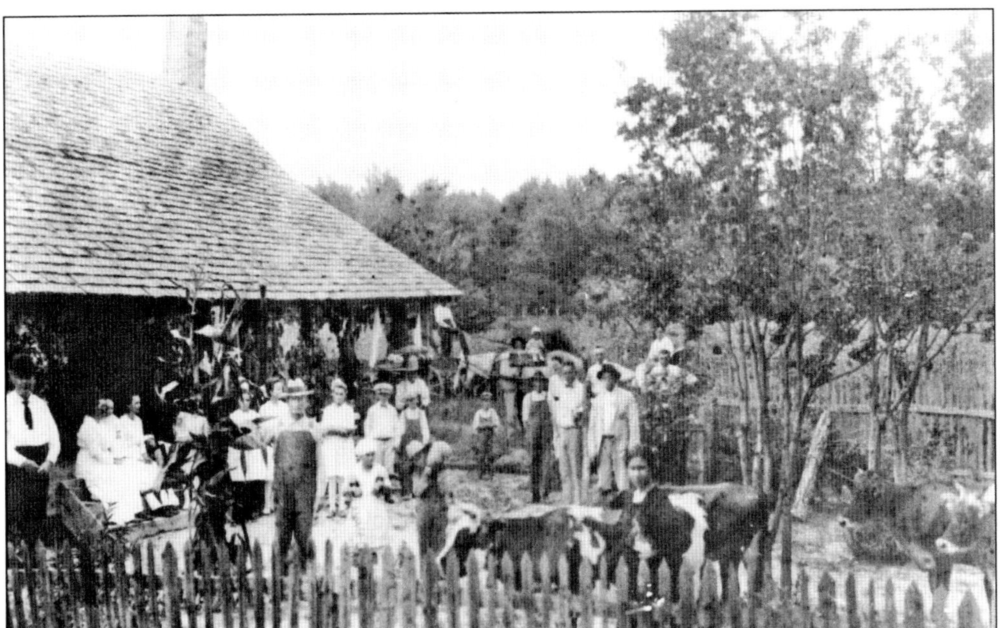

This photograph features harvesttime on the Wilson farm, located between Magnolia and Waldo, around 1918. From left to right in the foreground are J.B. "Munge" Wilson, holding corn stalks; Margaret Wilson (Saxon), holding jars; Smead Wilson, holding melon; and daughter-in-law Ida Cephus Wilson, standing beside the cow. (Mary Alice Colquitt.)

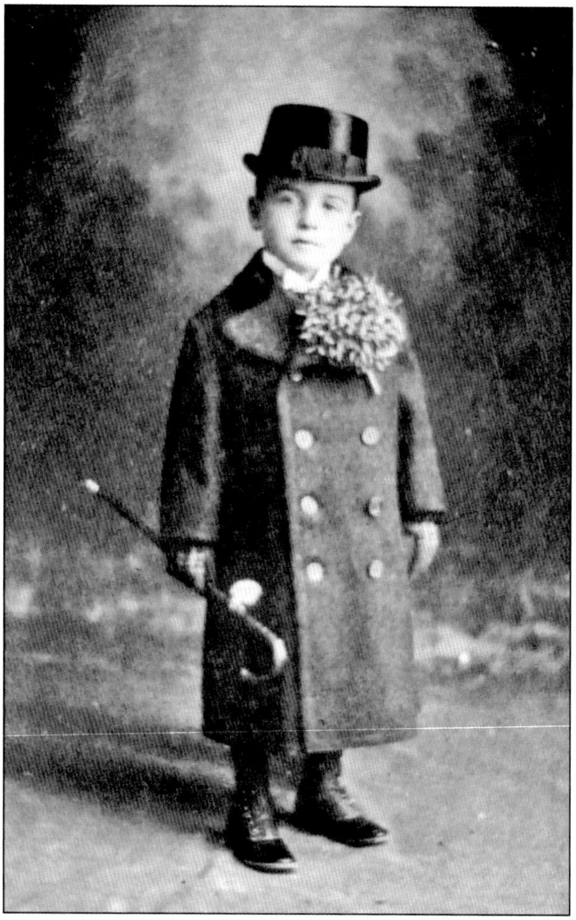

Joe L. Davis Jr. is pictured around 1904. Young Master Davis is dressed to the nines, from the tip of his top hat to the spats on his little leather shoes. Joe was the brother of Mary Davis Woodward Lewis, who was a lifelong resident of Magnolia. (Mary Davis Woodward Lewis.)

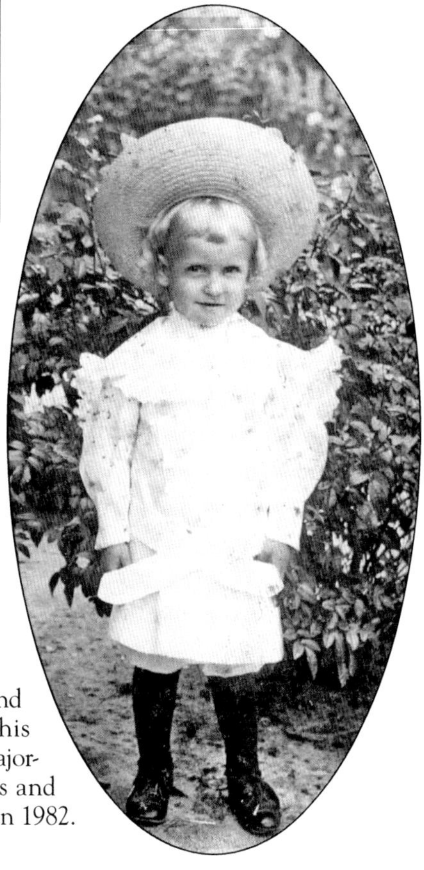

Three-year-old Travis Calvin Jackson is pictured around 1907. Jackson grew up in Waldo, and baseball was his interest from a very early age. He grew up to become a major-league shortstop for the New York Giants for 14 years and was inducted into the National Baseball Hall of Fame in 1982. (D.J. Fincher.)

This beautiful portrait is representative of the photographs popular of babies during the 19th century. The photograph is of Mary Jeannette Blackman, who is the mother of Dorothy Jeanne Jackson Fincher of Waldo, Arkansas. (D.J. Fincher.)

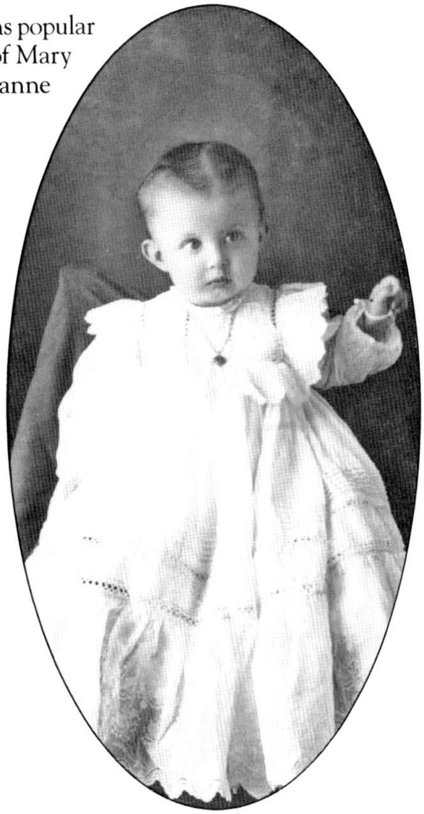

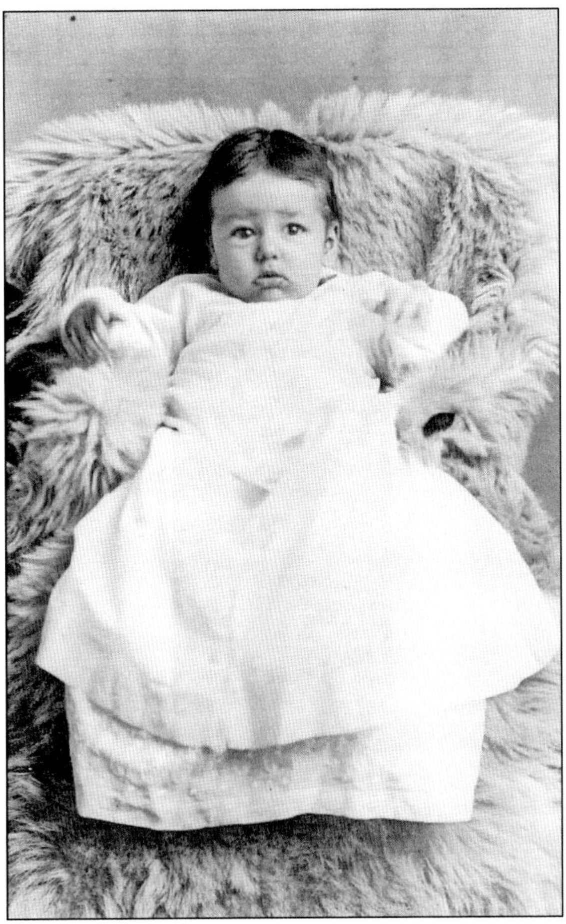

Young Clyde Pillow was the oldest son of George Anderson Pillow and Lurana Pillow (née Dorman). His mother's family, the Dormans, moved into Georgia Township in 1850 and built their first homestead in 1855, five miles east of Magnolia. They prospered and acquired additional land near Emerson in 1857 and 1859. This photograph was taken around 1905. Dorman descendants live in Columbia County today. (Michael Burk.)

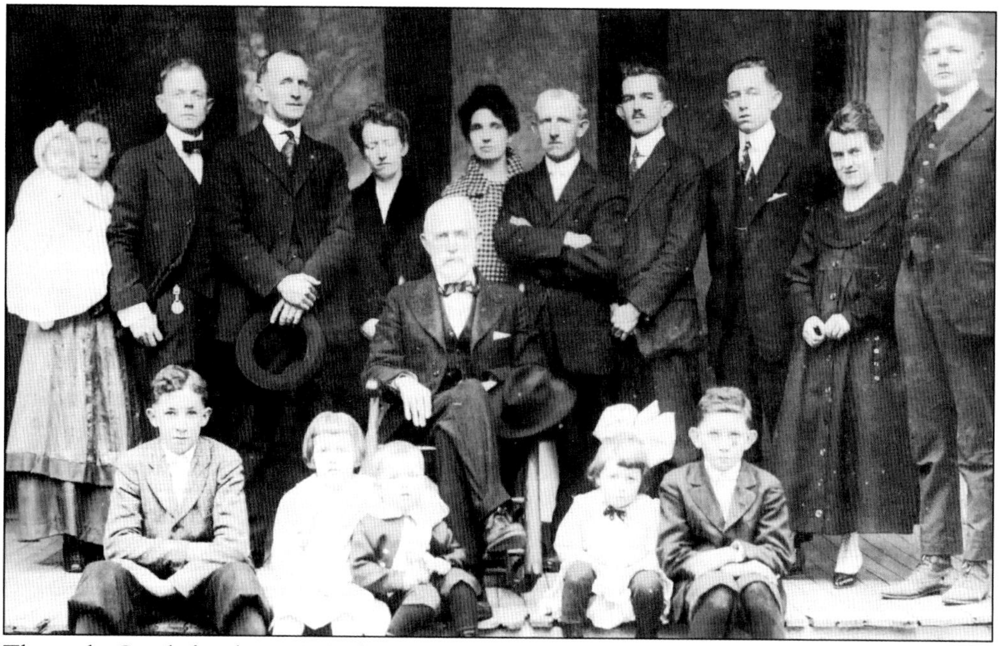

This is the Smith family in 1916. Shown are, from left to right, (first row) Erman Edward Smith, Doris Eddiline Reynolds, Harry Lord Smith, Marjorie Percy Smith, and Arren Osler "Bo" Smith; (second row) Mary Alice Smith (infant), Helen Savage Smith, Bee Reynolds, Daniel Edward Smith, Lora Smith, Lillie Buffington Smith, Parks Mathews Smith, Claude Lawrence Smith, Woodford Ransom Smith, Lillie Viva Smith, and Lann Bazemore "L.B" Smith; seated in the center is patriarch James Edward Smith. (Belva Smith.)

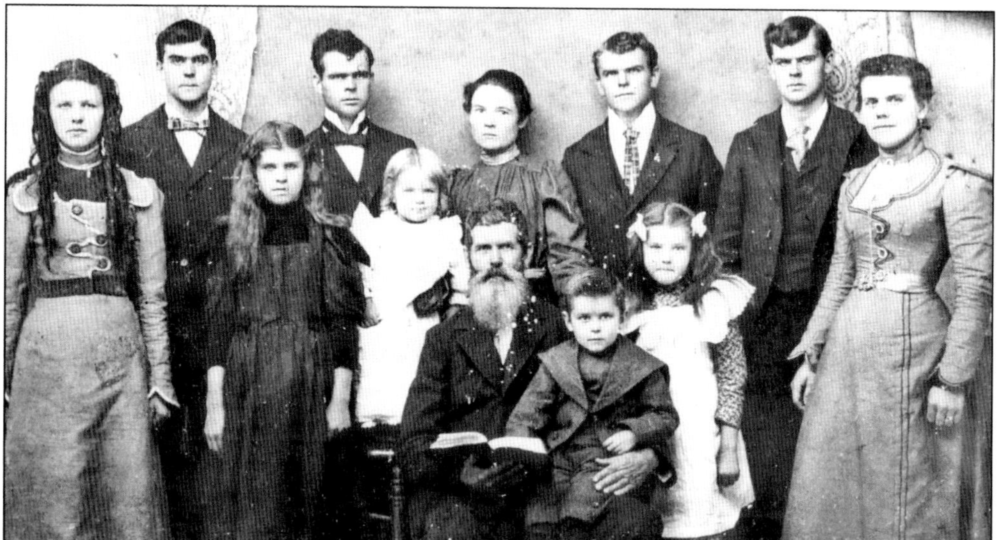

The C.R. Rudd family of the Antioch West community is shown around 1893. From left to right are (first row) Emma Rudd Dennis, Mattie Rudd Volentine, C.R. Rudd, Arthur Rudd, Eva Mae Rudd, and Anna Rudd Skinner; (second row) Jack Rudd, Jim Rudd, Brown Lee Rudd (child), Nannie Rudd, Claud Rudd, and Newt Rudd. C.R. donated land for both the Antioch West Baptist and the Kilgore Lodge Methodist Churches. The community is called Rudd's Crossing. (Herbert Skinner.)

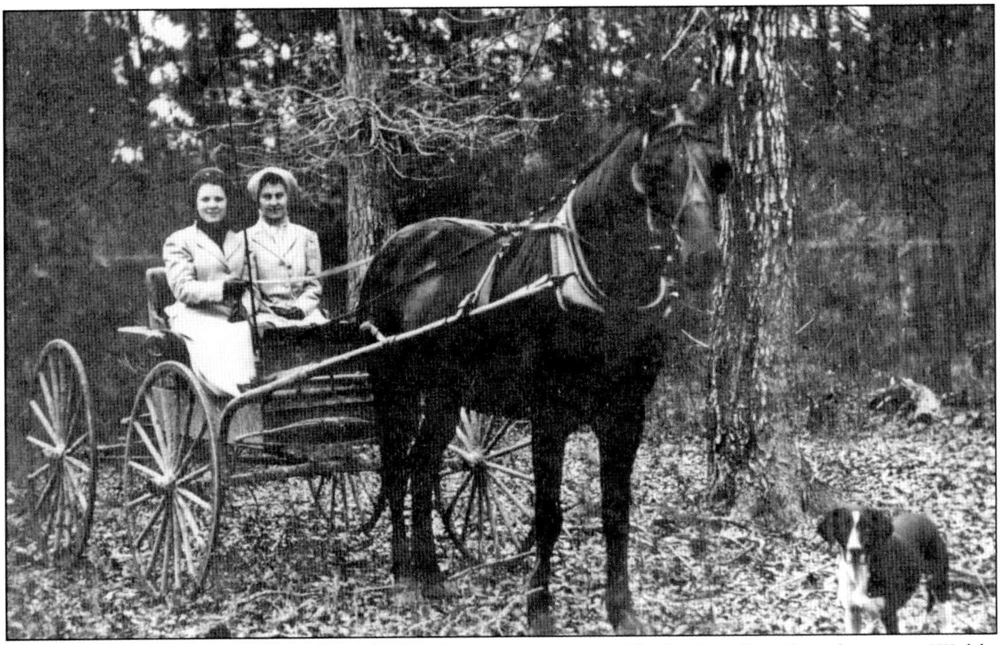

Lelia Beasley Beeson (left) and Ruth Hendrix are sitting in Dr. Joshua Beasley's buggy at Waldo in 1907. Minnie is the mare, and Prince is the dog. Ruth married James Askew, and they lived out their lives in the same house in Waldo. The home still stands today, and another family enjoys its shelter. (Betty Askew Genestet.)

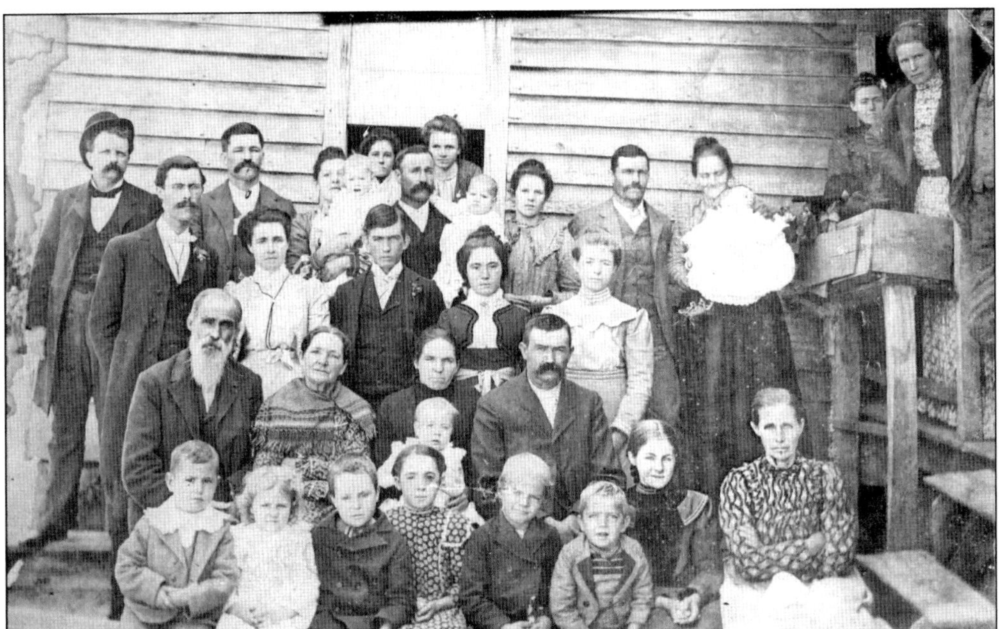

This is a photograph of the Souter and Whaley families gathered for a wedding in 1901. Married the evening before were Key Rogers and Georgia Souter. The couple is seen in the third row on the far left; the parson who married them is standing on the far left in the last row, wearing a bowler hat and bow tie. (Dorothy Whaley.)

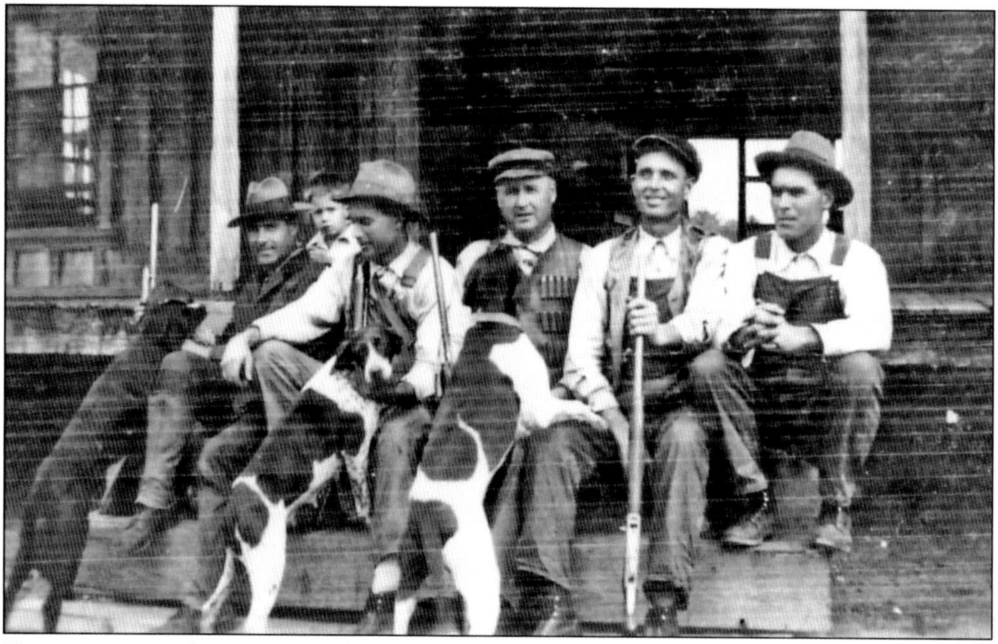

Hunting is serious business in south Arkansas. In front, from left to right, Burl Nipper, Roy Nipper, Artie Nipper, Parker Nipper, and Jody Nipper are resting on the front porch after a successful coon hunt about 1920. (Christine Butler Snider.)

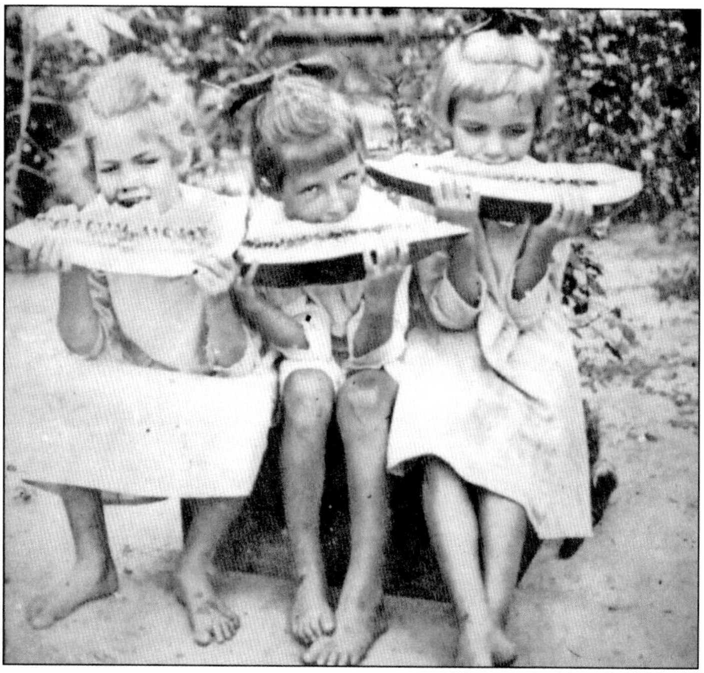

Here, a watermelon feast is taking place at Village, Arkansas, around 1918. Pictured are, from left to right, Lucille Jamerson Hyde, Bertha Jamerson Brasher, and Flavis Jamerson Cheatham. (Pam Cheatham Ravanscraft.)

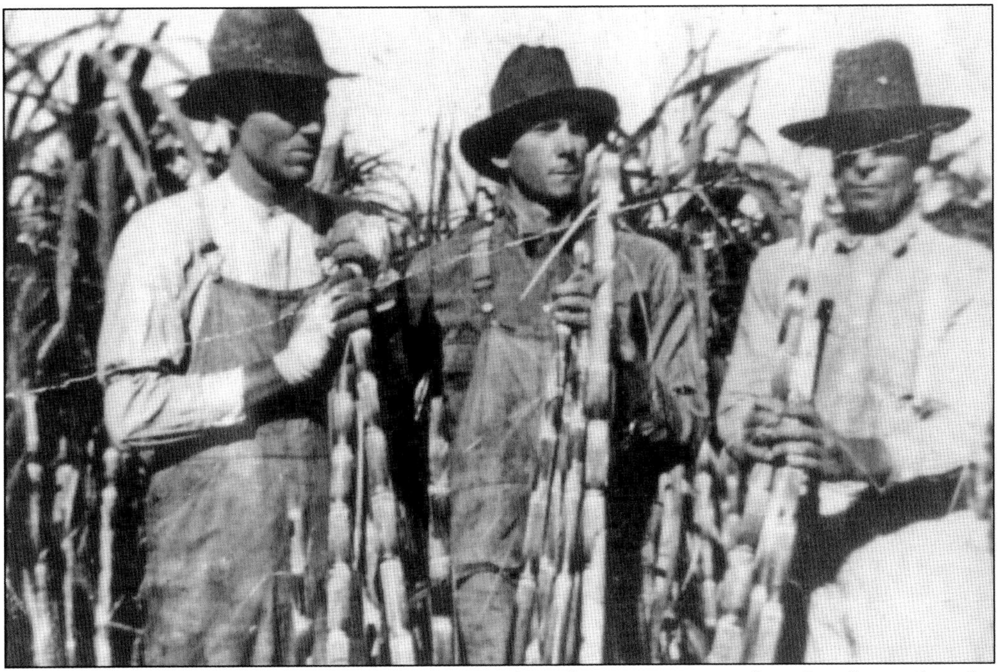

Philadelphia was largely a farming community when this picture was taken. It is located in the west central section of the county on Burnt Bridge Road (County Road 15). Here, from left to right, Granville, Wordie, and Charlie Elmore are inspecting a prosperous sugarcane crop near Philadelphia. (Dr. Robert Walz.)

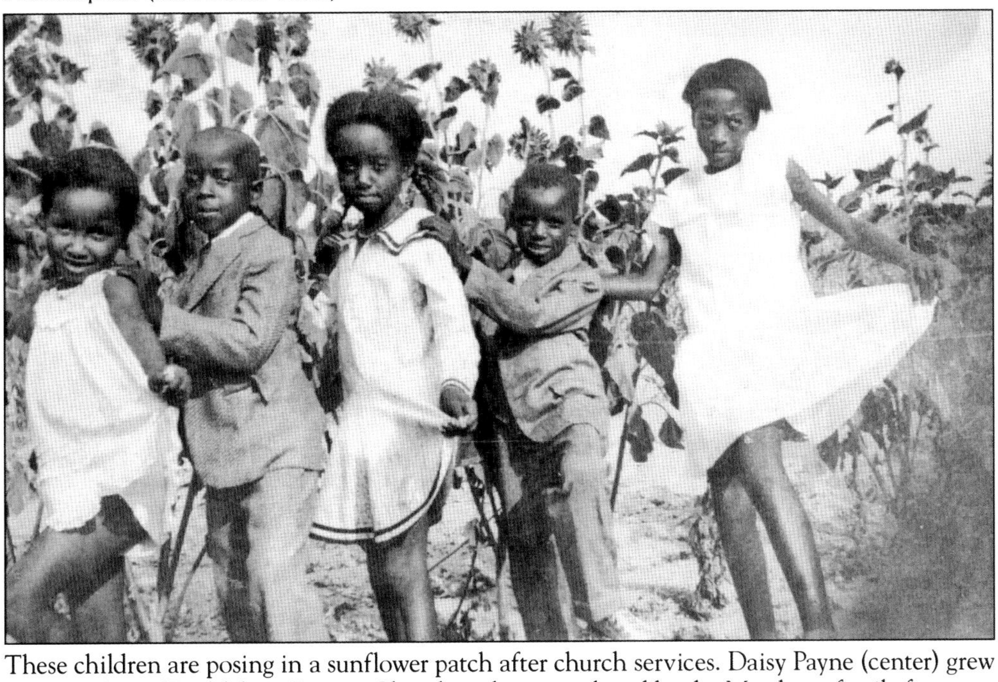

These children are posing in a sunflower patch after church services. Daisy Payne (center) grew up a member of Bethlehem Baptist Church and was employed by the Matthews family for many years. C.Z. Payne (second from the right) held the distinction of being the only porter or "Red Cap" at the Greyhound Bus Line in Magnolia. (Peggy Goode Ruff.)

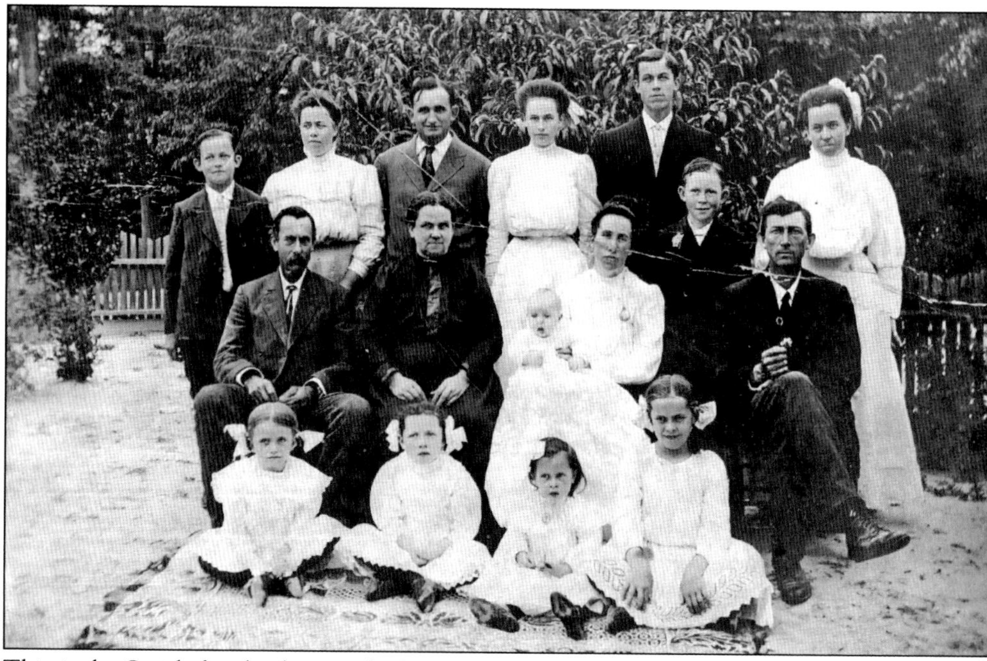

This is the Smith family close to the Mount Holly junction. From left to right are (first row) Esther, Docia, and Gertude Smith and Verda Richardson, who died young; (second row) W.H. Allen, Minnie O-Della Smith, and Emma (holding baby Hubert) beside husband Marcus Smith; (third row) Oswell ?, "Aunt Sis" (Loula Smith), Louie Smith, Netta Richardson, Anner Smith, unidentified, and Excell Smith. (Emma Jean Allen Gunnels.)

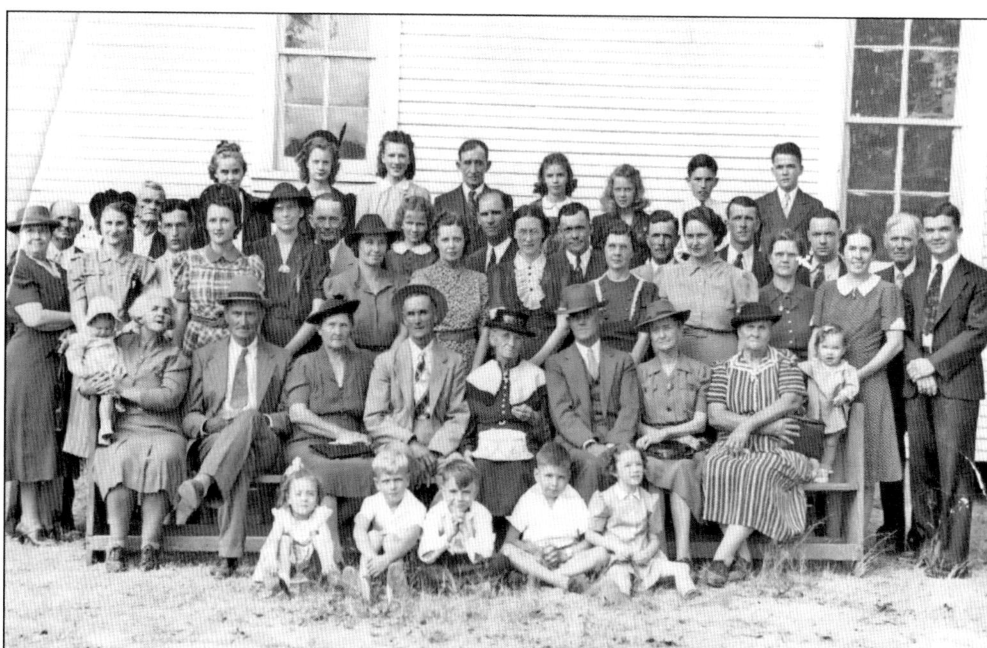

This is the family of William Henry Jackson and Martha Jane Baker Jackson of Waldo, Arkansas. The occasion for this 1944 photograph is Martha's 90th birthday celebration. (D.J. Fincher.)

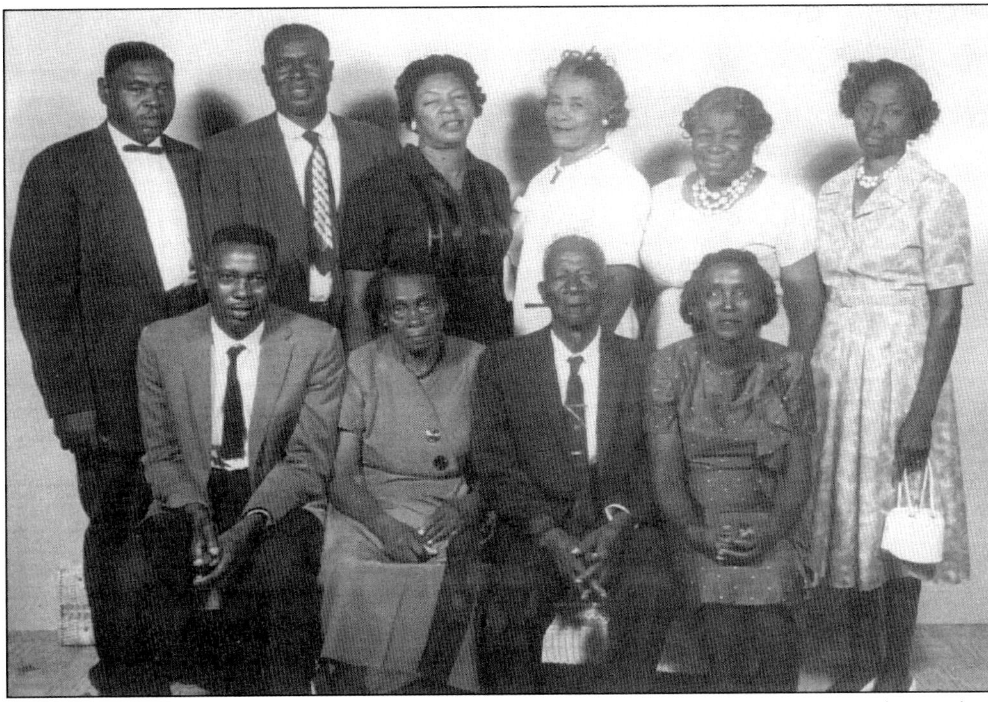

Jamerson family members pictured here are, from left to right, (first row) King, Martha, Walter, and Myrtis; (second row) John, James, Jose, Florida, Gurtha, and Mary Lee of the Free Hope community. (African Methodist Episcopal Church Directory.)

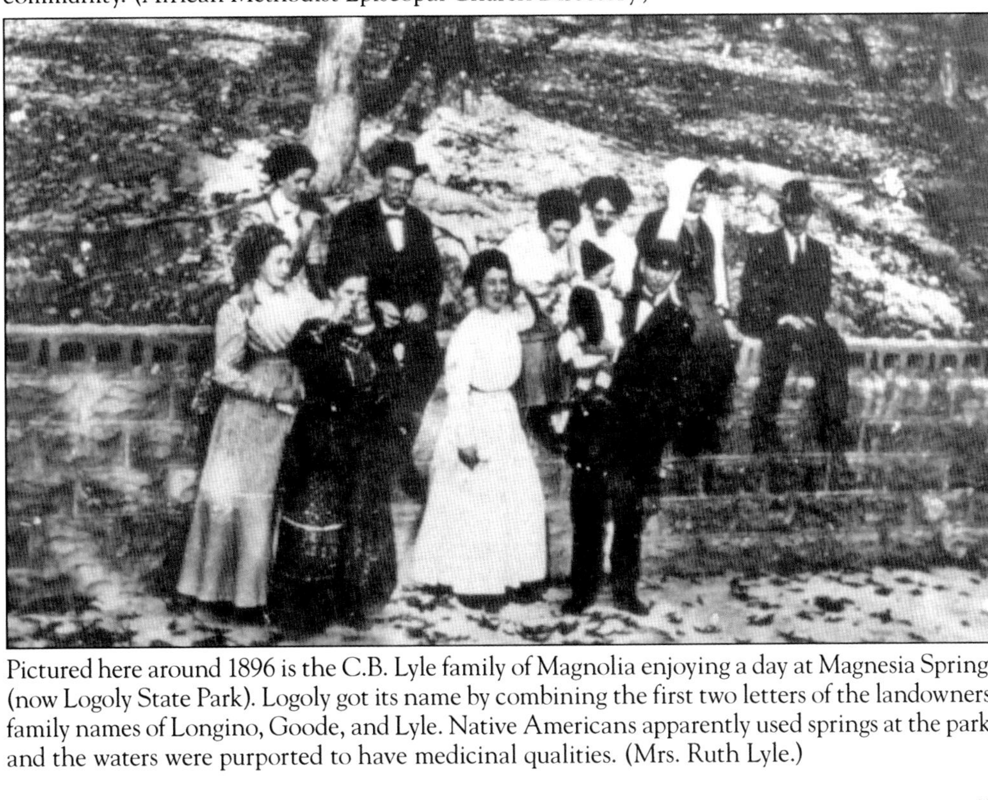

Pictured here around 1896 is the C.B. Lyle family of Magnolia enjoying a day at Magnesia Springs (now Logoly State Park). Logoly got its name by combining the first two letters of the landowners' family names of Longino, Goode, and Lyle. Native Americans apparently used springs at the park, and the waters were purported to have medicinal qualities. (Mrs. Ruth Lyle.)

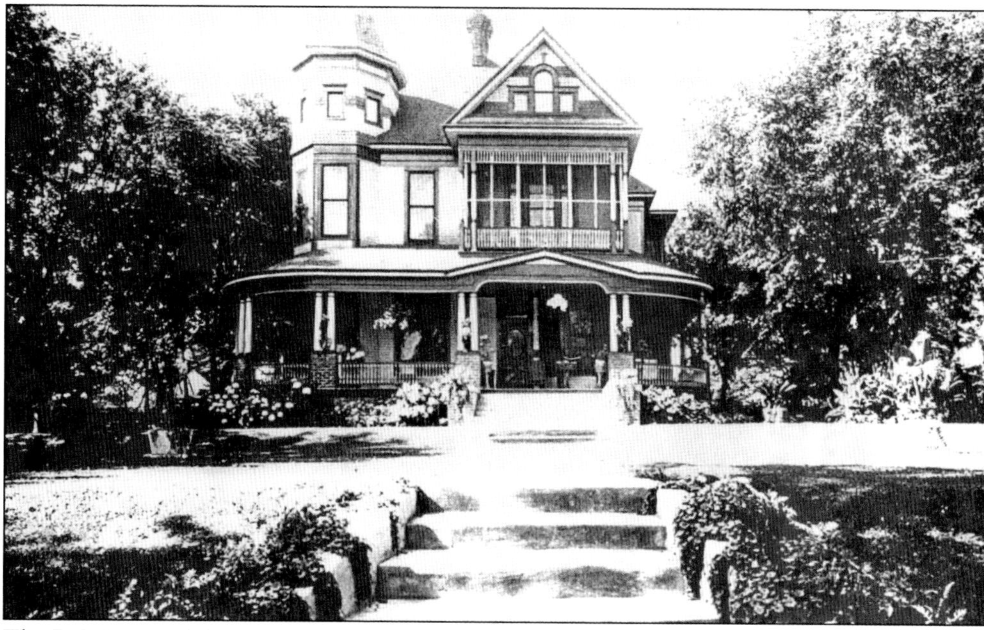

The R.S. Warnock home was a stately structure situated for many years on East Main Street in Magnolia. After the Warnocks moved from the house in the 1950s, the family graciously allowed the building to be used as the Boy's Club of Magnolia. The organization was housed there for several years. (Molly Harsh Burns.)

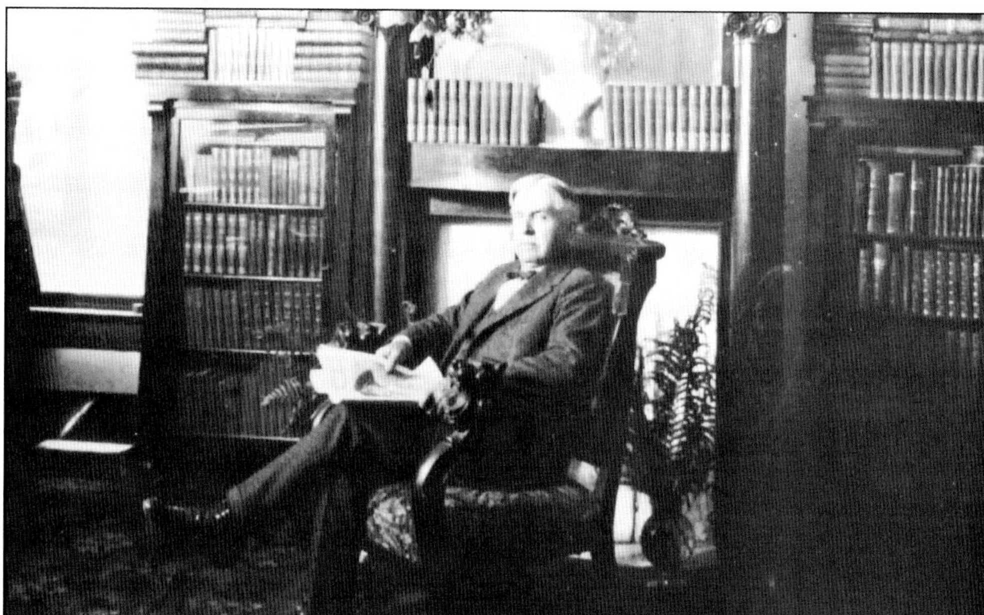

R.S. Warnock Sr. reflects in the library of the Warnock home on East Main Street in Magnolia. He was born in 1857 and, as a young entrepreneur, would eventually build a livery stable near the square. When he went to St. Louis to purchase and trade for mules, he took his family along on the train. He was an avid reader and, though largely self-educated, would eventually establish Farmers Bank, serve the people in the Arkansas Legislature, and guide the A&M College as a member of the board of directors. (Molly Harsh Burns.)

Two

CHURCHES AND CONGREGATIONS

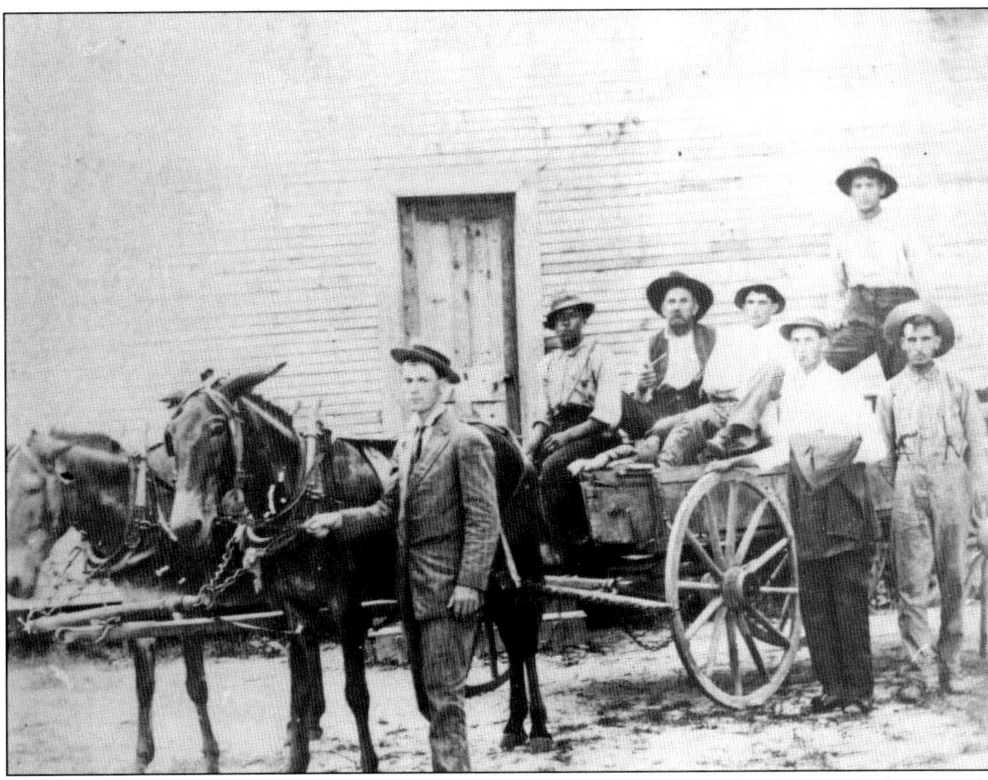

The New Vernon Methodist Church was located on Burnt Bridge Road in this 1915 photograph. Pictured from left to right are (standing) Boss Maness, Will Aldridge, and Charlie Tennis; (in the wagon) Sam Potts, Joe Pearce, and Levi Pearce, and an unidentified person. This church was at the Maness Cutoff and faced the present Pilgrim's Rest Baptist Church. (Nettie Pearce.)

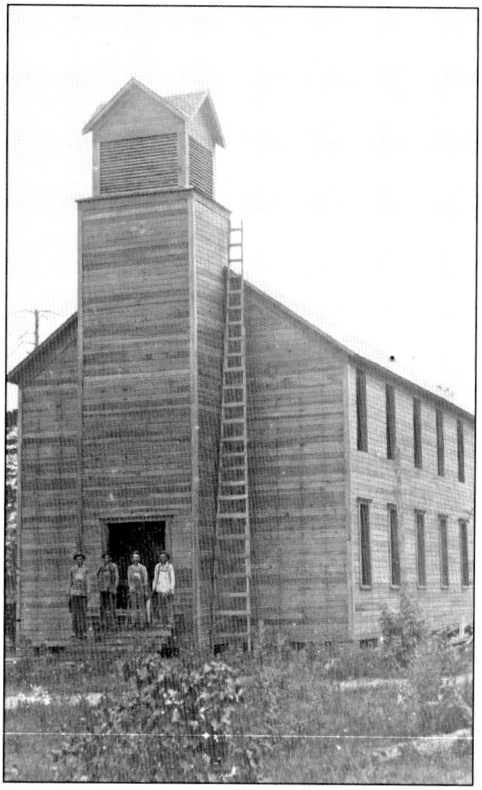

This is the First Baptist Church in Taylor around 1912. Both Baptists and Methodists used the building for services. The top floor was also used as a Masonic lodge. (Ronald Orrick.)

Mount Tabor Missionary Baptist Church was established in 1895 and has served the people of Magnolia from that time. The congregation celebrated its 117th anniversary with a commemorative celebration on October 7, 2012. (Authors.)

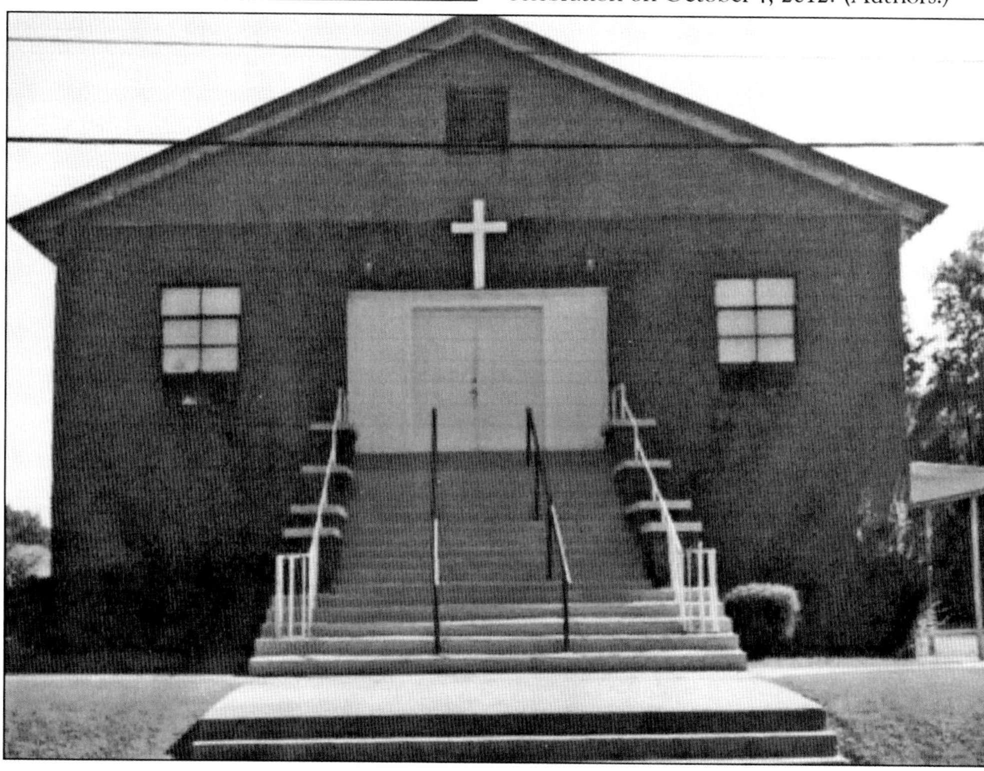

First Baptist Church of Magnolia was established in October 1854. The building pictured was constructed in 1888–1889. Dr. J.R. Graves, a very prominent Southern minister, was chosen to conduct the dedication service of the new church. He described the large steeple as resembling a Chinese pagoda. (Dr. Robert Walz.)

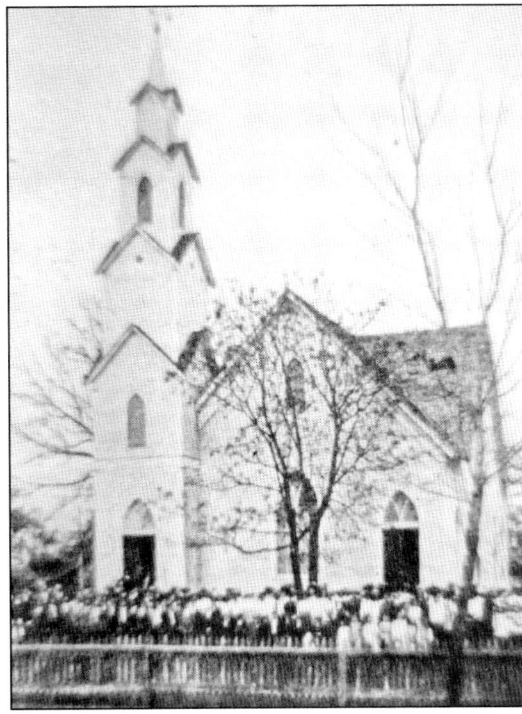

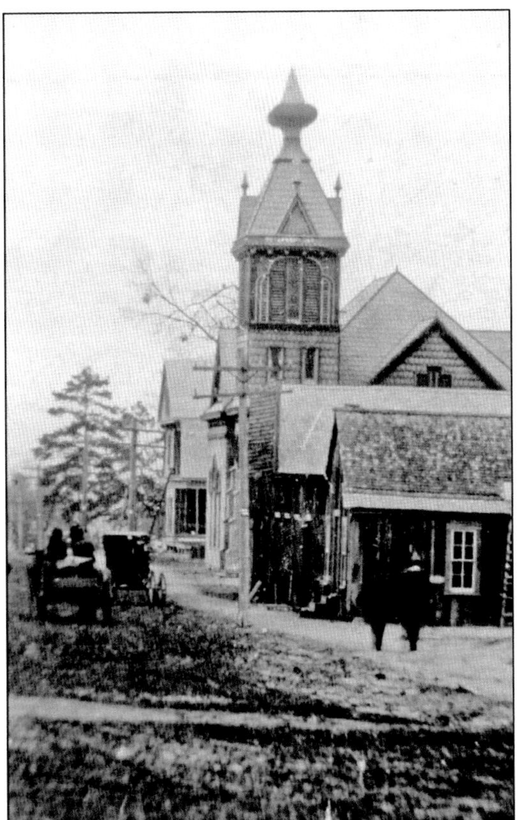

The First Methodist Church of Magnolia, located on East Main Street, was built in 1892. This church burned in an 1899 fire that destroyed the entire northwest block—from the town square to Madison Street. The new church was built in 1900 and remodeled in 1912. (Dr. Robert Walz.)

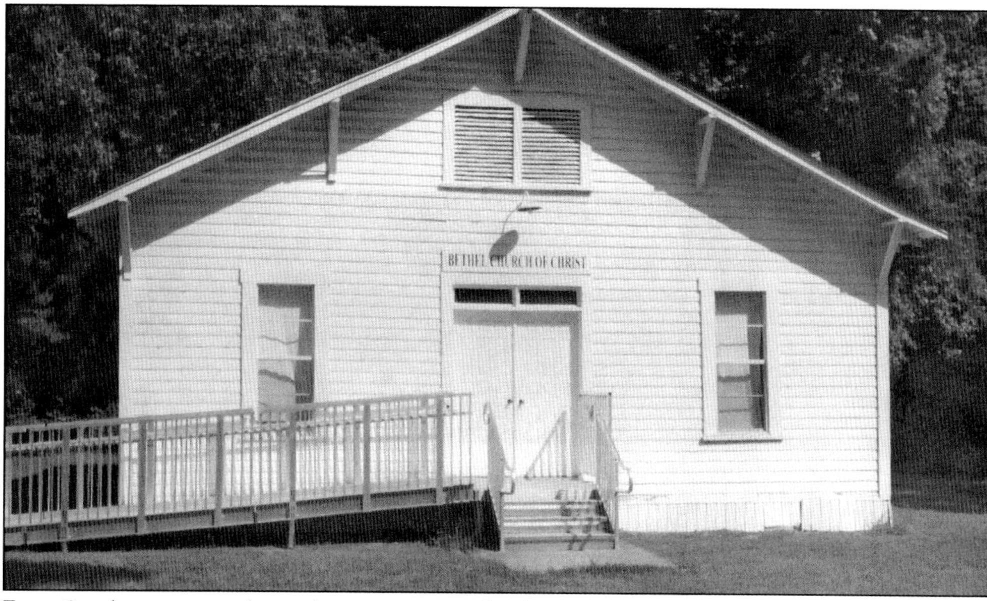

Every Sunday morning, devoted constituents make their way along winding roads and up and down rolling hills to finally settle among outstretched oak trees. There they embrace the welcoming sustenance found at Bethel Church of Christ. The church is located in the Bethel community in the northwest quadrant of Columbia County. This lovely old church is still in use and sits in a charming glade. On the day that this photograph was taken, the church had a beautiful new coat of white paint. (Authors.)

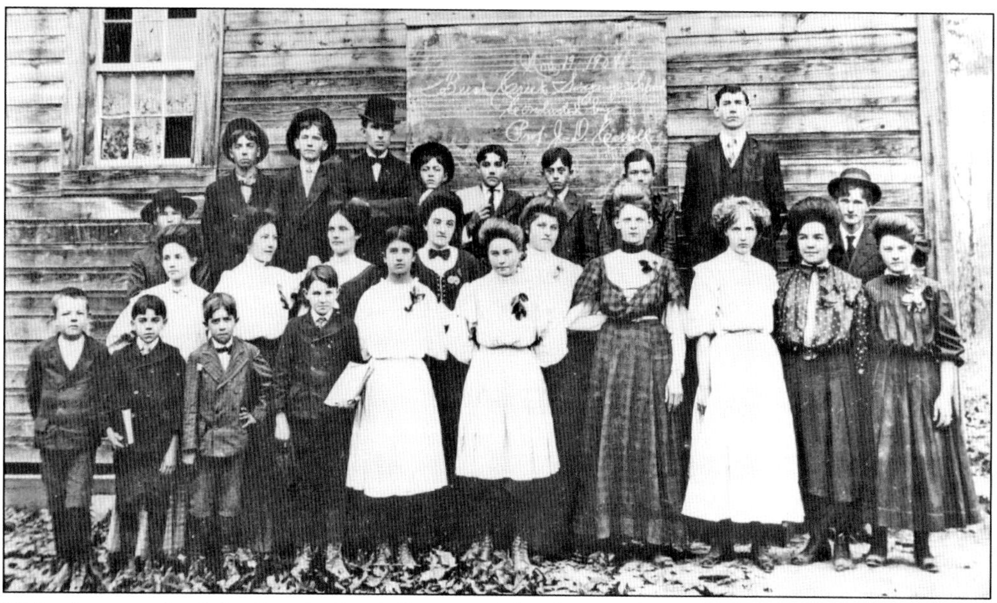

This photograph of the Beech Creek Singing School was taken on November 19, 1908. From left to right are (first row) Ben Warren, Earl Clark, Lloyd Waren, Albert Clark, Eunice Warren, and Edgel Sewell; (second row) Carrie Baird, Victoria Clark, Izzie Hudgens, Annie Clark, Lecie Kitchens, Emma Williams, Autna Dennis, Cleo Warren, and Laura Warren; (third row) Huse Lindsey, Clifton Warren, Calvin Carroll, John Morris, Cleveland Warren, Jesse Clark, Grover Warren, Jim Warren, teacher J.D. Carroll, and Roy Dempsey. (Louise Hudgens.)

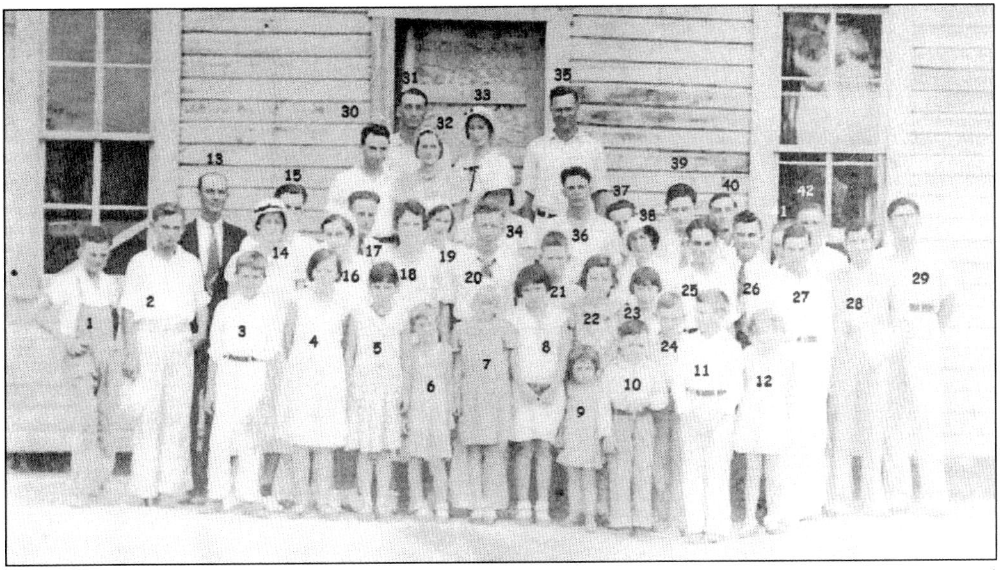

The Philadelphia Methodist Church Sunday school class is pictured here in 1934. In numerical order, they are from left to right Wesley Pearce, Dock Pearce, Raymond Pearce, unidentified, Ida Mae Elmore Sweet, Alta Mae Elmore Kirkpatrick, two unidentified, Kathleen Pearce Elmore, unidentified, Julious Elmore, Ernestine Gee, Ermon Campbell, Dorothy Willis Johnson, unidentified, Lola Camp Kirkpatrick, Curtis Willis, Frankie Elmore, Nettie Lou Camp, Willis M. Houck, Elbert Gee, Virginia Elmore, Mavis Houck, Maurice Gee, Hinton Elmore, Vernon Elmore, two unidentified, Pelton Nipper, Johnnie Camp, Vernon Johnson, Toye Camp, Bessie Elmore, unidentified, Myron Pearce, Courtney Pearce, unidentified, Vivian Elmore, Clifton Elmore, and three unidentified. (Barbara and William Powell.)

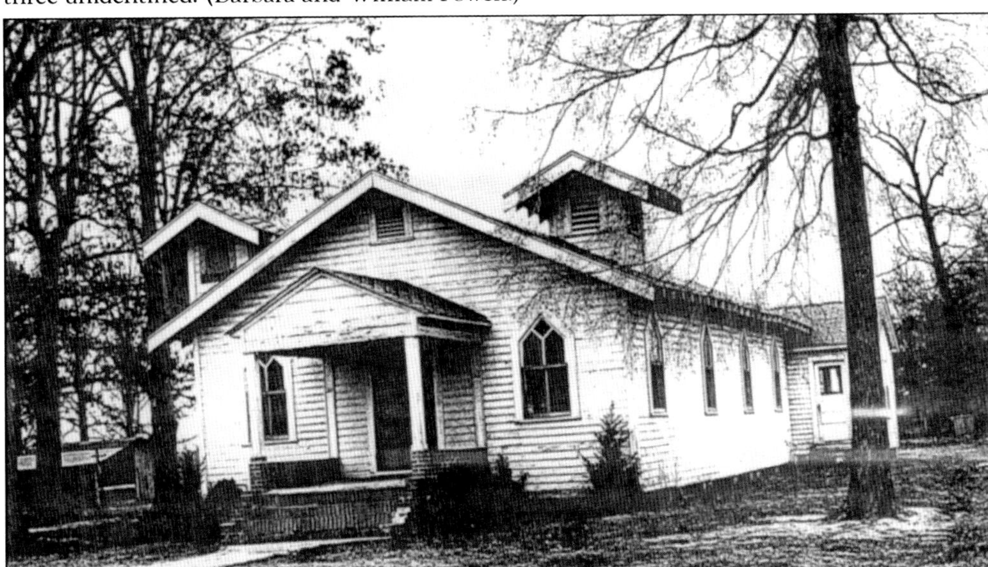

Taylor First Methodist Church was established in 1923 and had its beginnings in a small white frame building at the corner of Pope and Forest Streets. The congregation moved to new facilities in 1983. Early members included the Dodge, Gordon, Whitehead, Stuart, Hudnall, Beene, and Smith families. (*Southwest District.*)

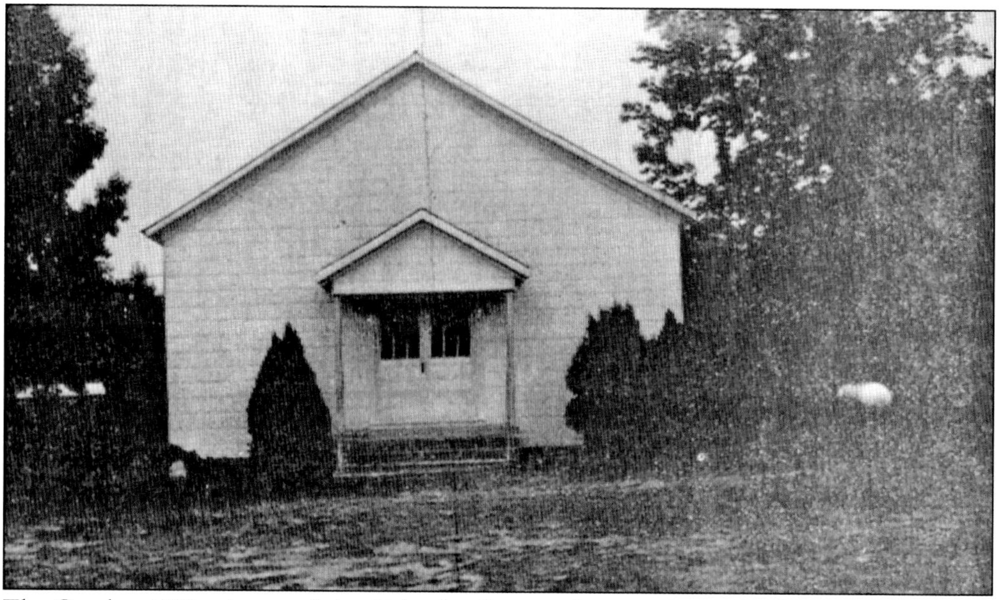

The October 1887 minutes of the Columbia Baptist Association read, "On motion a call for petitionary letters, the delegate from Brister Church presented a letter, which, after explanation was received, and the hand of fellowship was extended by the moderator." This photograph is from 1966. (*History of the Columbia Baptist Association.*)

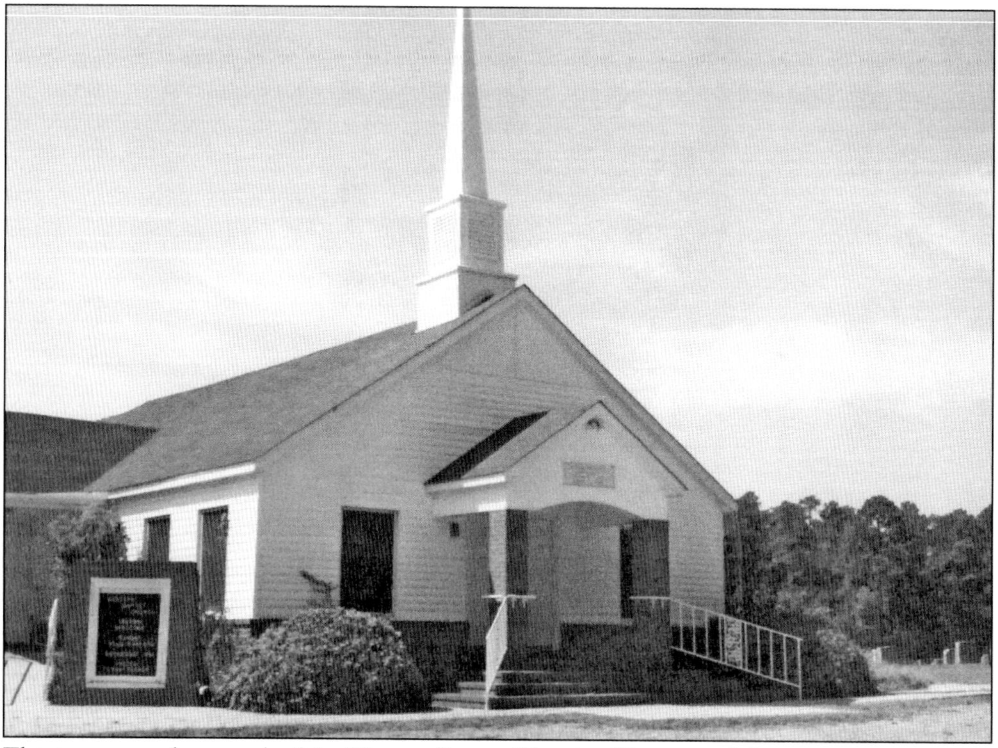

This is a recent photograph of the Western Baptist Church of Emerson, Arkansas. It was organized in 1863 with 19 charter members. The association records of 1866 show the membership to be 76 persons. (Authors.)

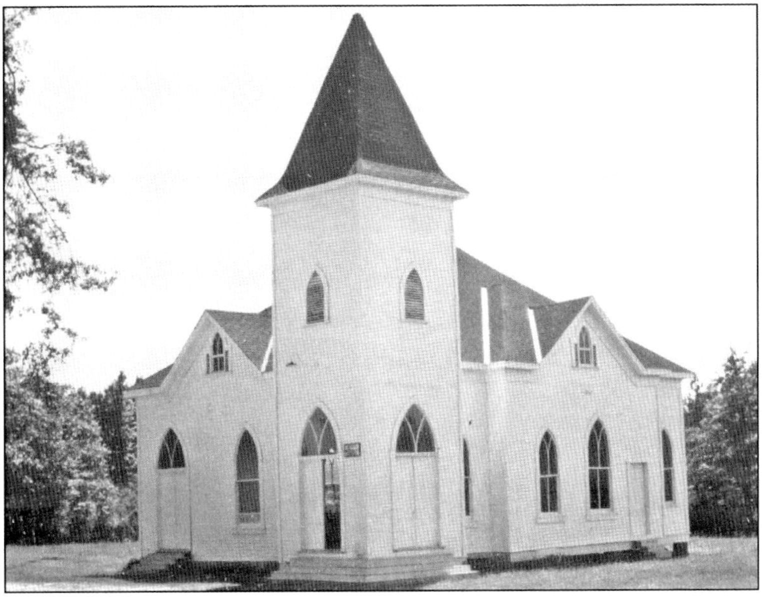

This classic building is the Atlanta Methodist Church, constructed in 1902. Church services were held here until 1967. The church was recently converted to a private home by Richard and Sarah Shepherd. (Marie Shepherd.)

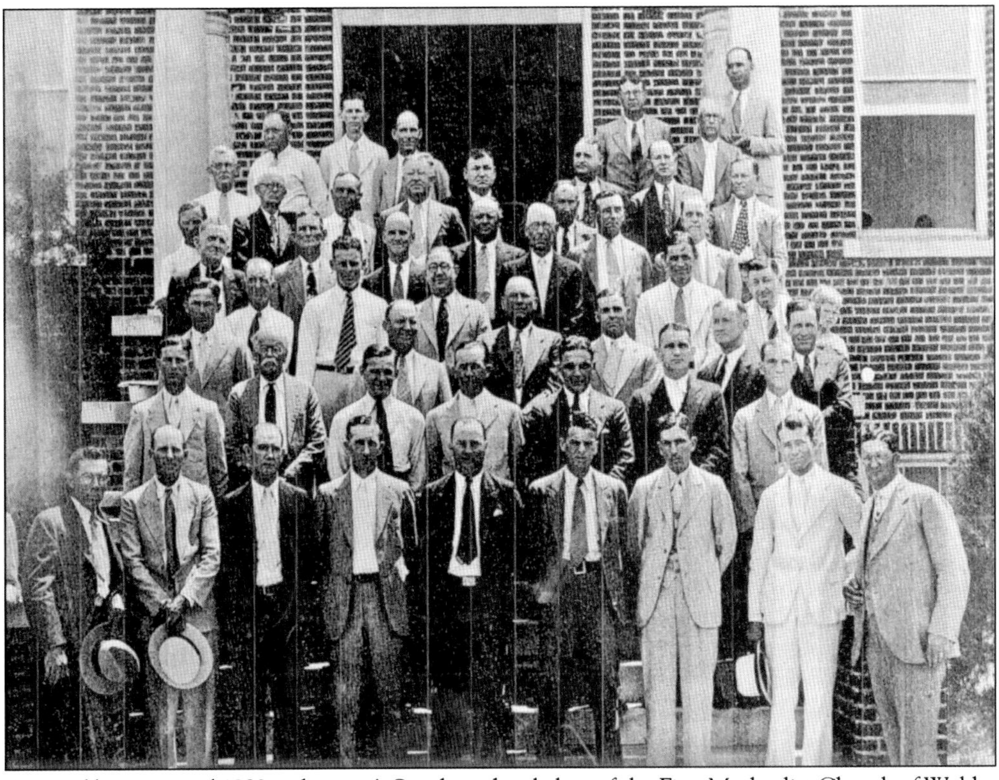

Pictured here around 1932 is the men's Sunday school class of the First Methodist Church of Waldo, Arkansas. Almost every man in the photograph is wearing a suit coat, all have on neckties, and many are carrying hats. (D.J. Fincher.)

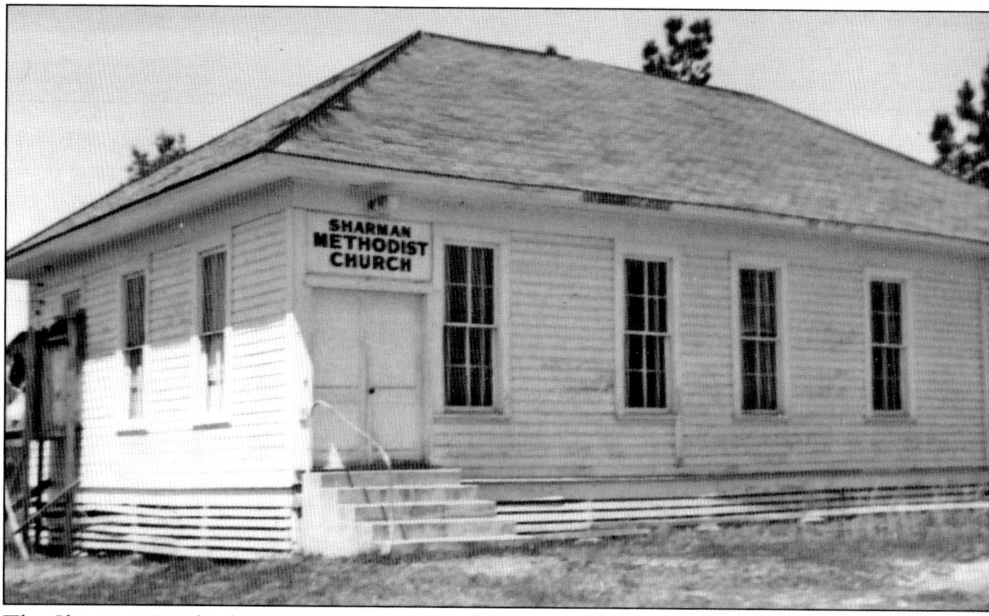

The Sharman Methodist Church was founded in the early 1900s. A new building was erected in 1926 on land purchased from the John Keith estate; it also served as a school for the community. Charter members included Lizzie Welbourn, Dr. J.J. Jack, Dr. A.W. Keith, and Mary Keith. New Hope and Sharman Methodist Churches merged in the 1960s, and at that time the joint church was called Unity Methodist Church. (Dorothy Whaley.)

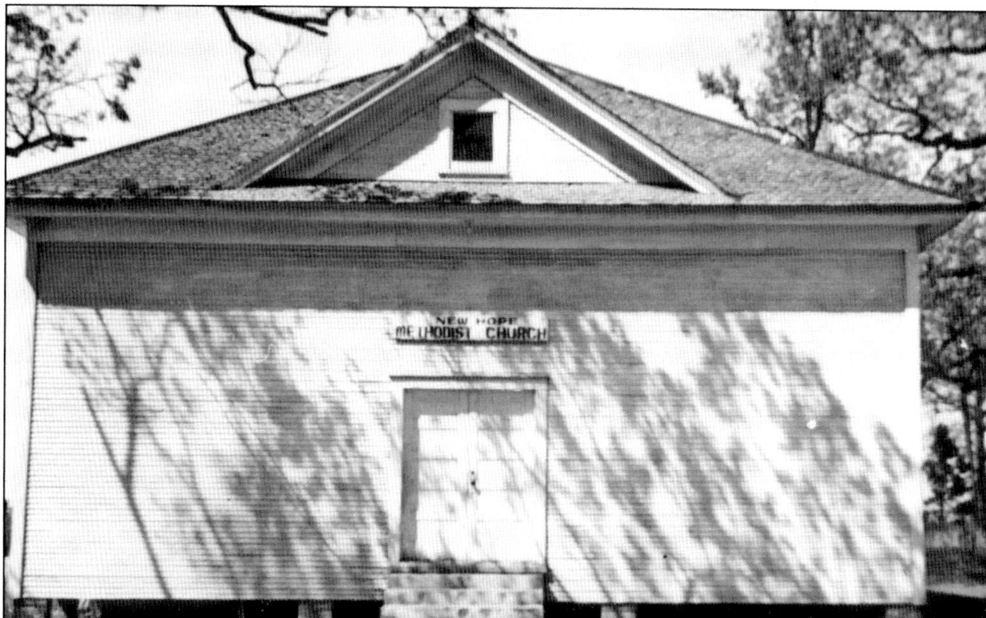

New Hope Methodist Church in Bussey, Arkansas, was founded before 1898. Indications are that a log building on the site served as the sanctuary before the church kept official records. Charter members recorded include A.W. Davis, Mary F. Davis, Lucretia Bussey, Jennie Garrett, Annie Barnett, Clara Christian, and G.B. Davis. Both Methodist and Baptist services were conducted in this church for over 30 years. (Dorothy Whaley.)

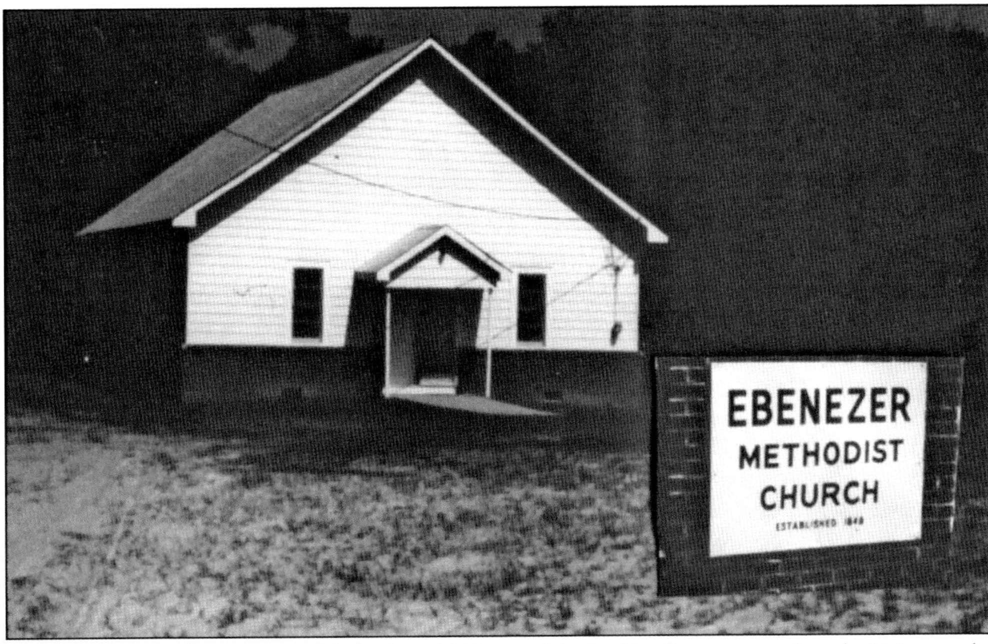

Ebenezer Methodist was established in 1849 as a Methodist Protestant church. Prior to the building of the church pictured here, members met in a New Hope schoolhouse two miles to the southeast. Early families included the Wells, Carterics, Myatts, Wilsons, Crumplers, Franklins, Shannons, and Allens. (Columbia County Library.)

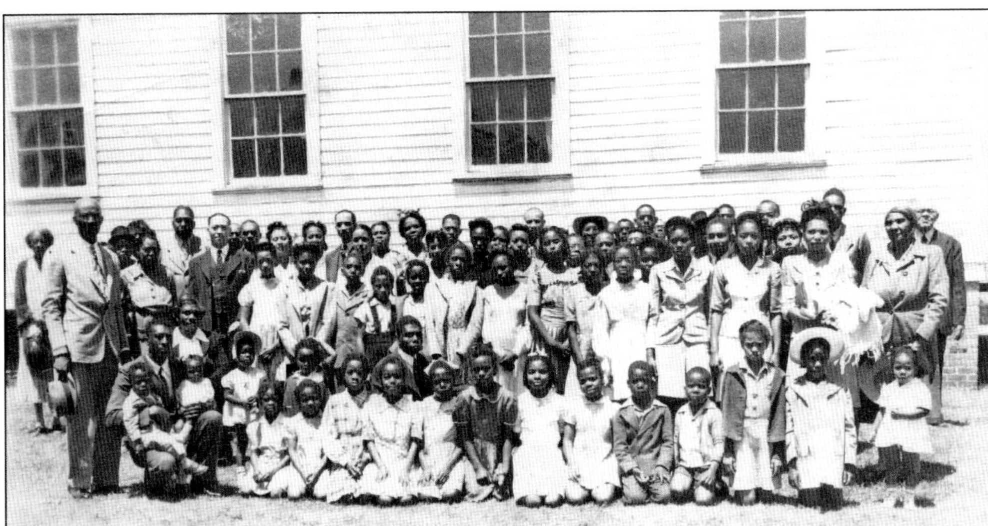

Bethlehem Baptist Church was established in 1868. Pictured in the back row, fourth from the left, is F.B. Buffington. Four persons to the right of Buffington is B.G. Williams, who started Walker School. On the far right in the second row, Mattie Brigham is holding a baby. The woman gazing over her right shoulder is Claudie Mae Shephard Hayes. (Helen Hildreth.)

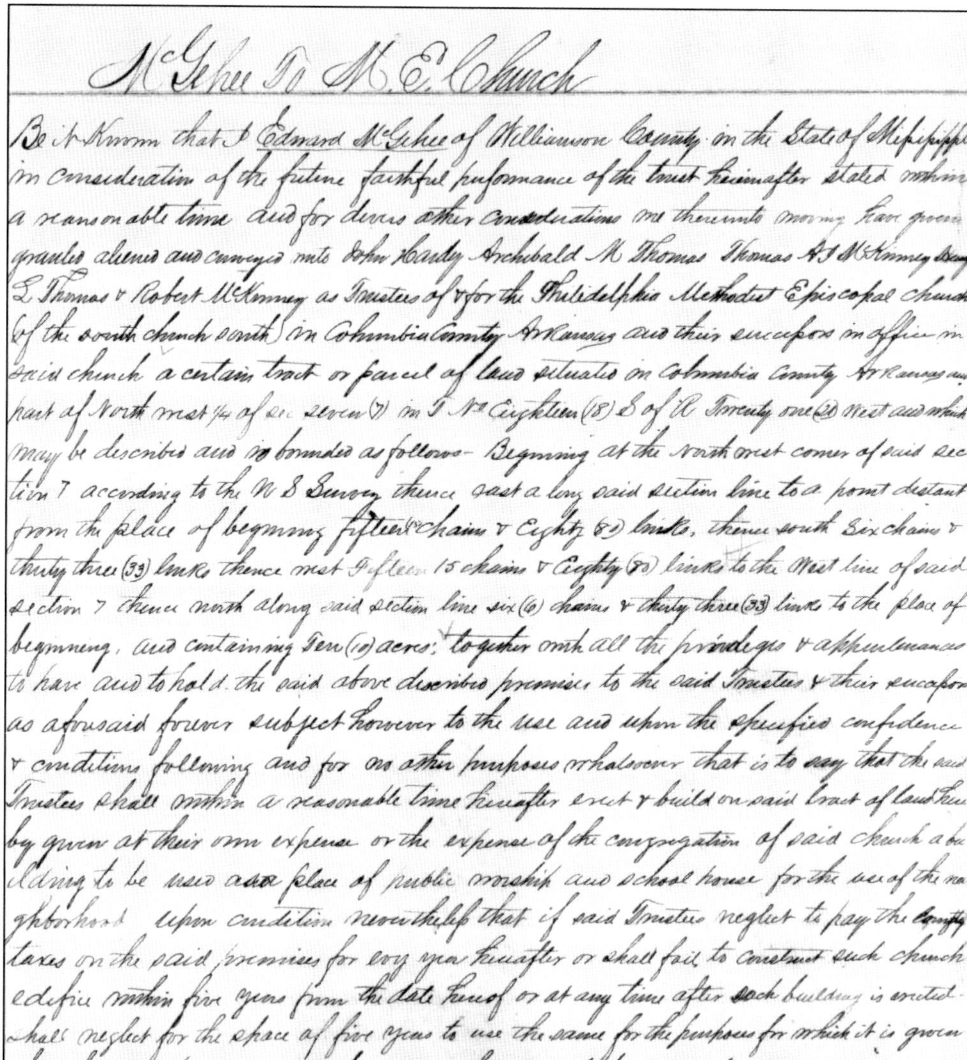

McGehee To M. E. Church

Be it Known that I Edward McGehee of Wilkinson County in the State of Mississippi in consideration of the future faithful performance of the trust hereinafter stated within a reasonable time and for divers other considerations me thereunto moving have given granted aliened and conveyed unto John Hardy Archibald M Thomas Thomas A J McKinney Benj L Thomas & Robert McKinney as Trustees of & for the Philadelphia Methodist Episcopal church (of the south church south) in Columbia County Arkansas and their successors in office in said church a certain tract or parcel of land situated in Columbia County Arkansas and part of North west 1/4 of sec seven (7) in T No Eighteen (18) S of R Twenty one (21) West and which may be described and is bounded as follows- Beginning at the North west corner of said section 7 according to the U S Survey thence east along said section line to a point distant from the place of beginning fifteen chains & Eighty (80) links, thence south Six chains & thirty three (33) links thence west Fifteen 15 chains & Eighty (80) links to the West line of said section 7 thence north along said section line six (6) chains & thirty three (33) links to the place of beginning, and containing Ten (10) acres; together with all the privileges & appurtenances to have and to hold the said above described premises to the said Trustees & their successors as aforesaid forever subject however to the use and upon the specified confidence & conditions following and for no other purposes whatsoever that is to say that the said Trustees shall within a reasonable time hereafter erect & build on said tract of land hereby given at their own expense or the expense of the congregation of said church a building to be used as a place of public worship and school house for the use of the neighborhood upon condition nevertheless that if said Trustees neglect to pay the County taxes on the said premises for every year hereafter or shall fail to construct such church edifice within five years from the date hereof or at any time after such building is erected shall neglect for the space of five years to use the same for the purposes for which it is given then the said premises & all buildings thereon are to be revert to & vest in me or my heirs & the same shall belong to me as fully & effectually as if this deed had not been executed & the same shall thereafter become null & void - And I do covenant with the said Trustees & their successors that so long as they observe the terms & conditions of this gift they shall hold the said premises free from all claims from me or my heirs for the use aforesaid forever As witness my hand & seal this 27th day of August AD 1859

Edward McGehee (seal)

Mary B McGehee (seal)

State of Mississippi

In 1859, Edward and Mary McGehee of Mississippi deeded 10 acres of land to the Philadelphia Methodist Church. The sanctuary was once used as both a church and a school and is located about seven miles southwest of Magnolia on County Road 15. The trustees were Archibald Thomas, Henry Thomas, and A.J. McKinney. The son of Archibald Thomas, Lewis Thomas, was the first preacher who served the church. Five churches have been erected on or near the original site. The present church was built in 1950. (Authors.)

Three

SCHOOLS AND ACTIVITIES

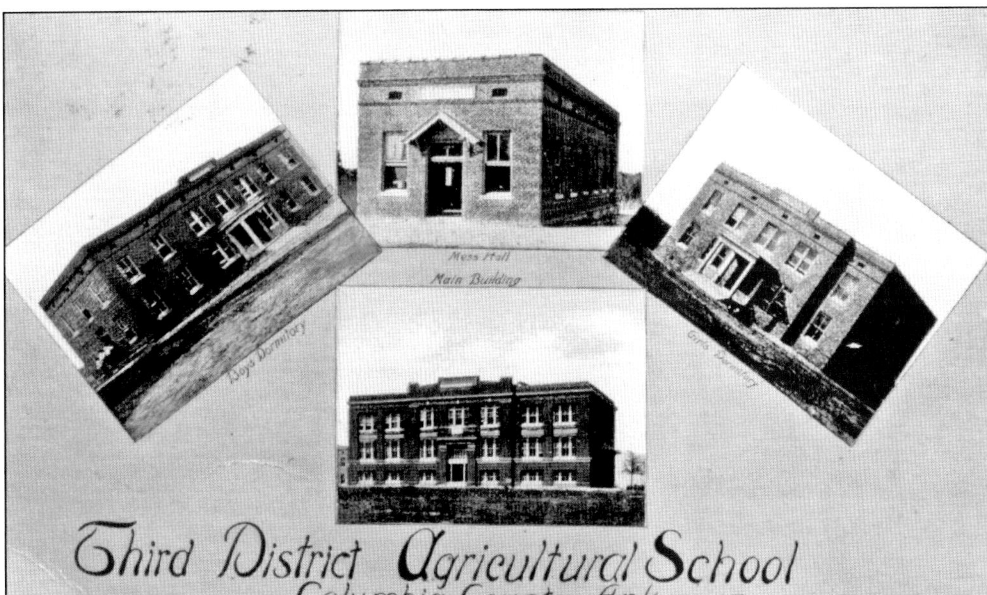

An interesting collage depicts the Third District Agricultural School as the campus appeared in 1912. This institution at Magnolia was one of four schools of agriculture established by authorization of Arkansas Act 100 of 1909. The institution served from January 3, 1911, to June 30, 1925, as a high school for boys and girls living in southwest Arkansas in school districts without four-year high school programs. In 1925, the state legislature authorized the school to add two years of college work to its curriculum and to change its name to Agricultural & Mechanical College, Third District. (Dr. Robert Walz.)

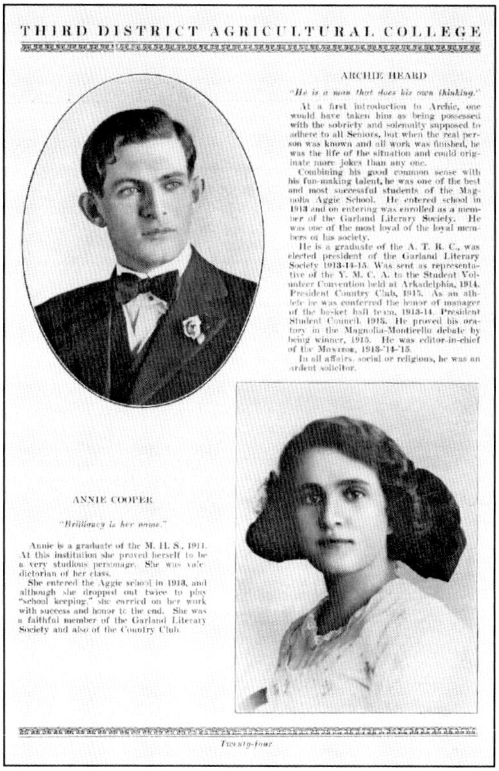

THIRD DISTRICT AGRICULTURAL COLLEGE

ARCHIE HEARD

"He is a man that does his own thinking."

At a first introduction to Archie, one would have taken him as being possessed with the sobriety and solemnity supposed to adhere to all Seniors, but when the real person was known and all work was finished, he was the life of the situation and could originate more jokes than any one.

Combining his good common sense with his fun-making talent, he was one of the best and most successful students of the Magnolia Aggie School. He entered school in 1913 and on entering was enrolled as a member of the Garland Literary Society. He was one of the most loyal of the loyal members of his society.

He is a graduate of the A. T. R. C., was elected president of the Garland Literary Society 1913-14-15. Was sent as representative of the Y. M. C. A. to the Student Volunteer Convention held at Arkadelphia, 1914. President Country Club, 1915. As an athlete he was conferred the honor of manager of the basket ball team, 1913-14. President Student Council, 1915. He proved his oratory in the Magnolia-Monticello debate by being winner, 1915. He was editor-in-chief of the MONITOR, 1913-'14-'15.

In all affairs, social or religious, he was an ardent solicitor.

ANNIE COOPER

"Brilliancy is her name."

Annie is a graduate of the M. H. S., 1911. At this institution she proved herself to be a very studious personage. She was valedictorian of her class.

She entered the Aggie school in 1913, and although she dropped out twice to play "school keeping," she carried on her work with success and honor to the end. She was a faithful member of the Garland Literary Society and also of the Country Club.

Twenty-four

The 1915 *Monitor* Third District Agricultural School's senior class, in its entirety, had four graduates. Archie Heard is on the left, and Annie Cooper is on the right. Elbert E. Austin was college president at the time, and the editor in chief of the annual was Archie. (Columbia County Library.)

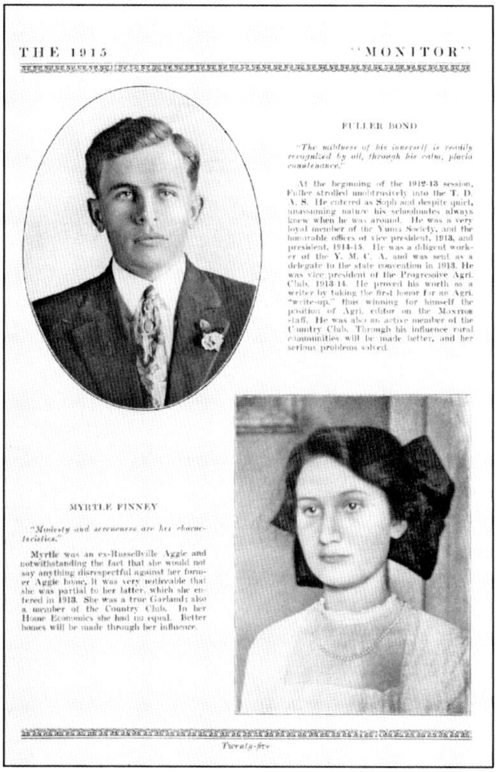

THE 1915 "MONITOR"

FULLER BOND

"The mildness of his innerself is readily recognized by all, through his calm, placid countenance."

At the beginning of the 1912-13 session, Fuller strolled unobtrusively into the T. D. A. S. He entered as Soph and despite quiet, unassuming nature his schoolmates always knew when he was around. He was a very loyal member of the Yuma Society, and the honorable offices of vice president, 1913, and president, 1914-15. He was a diligent worker of the Y. M. C. A. and was sent as a delegate to the state convention in 1913. He was vice president of the Progressive Agri. Club, 1913-14. He proved his worth as a writer by taking the first honor for an Agri. "write-up," thus winning for himself the position of Agri. editor on the MONITOR staff. He was also an active member of the Country Club. Through his influence rural communities will be made better, and her serious problems solved.

MYRTLE FINNEY

"Modesty and sereneness are her characteristics."

Myrtle was an ex-Russellville Aggie and notwithstanding the fact that she would not say anything disrespectful against her former Aggie home, it was very noticeable that she was partial to her latter, which she entered in 1913. She was a true Garland; also a member of the Country Club. In her Home Economics she had no equal. Better homes will be made through her influence.

Twenty-five

The 1915 *Monitor* Third District Agricultural School's remaining senior class members are shown here, with Fuller Bond on the left and Myrtle Finney on the right. The motto of the class was the following: "Not the end but the beginning." Their colors were turquoise-blue and steel-gray, and the class flower was the white rose. (Columbia County Library.)

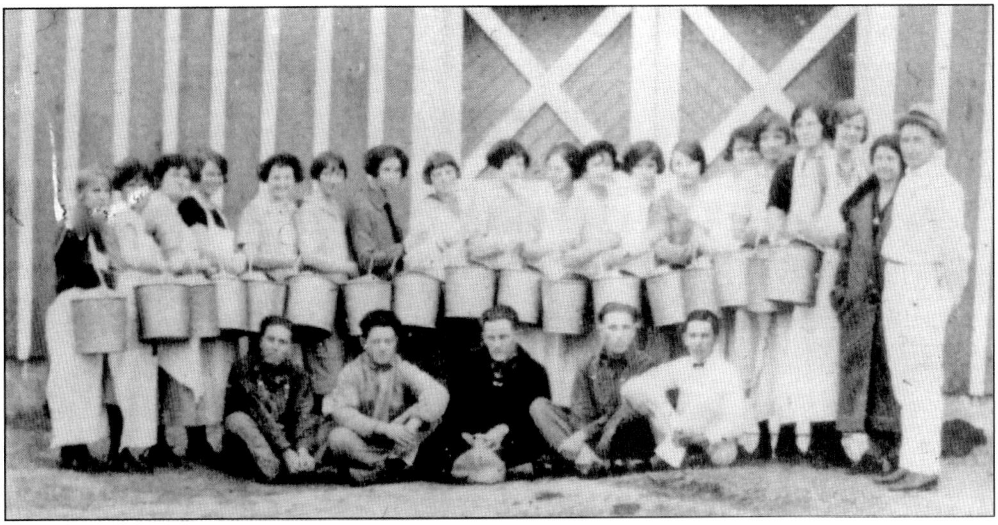

The 1925 A&M milking squad's theme was "earning and learning." Beneath this photograph, the caption reads: "It has been the policy of the College to lend deserving boys and girls one or two cows from the dairy herd, so long as these lasted, and to permit other students to bring profitable cows and milk them at the dairy barn. Each cow is charged with the feed she consumes and the profit goes to the boy or girl who milks her. Most of these boys and girls have been making their board the past year by so doing. Considerable fortitude and energy are required to enable a young man or a young lady to go to the dairy barn three times a day and milk a cow; however, that kind of a boy or girl will succeed in educating himself or herself and will develop into the men and women who prosper in this world." (*Mule Rider.*)

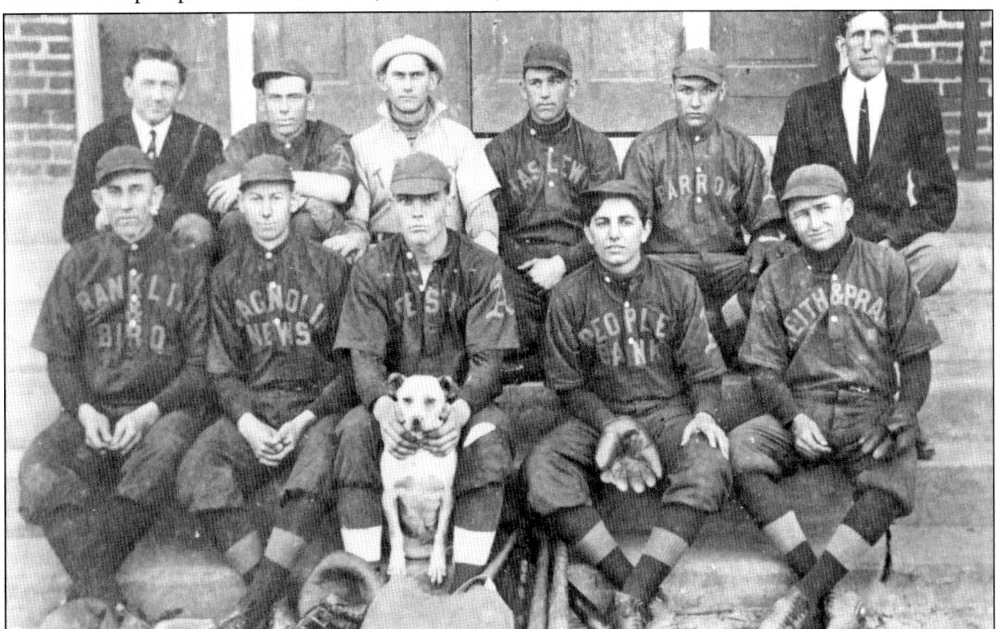

The Third District Agricultural School boasted a very impressive baseball team during the 1913–1914 school year. The players included, from left to right, (first row) Chester Green, Alton Sawyer, Francis W. Dawson, Henry Tate, and Bennie Chaffin; (second row) coach G.R. Turrentine, ? Souter, Conrad Lewis, Earl Stonecipher, Madison Sturgis, and manager Tal Picket. (Ruth Tate.)

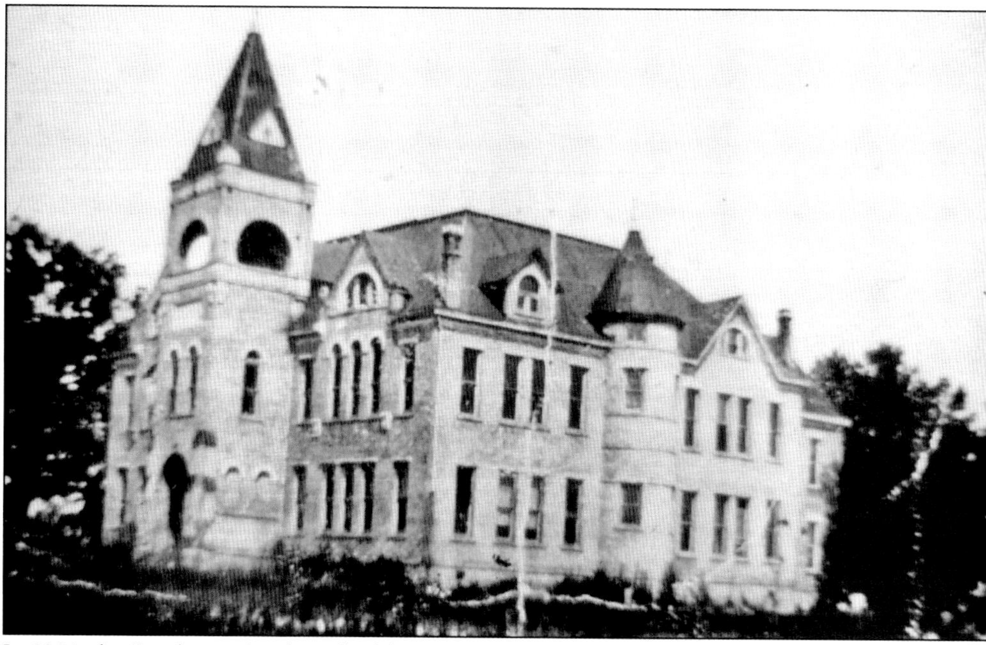

In 1904, the Southwest Academy building had 500 books in the library. Eleven grades were taught in 1903, seven in the lower grades and four in the high school. Six grades were paid from public funds, and the others were supported by tuition. There were from 310 to 365 students in daily attendance, with the total enrollment reaching 435. (Huddy Baker.)

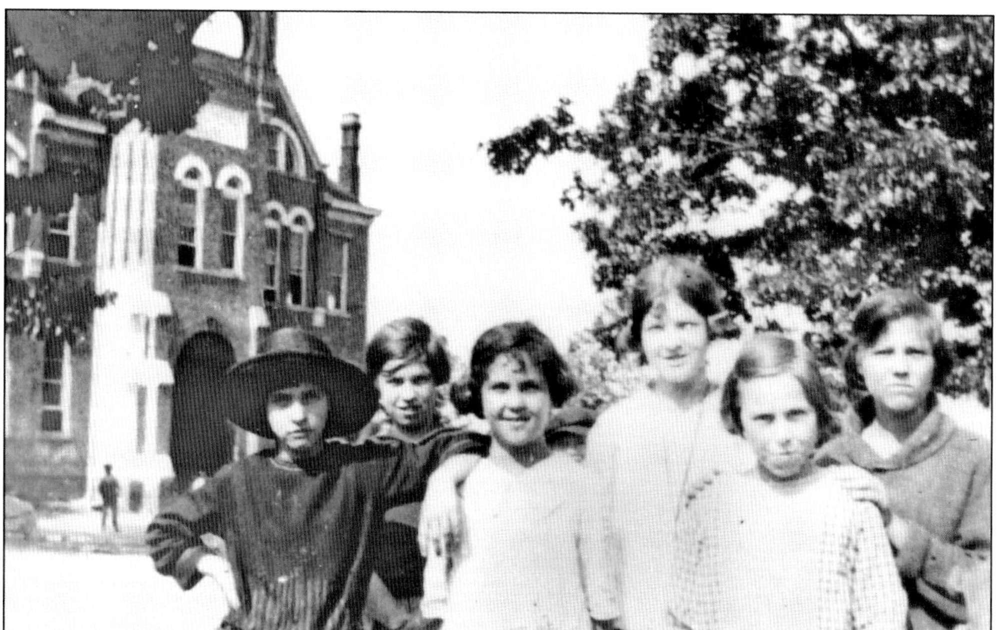

Schoolgirls pose outside the Southwest Academy in 1923. From left to right are Mary Helen Pittman Dodson, Mary O'Banion, Glenda Burns, Evalena Stevens, Lois Elmore Clayton, and Mary Hughes Gill. The Southwest Academy building was later used as the Magnolia Elementary School until it was destroyed by fire. (Walker Pittman.)

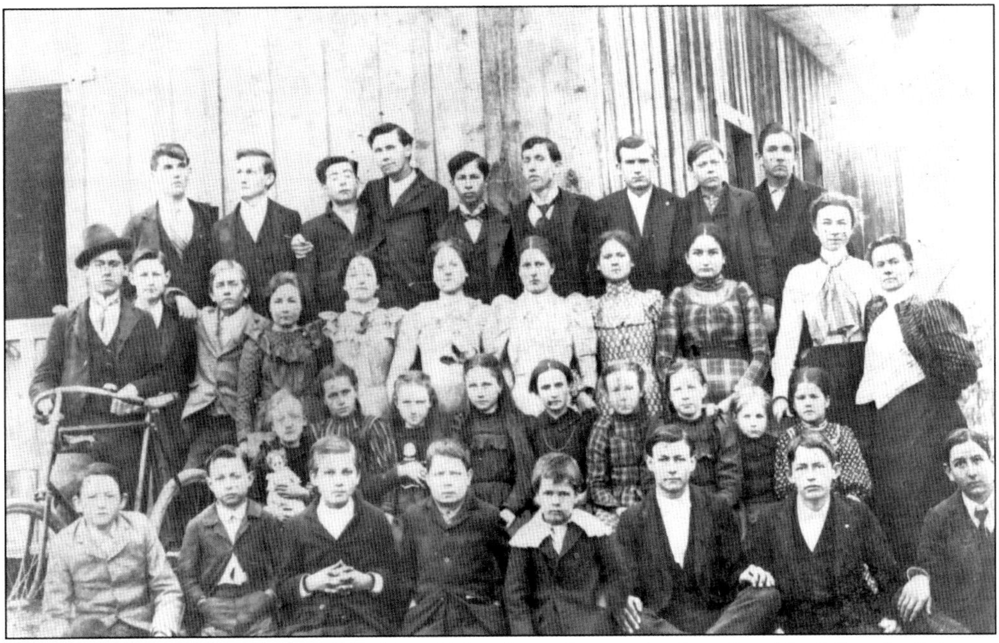

The 1895–1896 student body of the Zion School stands outside the school building for "picture taking" day. Ben Clary (third row, far left) shows off his mode of transportation. The Zion School was located between Calhoun and Atlanta. (Viola Hanson Clary.)

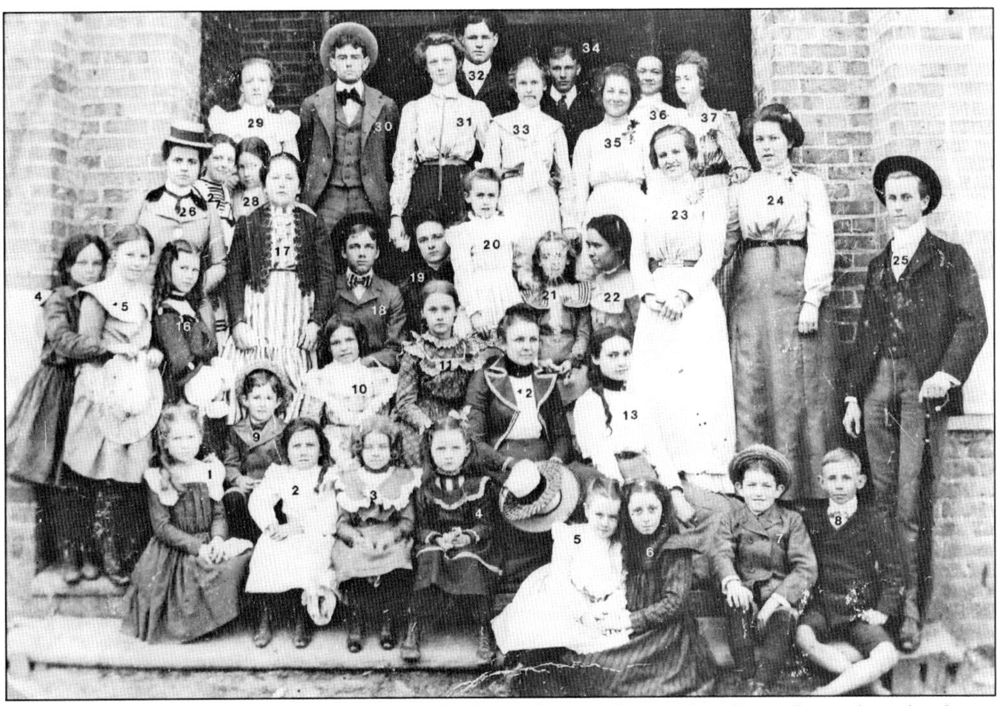

This photograph shows the 1898 student body of the Southwest Academy dressed in the finest fashion of the day. The decision to build the large, two-story brick building was made in 1894, and the academy became a preparatory school of high standard. (Nettie Hicks Killgore.)

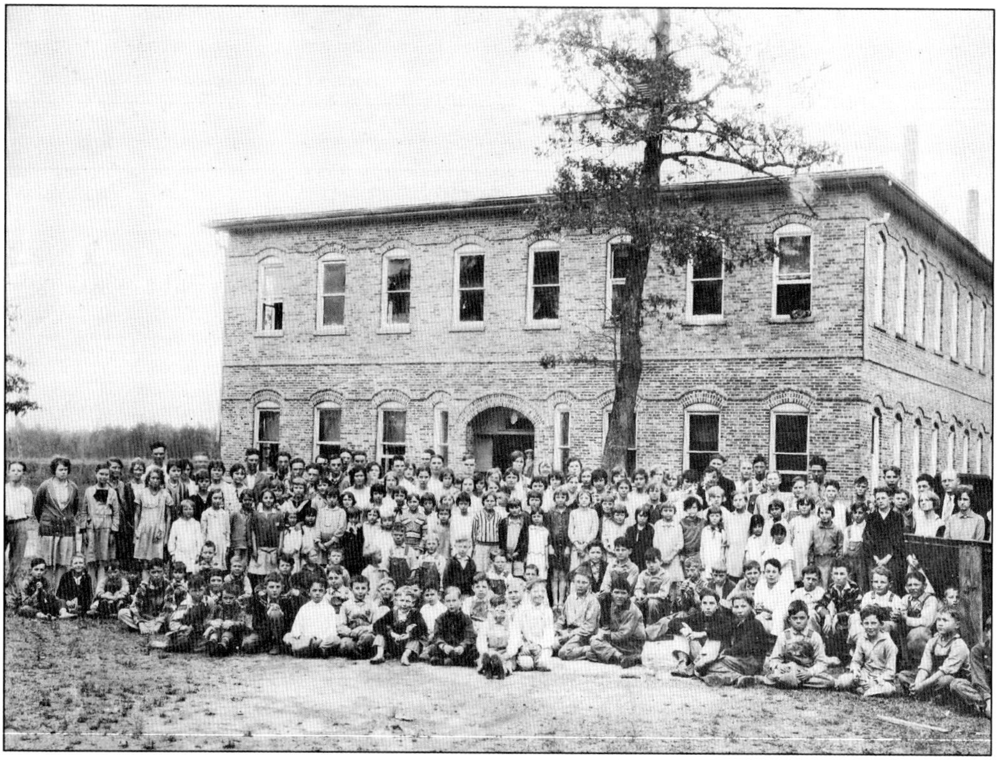

Taylor, Arkansas, was among the latter towns settled in Columbia County, but as evidenced by the large student body, the school built in 1900 was a welcome addition to the community. Classes were held in the two-story building until it was destroyed by fire in 1931. (Ronald Orrick.)

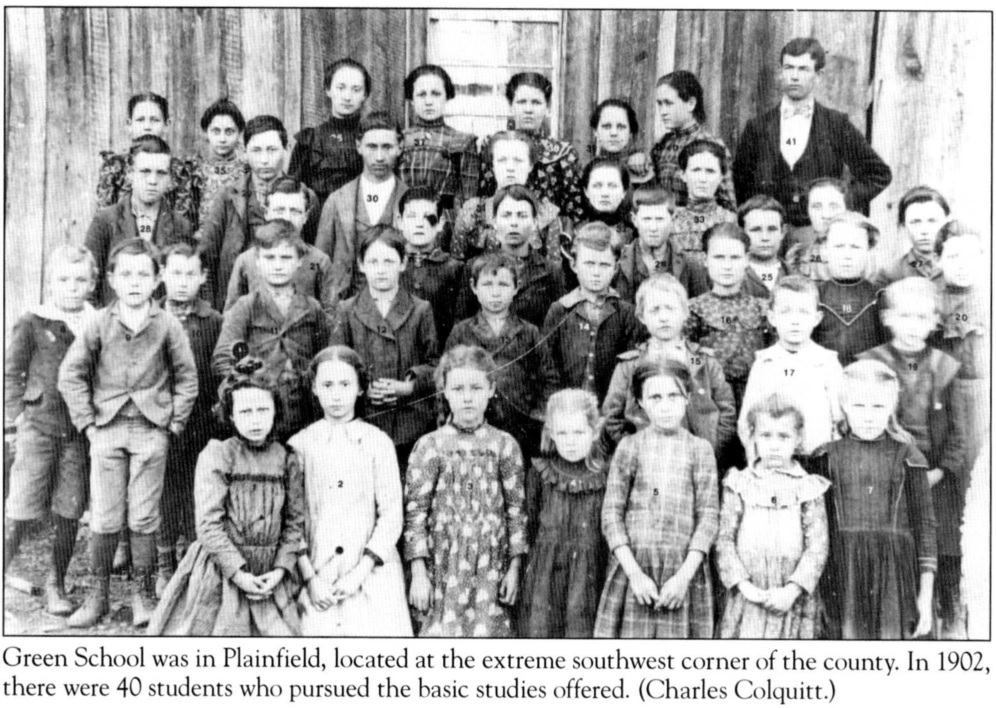

Green School was in Plainfield, located at the extreme southwest corner of the county. In 1902, there were 40 students who pursued the basic studies offered. (Charles Colquitt.)

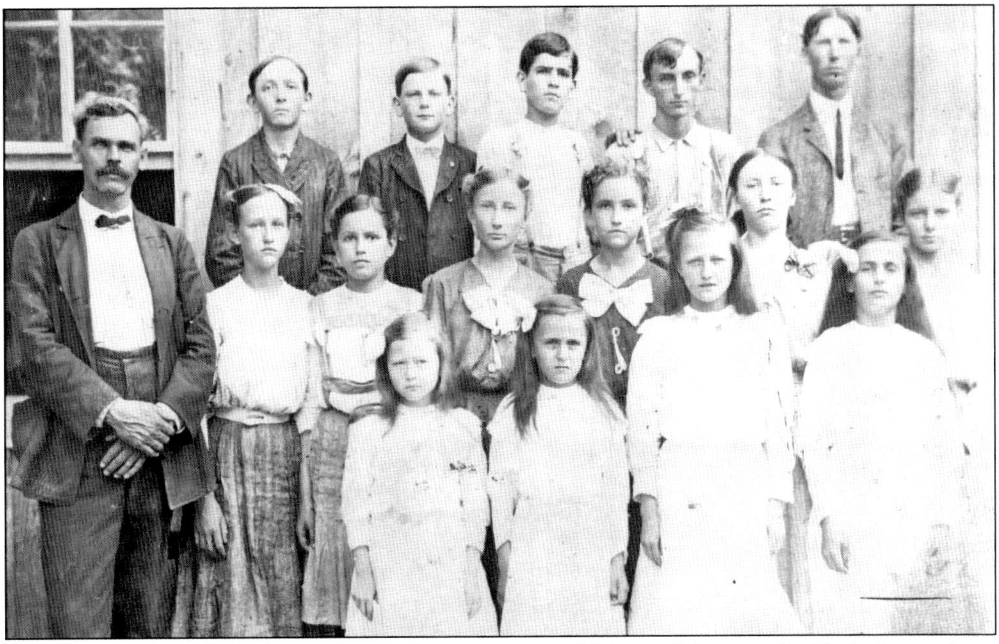

Holly Grove School was located six miles southeast of Village, Arkansas. In 1905, the students included, from left to right, (first row) Cassie Braswell, Eva Lewis, Ola Braswell, and Gladys Lewis; (second row) Mr. Dixon (teacher), Marcy Vinson, Lily McCall, Ruth Lewis, Mary McCall, Jessie Lewis, and Minnie Vines; (third row) Earnest Timmons, Barney Giles, Lawrence McCall, Percy Vines, and John Lewis. (Ruth Lewis Hughes.)

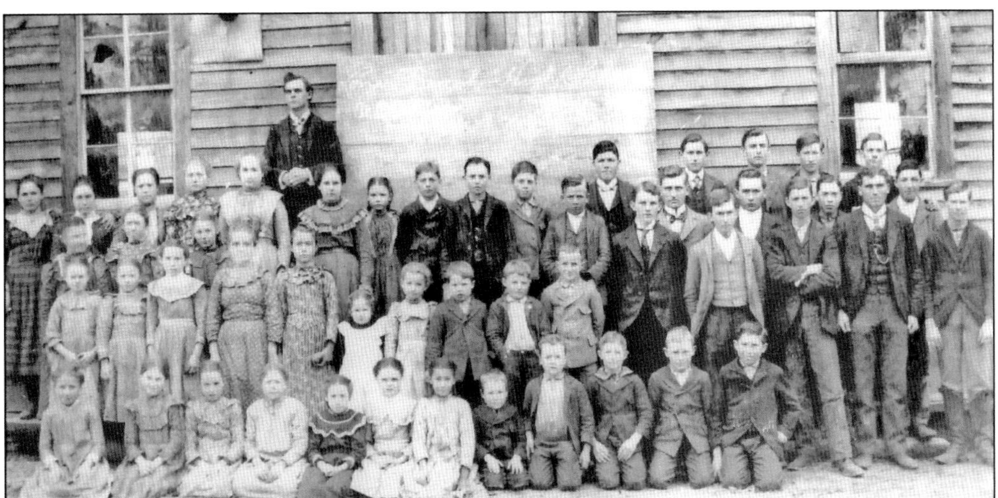

Lone Beech High School was located 10 miles from Magnolia on Burnt Bridge Road. The school term from 1899 to 1901 boasted an attendance of 35, and the teacher was W.E. "Emmet" Atkinson. Atkinson would later become county judge, serving from 1927 to 1930. (Dorothy Whaley.)

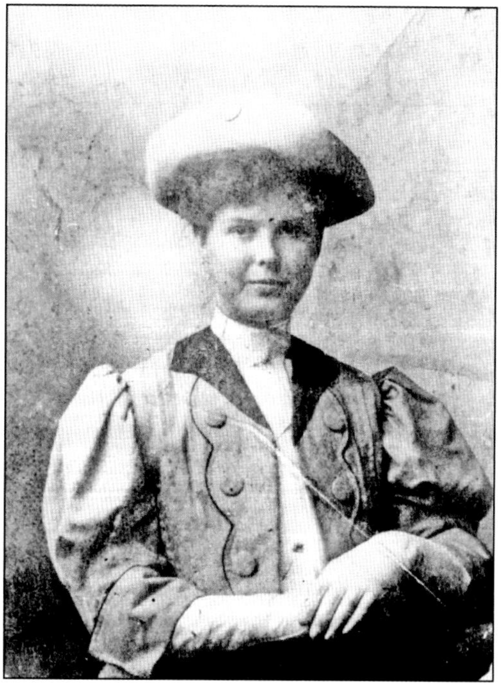

Dressed in the style of the era, lovely Maud Wilson is pictured in her graduation dress; she was part of Southwest Academy's class of 1907. She later married J.M. "Buck" Bird. (Dr. Robert Walz.)

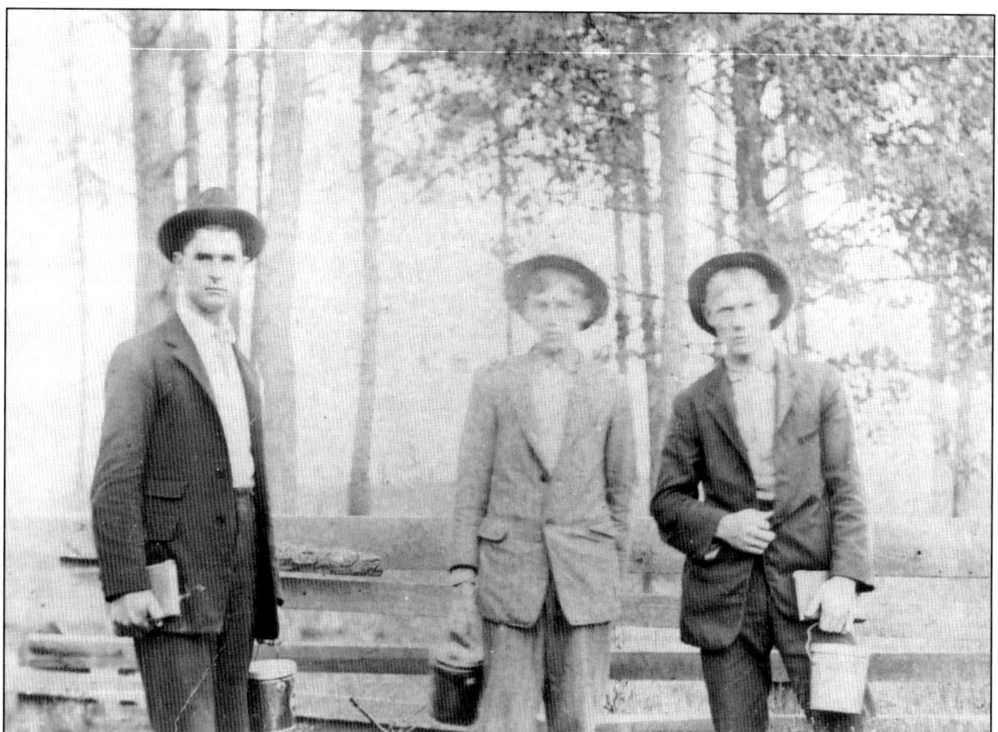

An instructor and students pose for a photograph outside of Cypress Fork/Mount Pisgah School. The image, taken in the summer of 1908, includes from left to right, Prof. Jim P. Litton, Ruby Clifton Pharr, and William Bert McDonald out on the school grounds for lunch. Note the fancy lunch pails! (Ivan V. Pharr.)

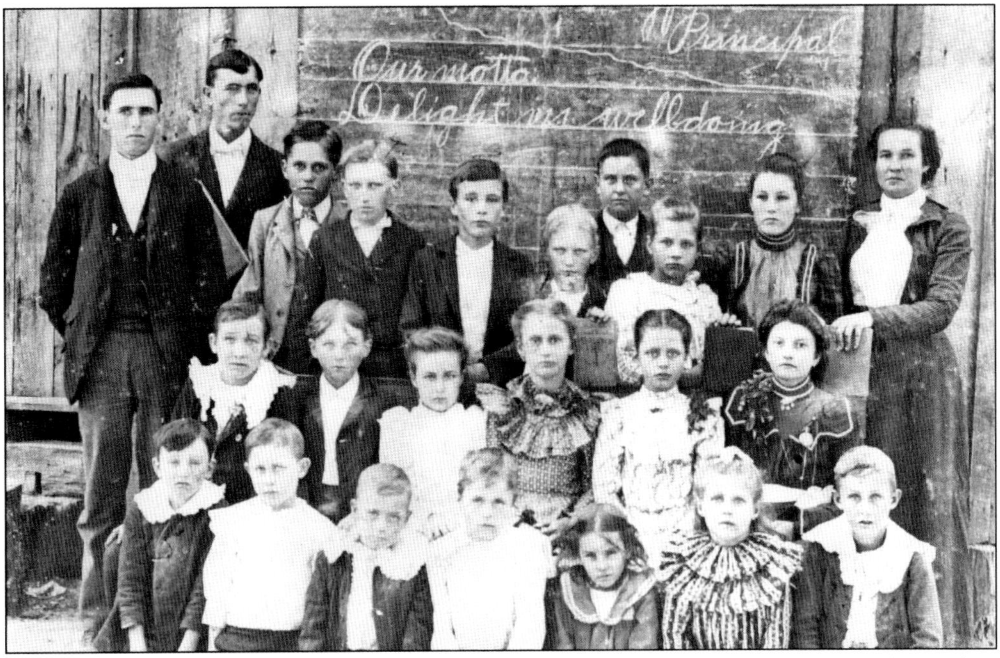

"Delight in well doing" was the high-minded motto of the New Prospect School, located in south central Columbia County. The student body is pictured in front of the school building on September 20, 1901. (Melbalene Olds Benefield.)

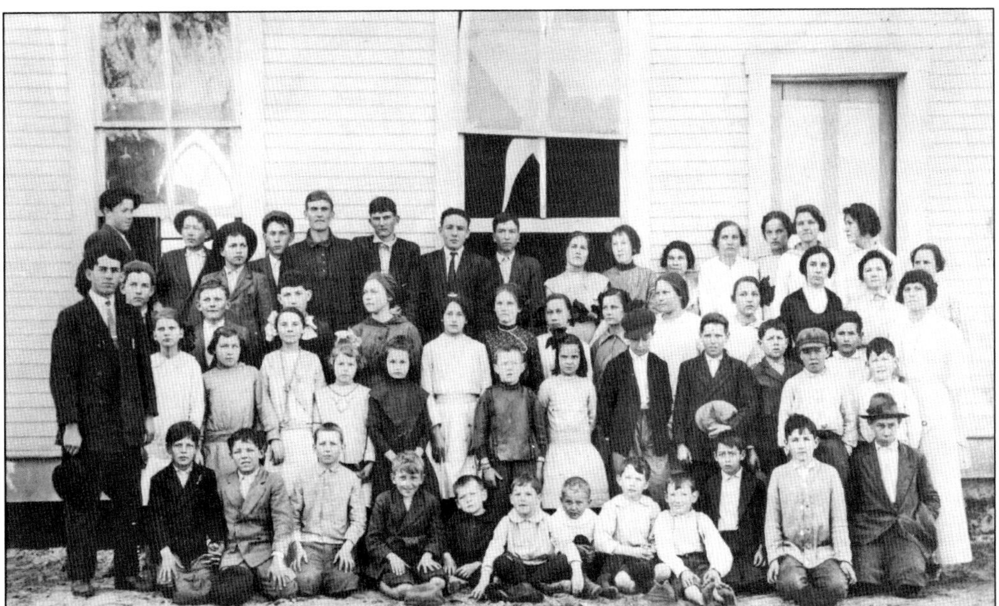

Pupils at the Atlanta School pose in front of the church that served as their school in 1914. The student classes ranged from primary to young adult men and women. Annie Mae Messer was the primary teacher, a daughter of a Methodist minister. (Irma Doss.)

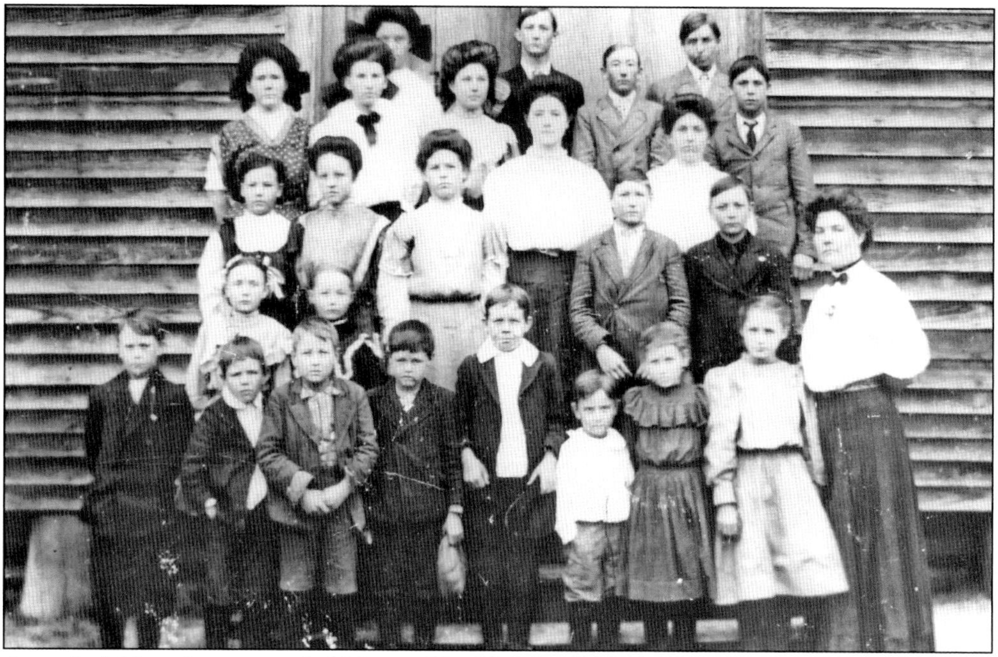

A total of 26 students attended Union Chapel School during the 1907–1908 term, and their teacher was Ethel Pittman. Union Chapel was located about four miles east of Magnolia. (Nora Jones Paschal.)

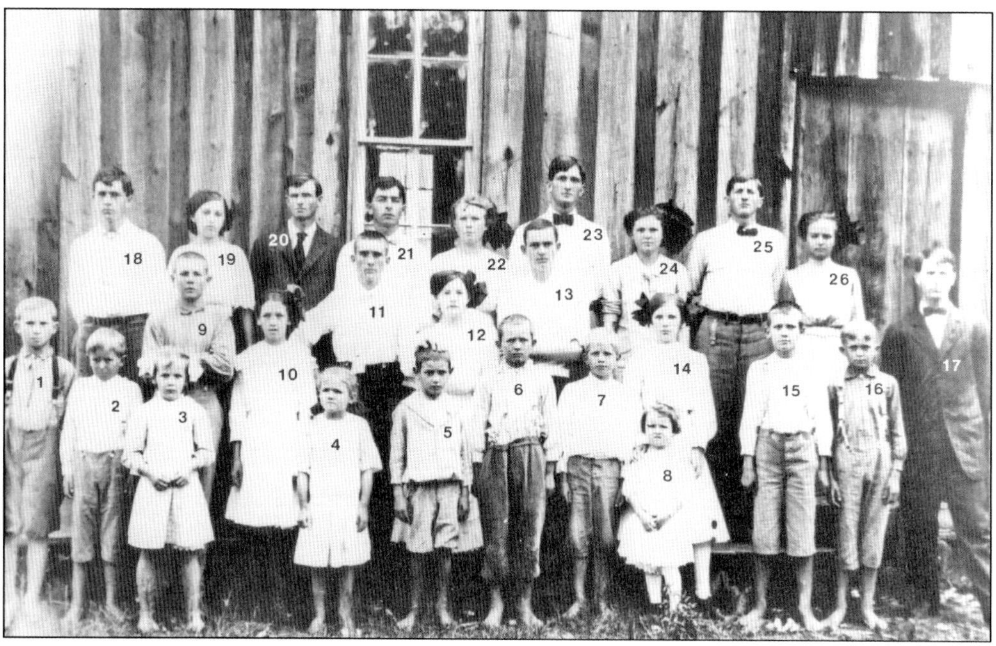

Center School was located three miles east of Calhoun. In 1910 and 1911, students with the surnames of Bird, Dees, Booth, Crisp, Gunnels, Baker, and Taylor attended classes at this rural school. The teacher was Jim Jones. Descendants of these early scholars continue to live and work in Columbia County. (Elvie Baker Booth.)

Ephram Brooks is believed to be the first African American educator in Columbia County. According to an interview with "Uncle" Alfred Monroe Frierson (a former slave), the first black educators in Columbia County were Joe Statley, who taught at Magnolia; Joe Brooks, who taught at Calhoun; Mary Brooks, who taught at Reid's Schoolhouse (located two or three miles from Magnolia on Calhoun Road); and B.G. Bryant, the instructor at College Hill. (Rachael Lowe.)

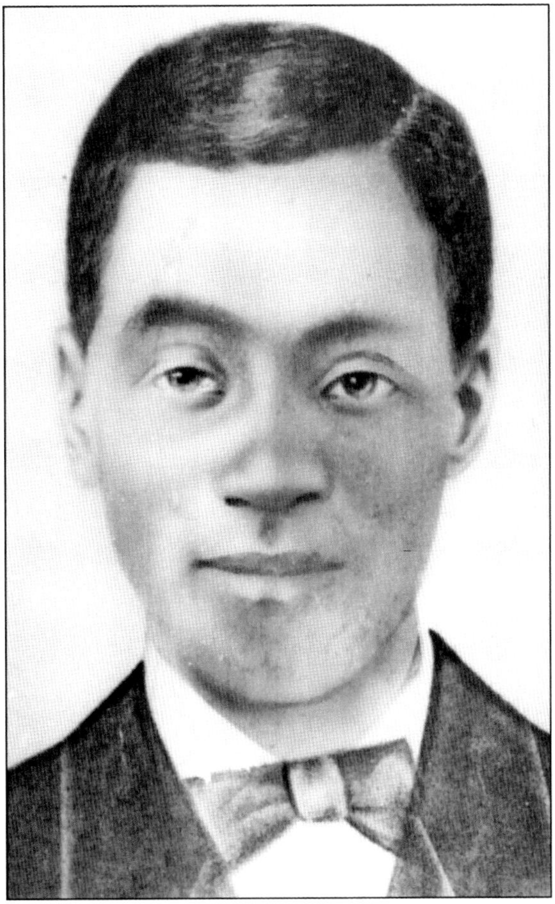

Here is one of the very few photographs of African American schoolchildren, discovered and copied by Dr. Robert Walz. This image of the students at the old Magnolia Public School was taken in 1919. The school was located in the same vicinity as the Columbia High School on Madison and School Streets, according to Mattie Brigham, the photograph's owner. She has identified Calvin Shepard (first row, third from the left), Leon Shepard (first row, sixth from the left), and Hattie Green, the teacher (second row, far right). (Dr. Robert Walz.)

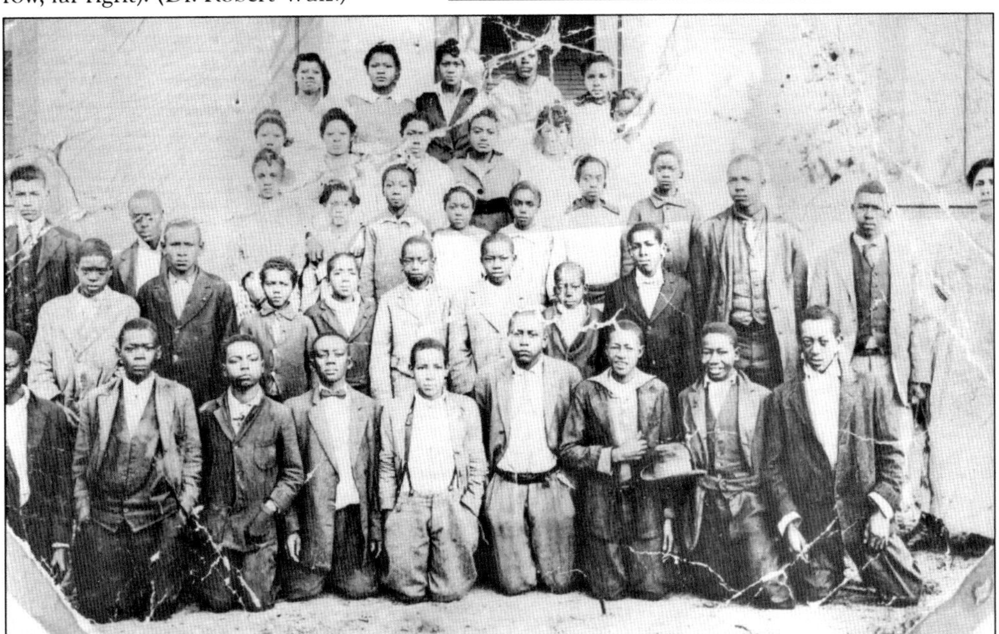

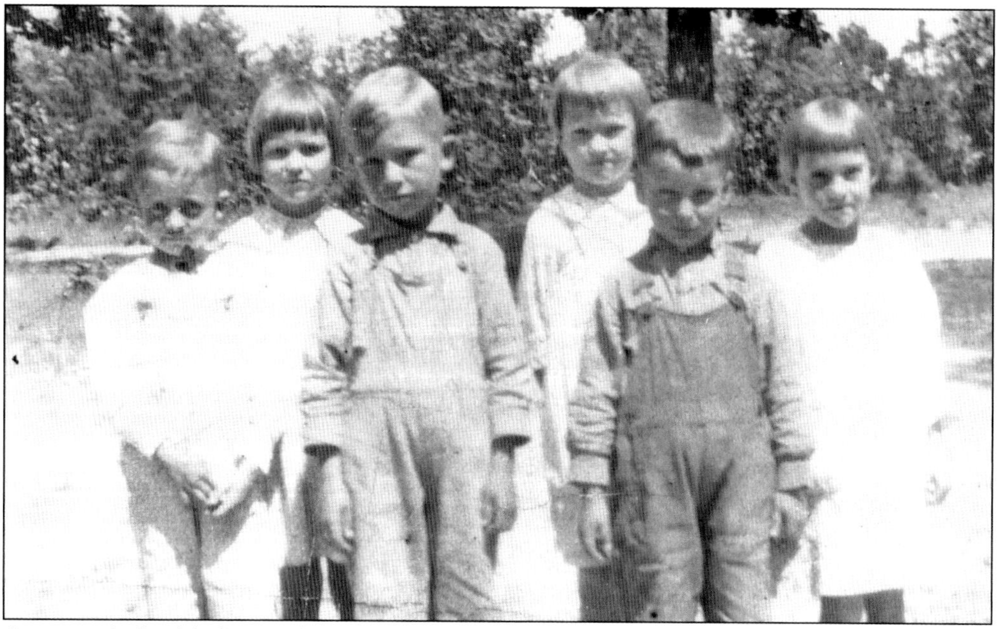

A group of adorable first graders is pictured at the Trickum School, which was located between Beech Creek and Bethel in the northwest corner of Columbia County. The photograph is believed to have been taken in 1918. From left to right are J.B. Malone, Ruby Bryan Collier, Thurston Puckett, Vera Horton Purtle, Bill Millican, and Sue Lindsey Crabtree. (Vera Horton Purtle.)

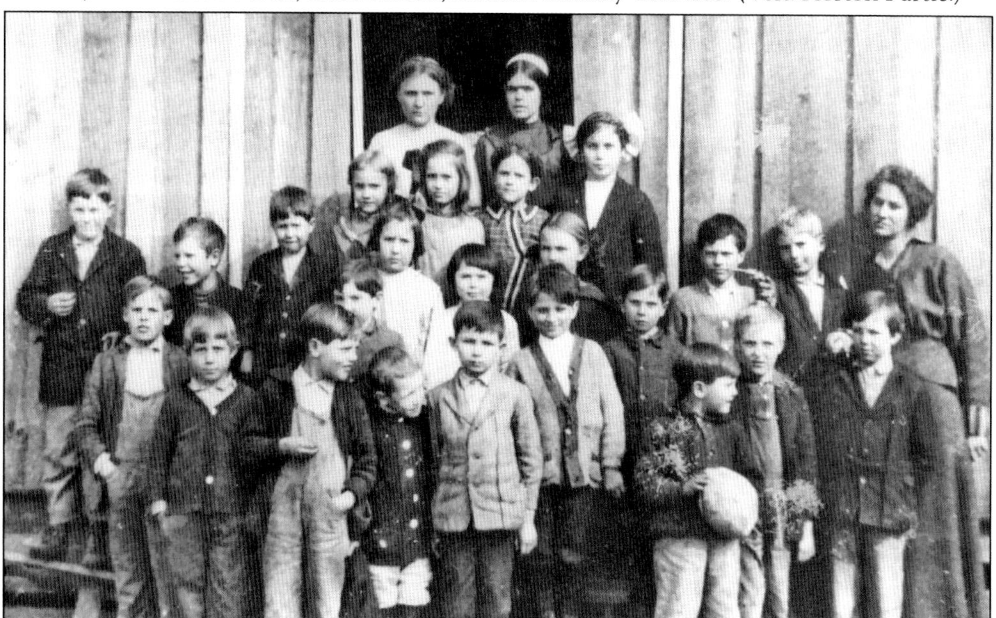

The students pictured here, who attended school in Bussey during 1915, include, from left to right, (first row) Jim Thompson, Robert Crain, Horace Thompson, Knight Norwood, Lester Souter, unidentified, Francis Rose, Harvey Thompson, Chester Whaley, R.E. Burnett, and George Souter; (second row) Freddie Bussey, Cecil Bryan, Louise Shepherd, Josephine Alden, Zora Powers, Othel Burnett, Sid McMath, Eddie Crain, and teacher Annie Harris; (third row) Flora Mae Davis, Ernestine Keith, Ofa Davis, Estelle Davis, Myrtle Powers, and Willie Lightning. (Eunice Burnett Mize.)

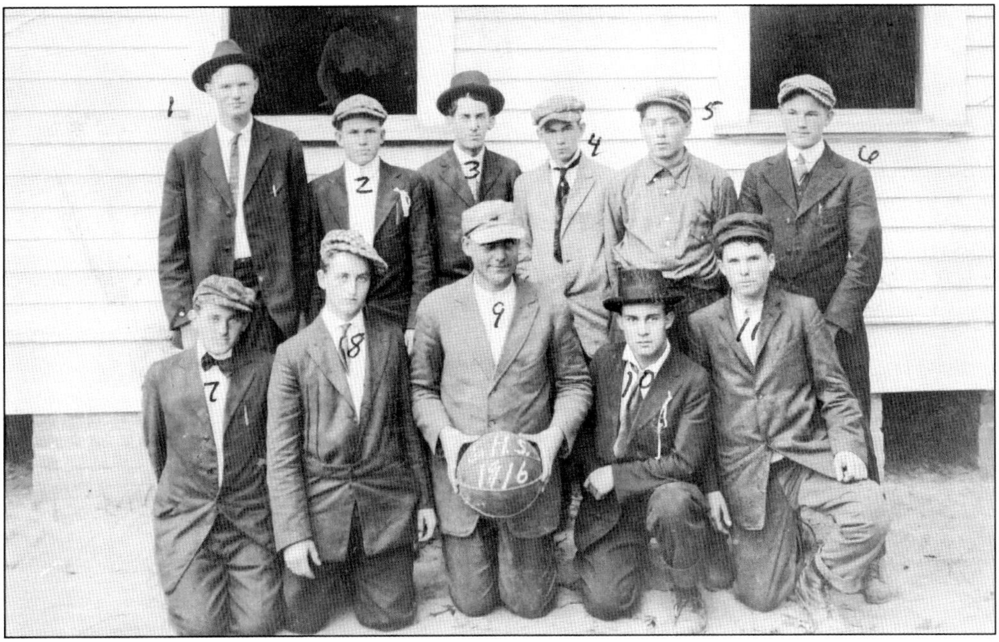

These Emerson boys' basketball team members in 1915–1916 are, from left to right, (first row) Littrell Stonecipher, Walter Wood, Hugh Stevens, Jim McWilliams, and Floyd Butler; (second row) Johnny Christie, Diffie Warren, principal Virgil Hardin, Russell Hawkins, Dewey Pharr, and Bran McMahen. (Christine Butler Snider.)

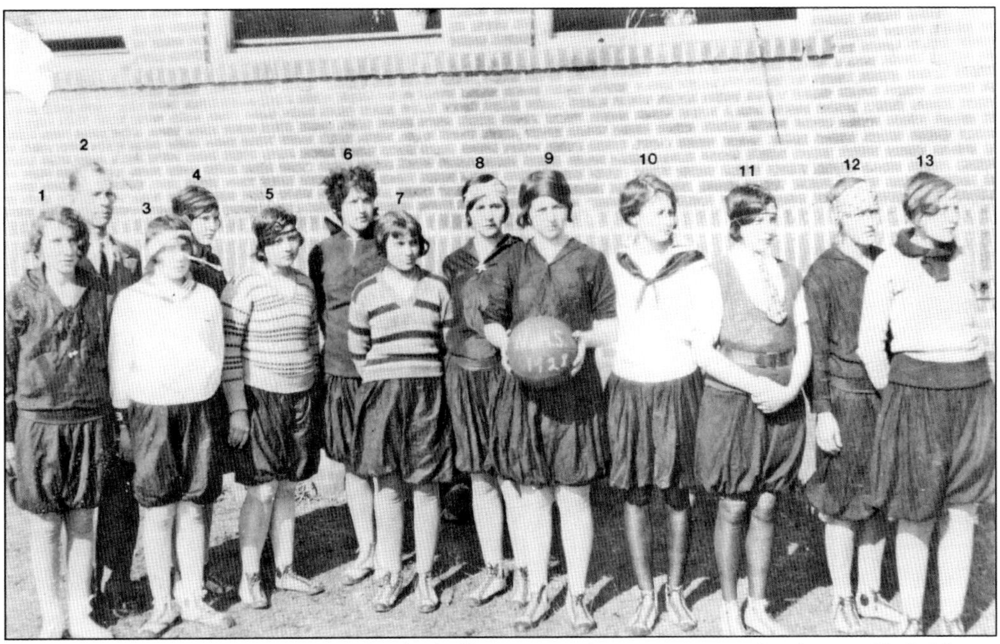

The Waldo High School girls' 1928 basketball team members in numerical order are Clyde Hayes, coach M.G. Richardson, Mavine Bright, Margaret Neill, Nellie McGowen, Ruth Black, Nora Crane, Ollie Young, Francille Rhea (team captain), Mary Lou Watkins, Louise Wallace, Lena Spradlin, and Lecy Spradlin. (Margaret N. Rowe.)

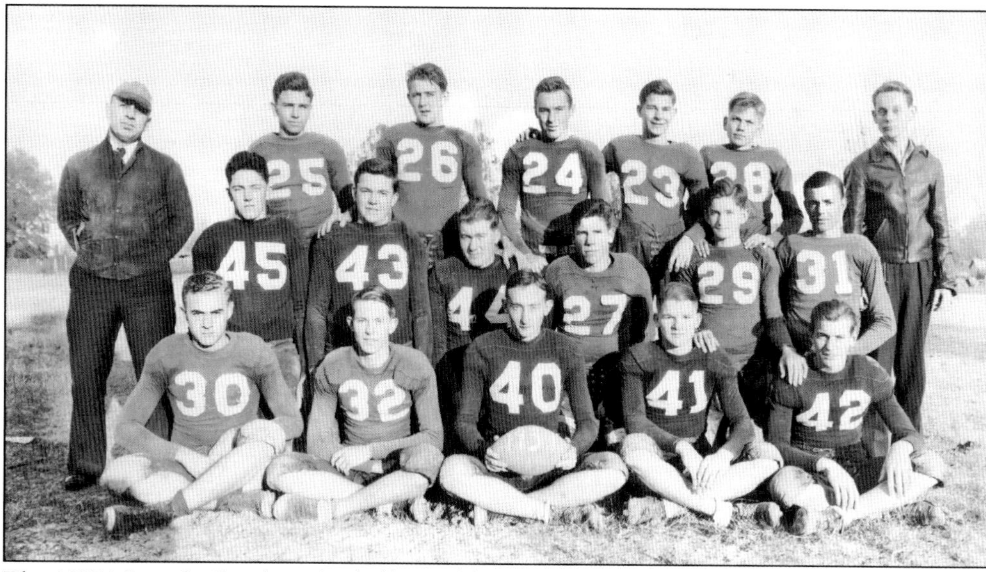

The 1937 Magnolia Panthers football squad had 16 members. From left to right they are (first row) Claude Whitlow, Lamar Dingler, Dale Booth, Martin Burns, and Buddy Jones; (second row) coach Gordon B. Gilbert, William Dunn, Charles Dunn, unidentified, Monroe Kirkpatrick, Lymon Maloch, and unidentified; (third row) John McMahen, Jimmy "Red" Jones, James Hudson, R.W. Wiley, William Talley, and Doyle Dingler. (Partee Tuberville.)

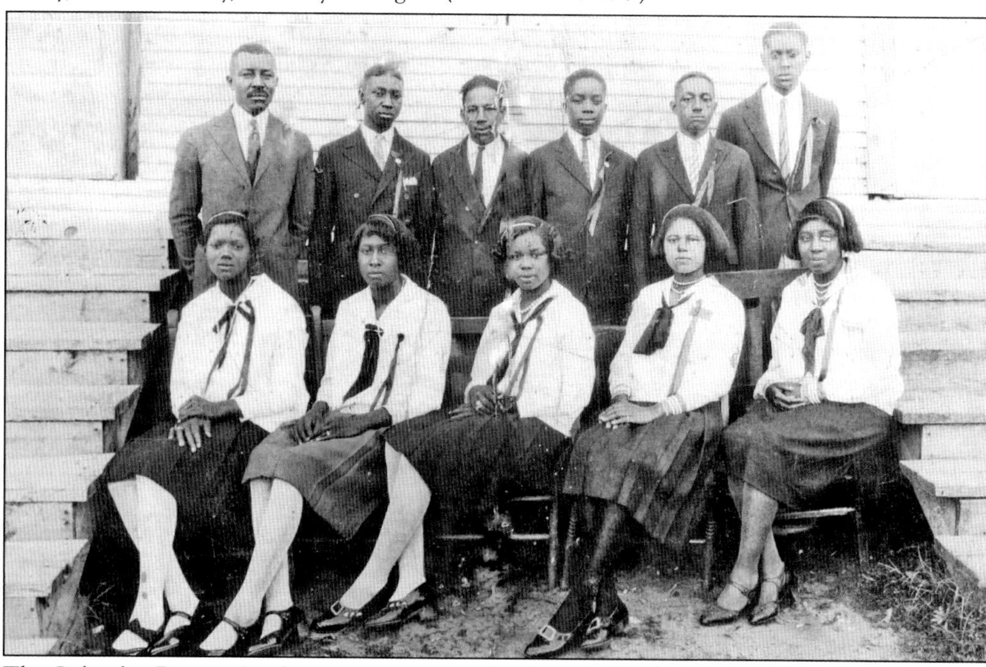

The Columbia Baptist Academy was a private school run by William J. Brigham Sr., the principal, and his wife, Fanny [*sic*] Brigham, the matron, with other teachers as assistants. Sadly, the names of many of these students have been lost over time. The young people pictured are, from left to right, (first row) two unidentified, ? Brigham, and two unidentified; (second row) Principal (or Professor) Brigham, two unidentified, William J. Brigham Jr., J. Watkin, and Hamp Brown. (Helen Hildreth).

Members of the 1930 graduating class of Columbia Baptist Academy are, from left to right, (first row) Annie Perry, Kennie Jones, and Addie Mae Correll; (second row) L.V. Jackson (secretary) and Maggie Curry (assistant secretary); (third row) Thurston Green (vice president), Madge Lee Rabb (treasurer), and Odis Preston (president); (fourth row) Othella Brigham, W.J. Brigham, and Flotiler Curry. (Helen Hildreth.)

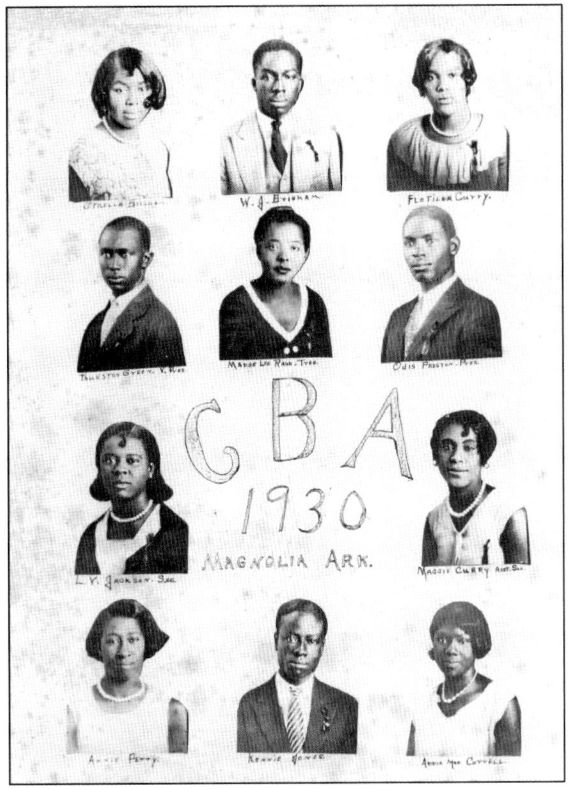

This photograph is of the Macedonia Grade School girls' athletic class as they appeared in 1940–1941. From left to right are Wilma Franks (Pearce), Bonnie Nipper (Keith), Haze Dodson (Conway), Ruby Thornton (Hudson), Audrey Ellison (Ford), Winni Dodson (Rose), and coach Arline Franks Young. (Arline Franks Young.)

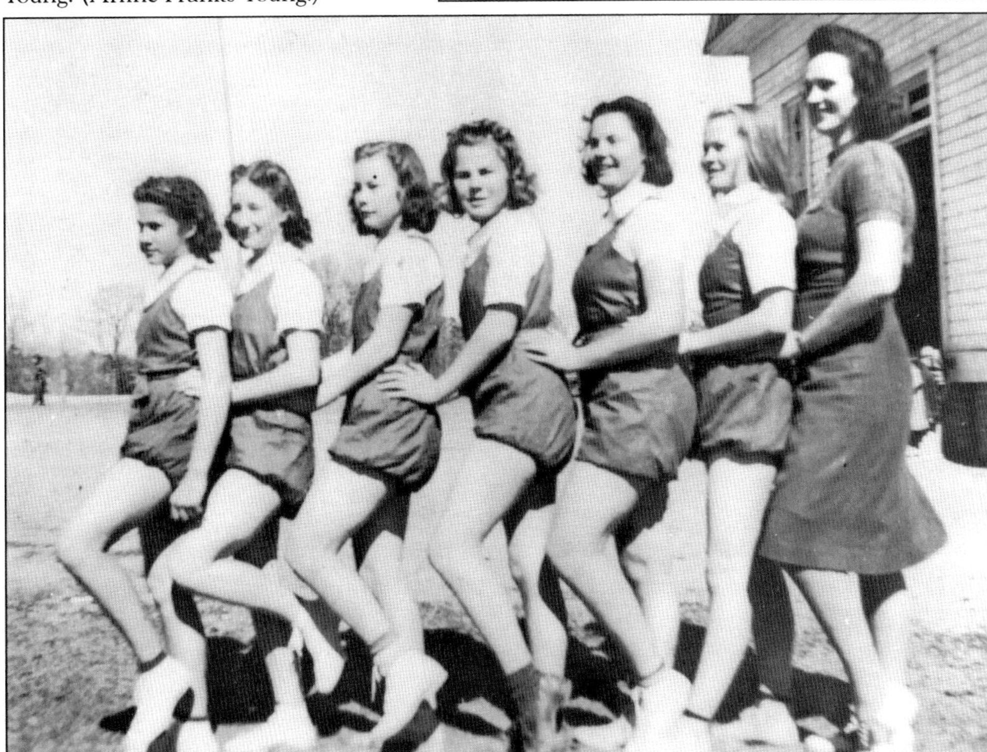

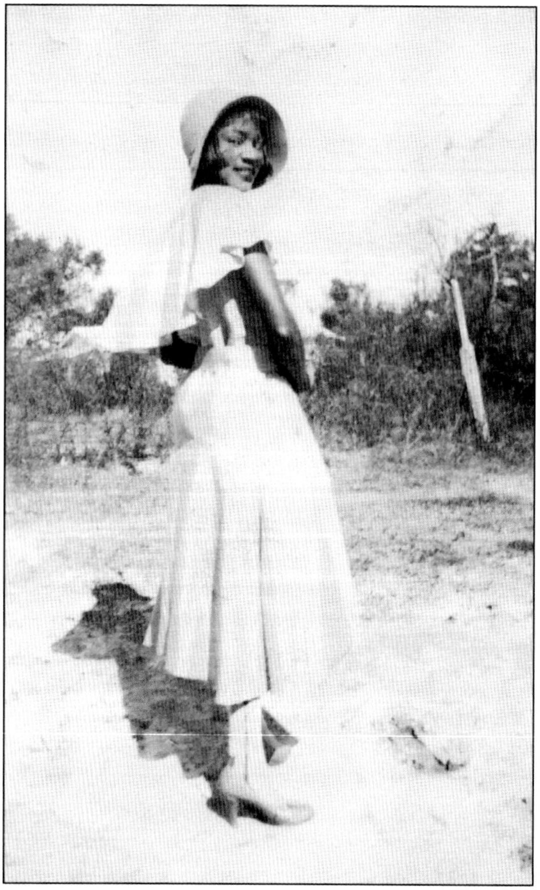

Pansy Payne Goode graduated in 1928 from Columbia Baptist Academy High School. She attended Pine Bluff AM&N College and, after graduation, taught school at C.S. Woodard. She also taught in McNeil, Damascus, and Bradley. She worked as a teacher under the supervision of Fannie Brigham and was director of the first government-funded Head Start, located in the Old Columbia High School home economics building. She was a member of Bethlehem Baptist Church in Magnolia and loved and taught vacation Bible school. (Peggy Goode Rudd.)

This photograph is of an unidentified student group attending Columbia Baptist Academy. The school was located on the corner of Arkansas State Highway 19 and Ross Street. On the north side of Bethlehem Baptist Church, it was positioned across from the city cemetery. (Helen Hildreth.)

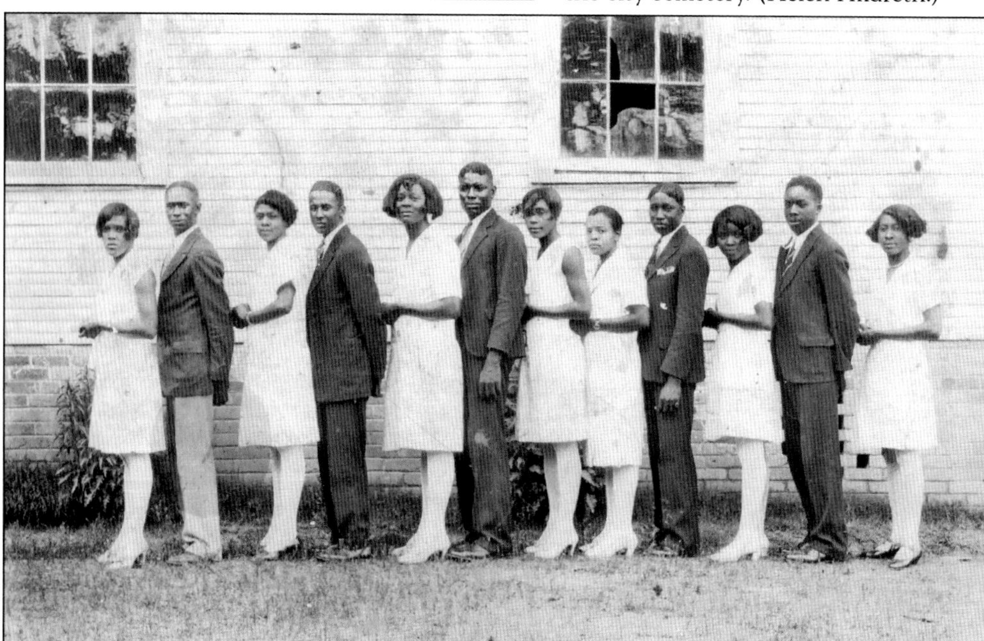

This is an engaging photograph taken in 1925 of a local A&M "Flapper." The daring young woman is only identified as Velma S., and according to the caption, she is waiting for her fiancé Bud Tucker. (Dr. Robert Walz.)

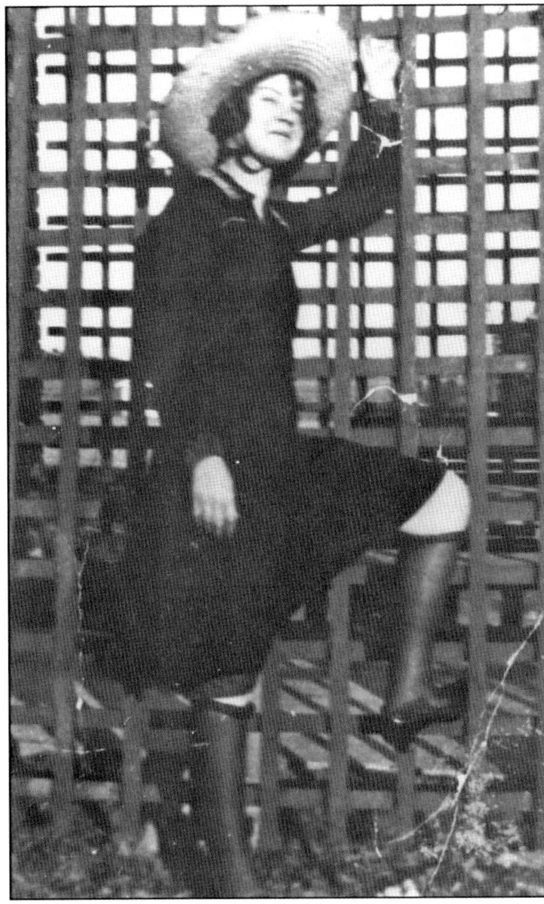

This 1916 photograph is of a school group being educated at Emerson, Arkansas. Virgil Hardin was the principal, and family names listed with the group are Christie, McMahen, Hammack, Rushton, Butler, Mcilveene, Hartsfield, Maloch, Stevens, McWilliams, Wingfield, Selvidge, Warren, Pharr, Hawkins, Wood, Gunnels, Stonecipher, Stewart, Tucker, Stell, and Beaty. (Dr. Robert Walz.)

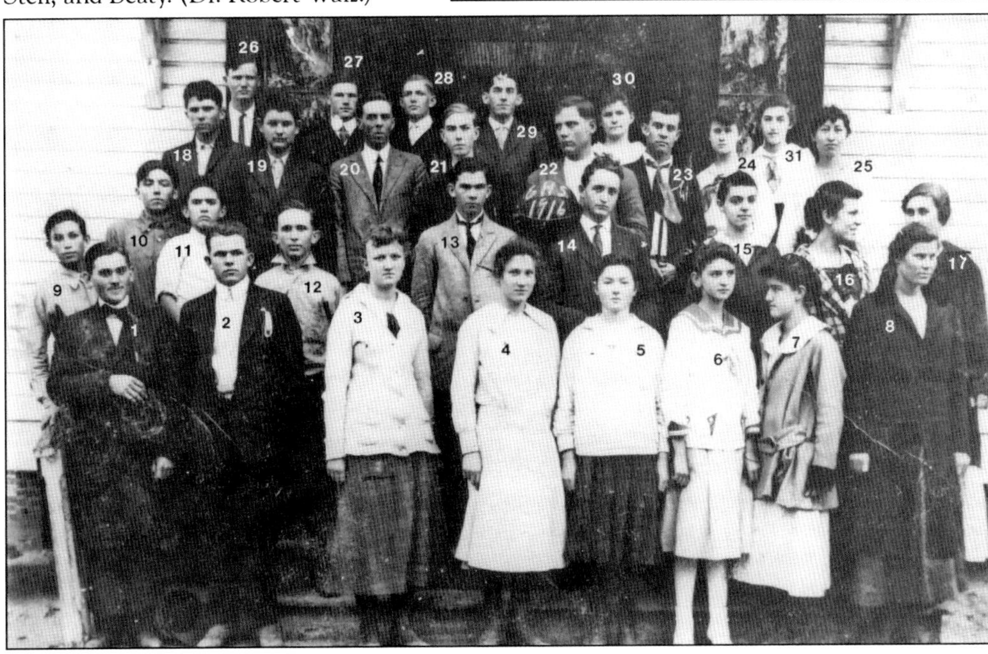

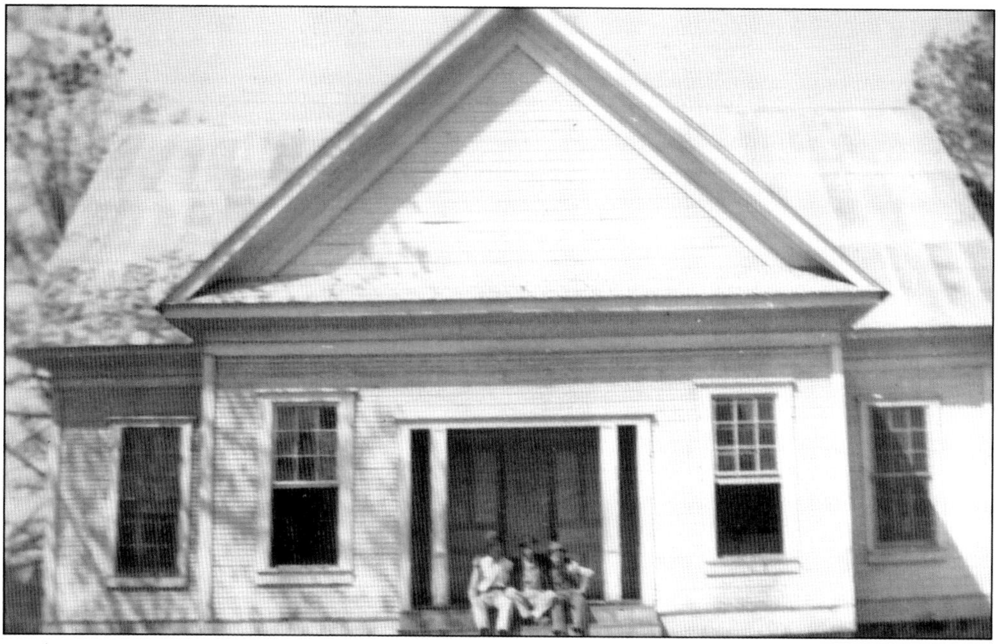

Rocky Mound is a rural community still in existence today. The Rocky Mound School was located between the Harmony community and Taylor on the current Arkansas Highway 160. The last graduating class was 1943–1944. (Christine Butler Snider.)

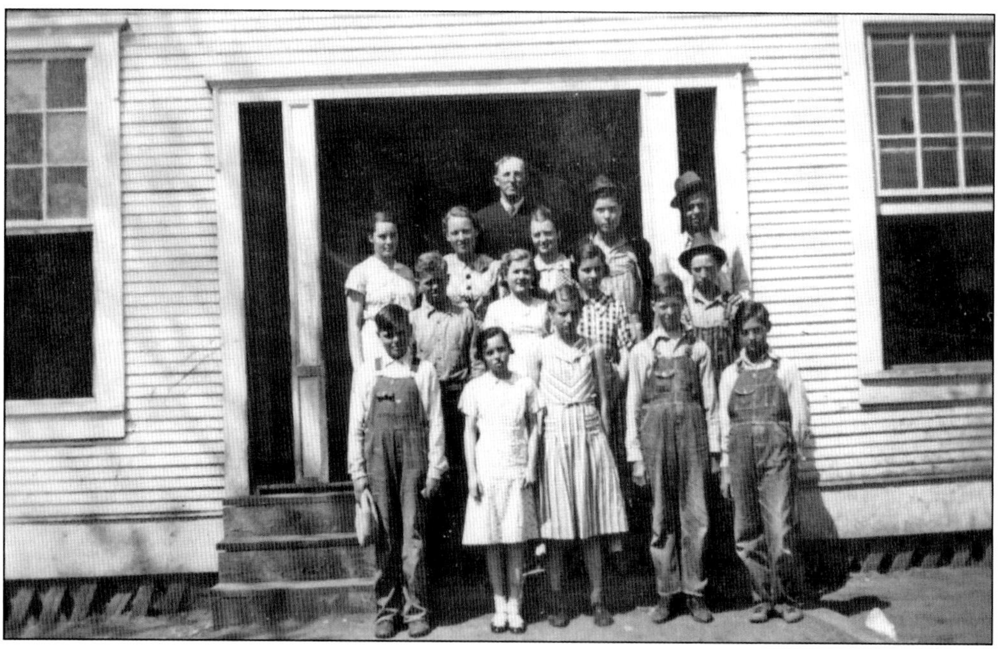

A group of unidentified students in 1937 is pictured on the steps of the Rocky Mound School. Through the years, records become lost and memories fade, but with a little imagination one can conjure up a spring day and see the sun, filtered through the trees, casting a shadow on the schoolhouse. In this setting, one might wonder who these young scholars were, what their dreams were, and only hope that all of those dreams came true. (Christine Butler Snider.)

Four

Businesses and Occupations

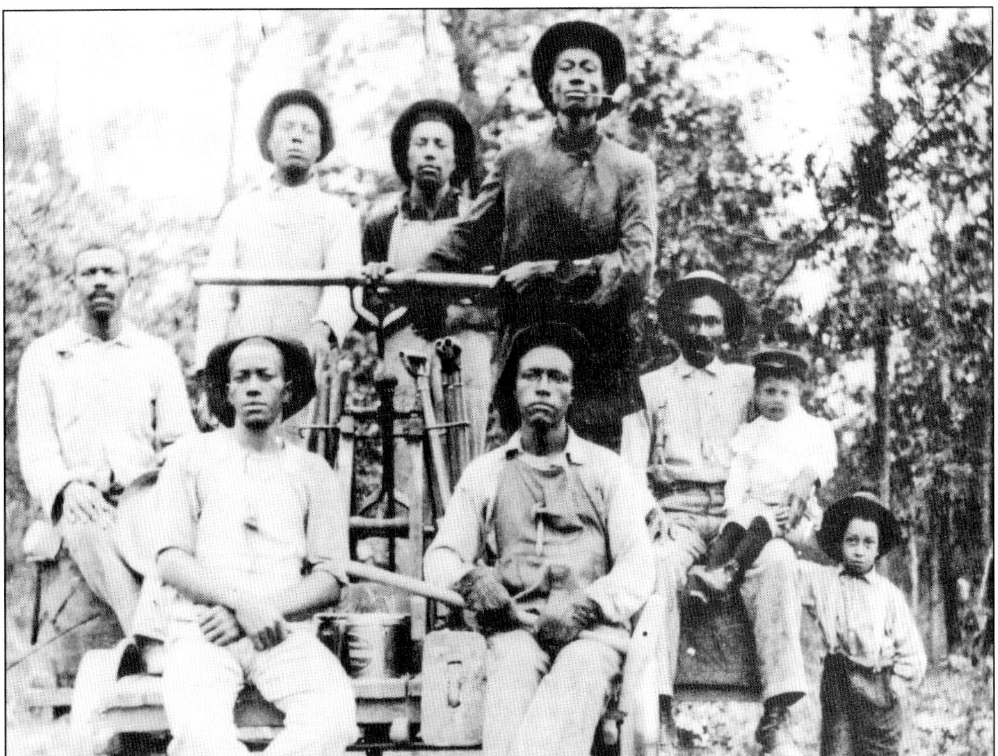

Pictured here is a section gang on the Louisiana & North West Railroad. This 1940s group checked and repaired the railroad tracks. In 1898, the 36-mile line was constructed from Homer, Louisiana, to Magnolia, Arkansas, and in November 1898, it was opened for traffic. (Mildred Ruff.)

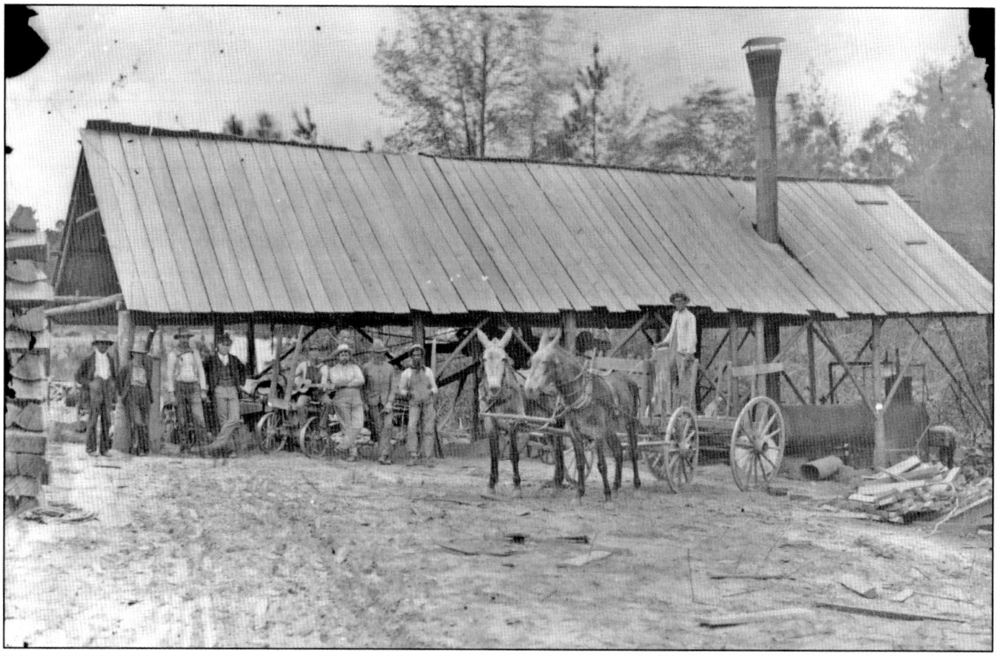

This 1914 photograph shows Ben Phillips's sawmill near Village. The man with the guitar is Phillips, and the man fourth from the left with the dark coat and vest is Dewey Wilson. (Hudson Phillips.)

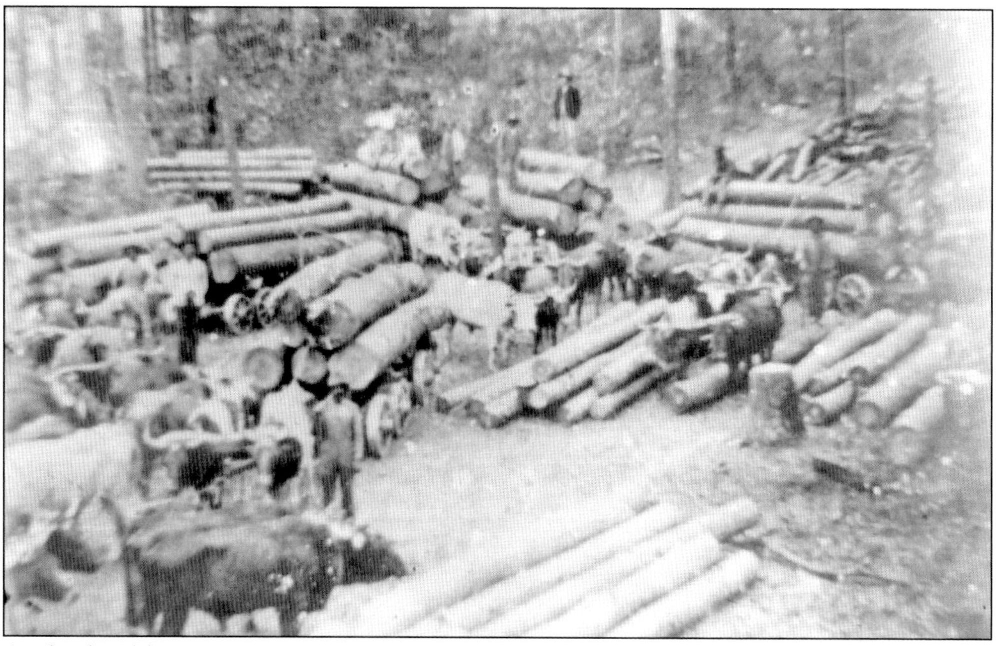

At this local logging site, ox teams were used to pull wagons hauling cut logs. Undated, this photograph is believed to have been taken in the late 1800s or early 1900s. (Dr. Robert Walz.)

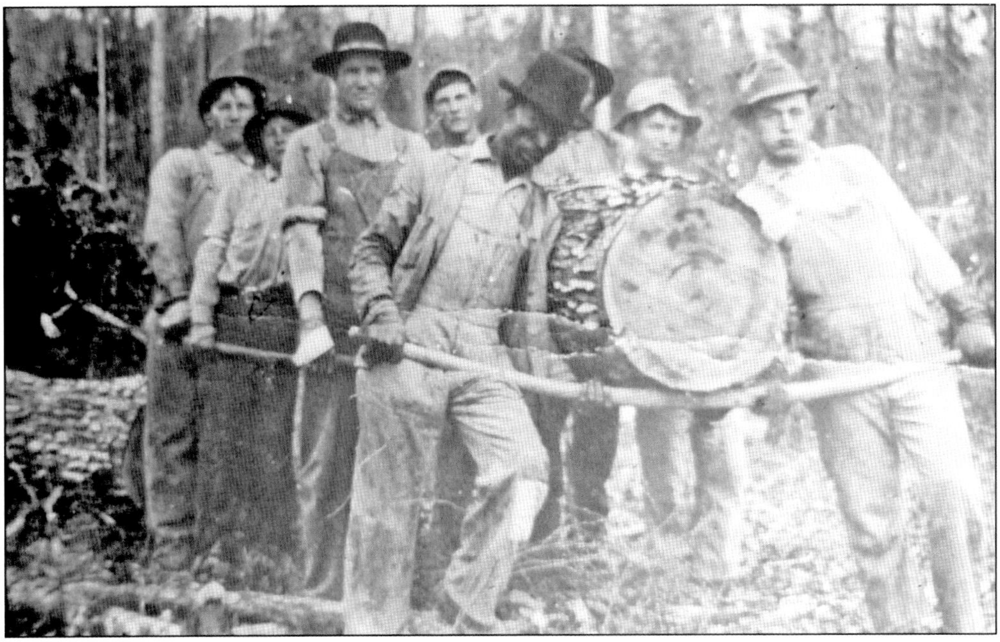

This photograph depicts a group of men as "log rollers." The image is believed to have been taken at a logging site in the Taylor, Arkansas, area. A team of eight men is using strong wooden poles to transport cut logs to the mill to be rough cut into planks. (Dr. Robert Walz.)

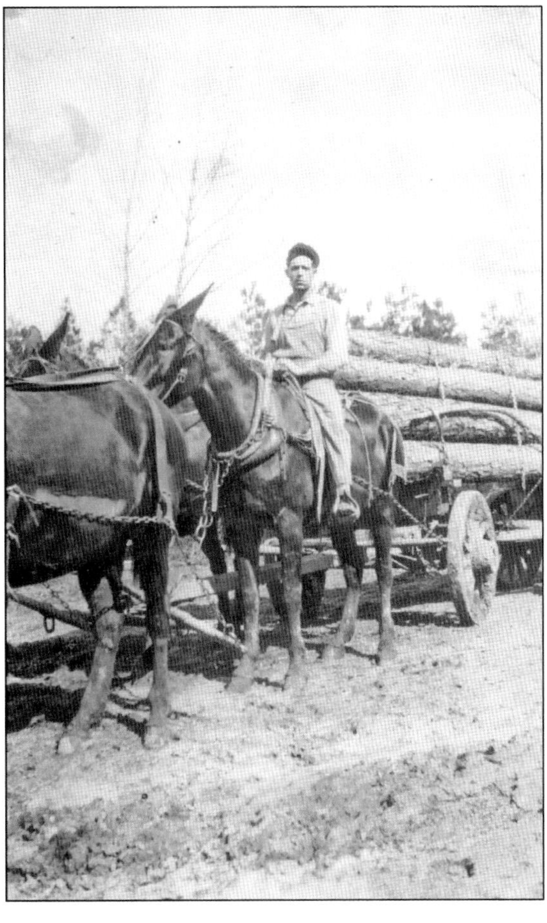

By far the most common conveyance used to deliver logs to the sawmill was the mule-drawn wagon. The time, as well as the manpower, necessary for accomplishing the removal of cut logs from forests and transporting them to the sawmill for processing was gargantuan. Seen here is Carl Wyrick with a team of at least four mules pulling a wagonload of timber. (Betty Faye Lewis.)

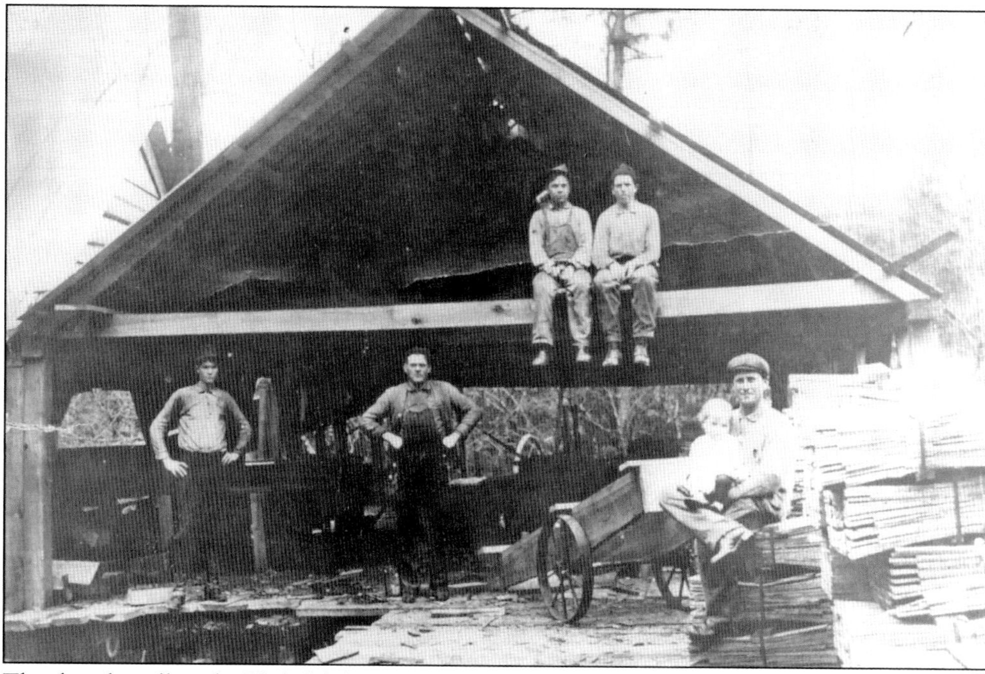

The shingle mill in the Philadelphia community is pictured here around 1910. From left to right are (on the ground) ? Woodard, Levi Pearce, and James Franklin Pearce holding Mary Josephine Pearce Burdine; (above) Oscar Aaron Pearce and Will Aldridge. (Kathleen Elmore.)

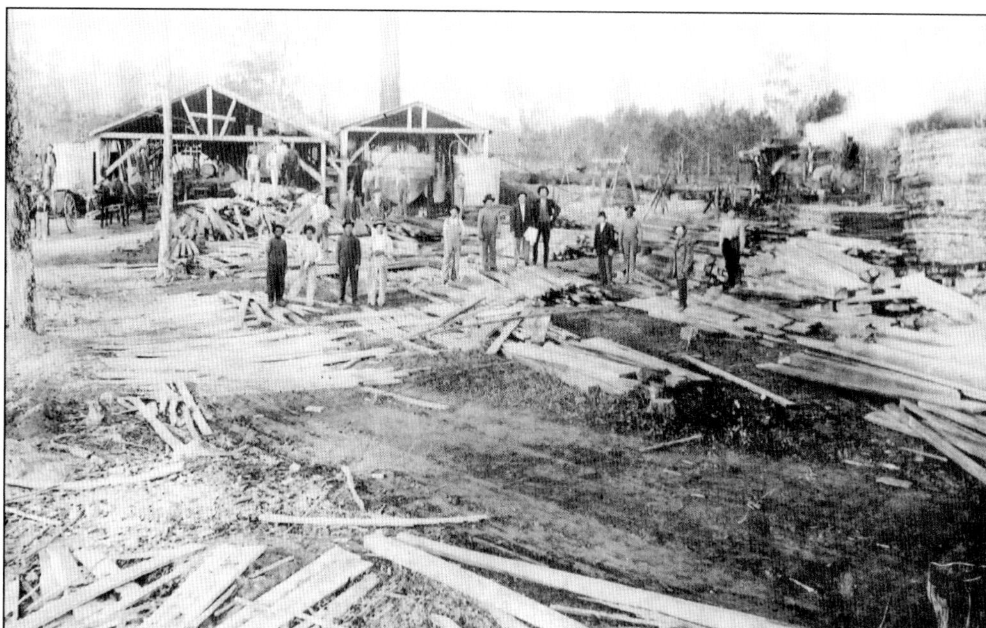

Columbia County was blessed with the natural resources of thick hardwood and pine forests. As the citizenry grew, so did the need for raw materials to build homes, churches, and businesses. Thus, numerous lumber enterprises sprang up throughout the county. This busy work yard is an early sawmill in Taylor, believed to be on the north side of town. (Ronald Orrick.)

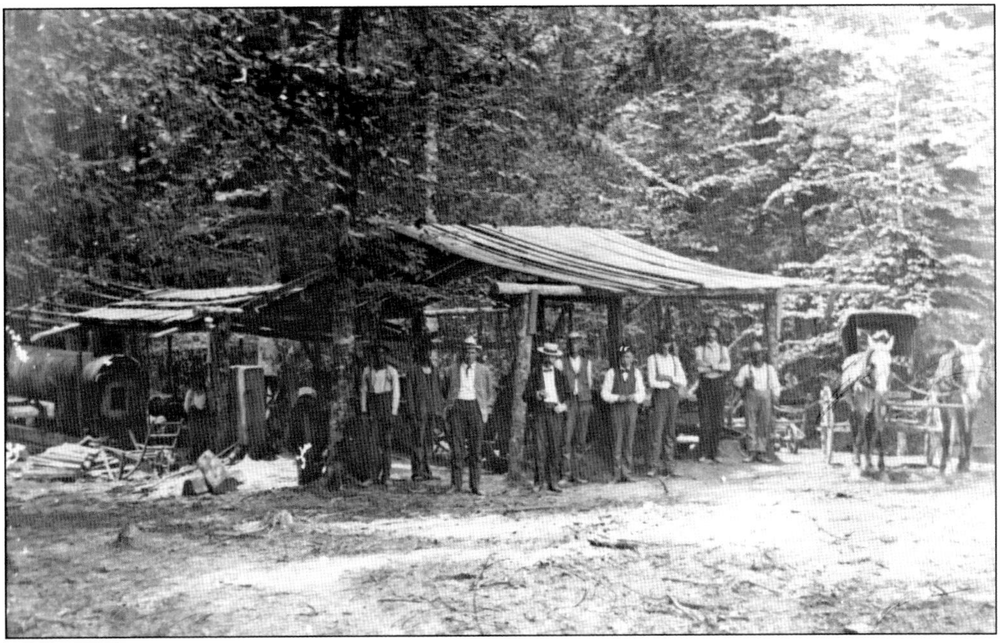

This sawmill was located at Mohawk, Arkansas. The Mohawk community was situated between Emerson, Arkansas, and Haynesville, Louisiana, just east of the railroad tracks. At one time, there were a large number of Bulgarian immigrants in Mohawk who had fled Europe during World War I. They were brought to this area by a woman named Betty McMarilla. (Dr. Robert Walz.)

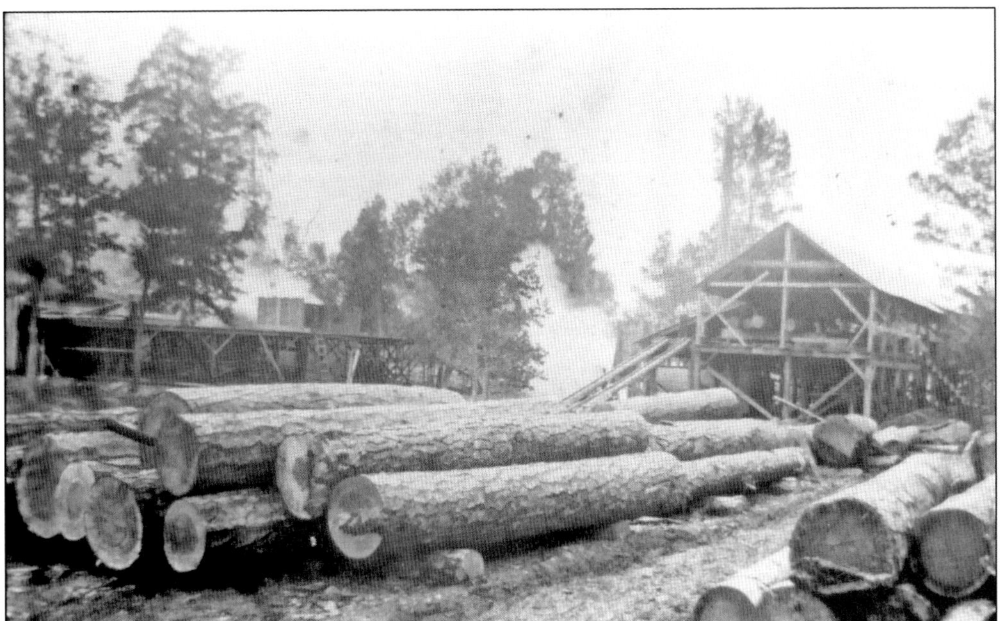

Because the Mohawk community was situated near the railroad tracks, it was a prime location in which to establish logging and milling operations. Sam Grayson, a leading citizen of the time, was the owner and operator of the Grayson Sawmill. (Dr. Robert Walz.)

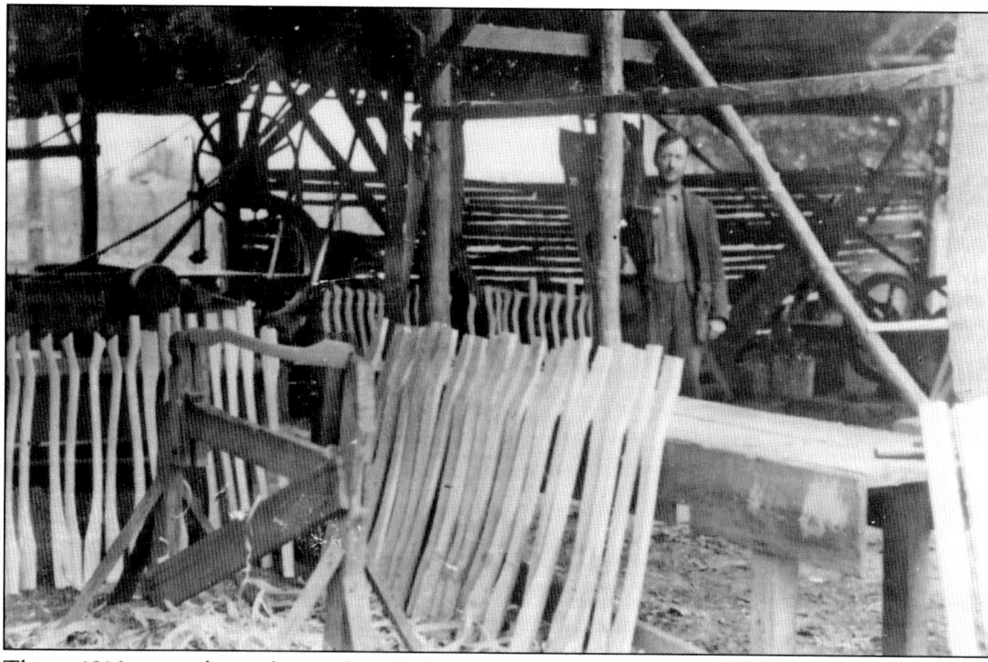

This c. 1916 image shows the axe-handle factory owned by Forrest Adair Lewis. The business was located in the New Hope community, just north of Magnolia. (Betty Faye Lewis.)

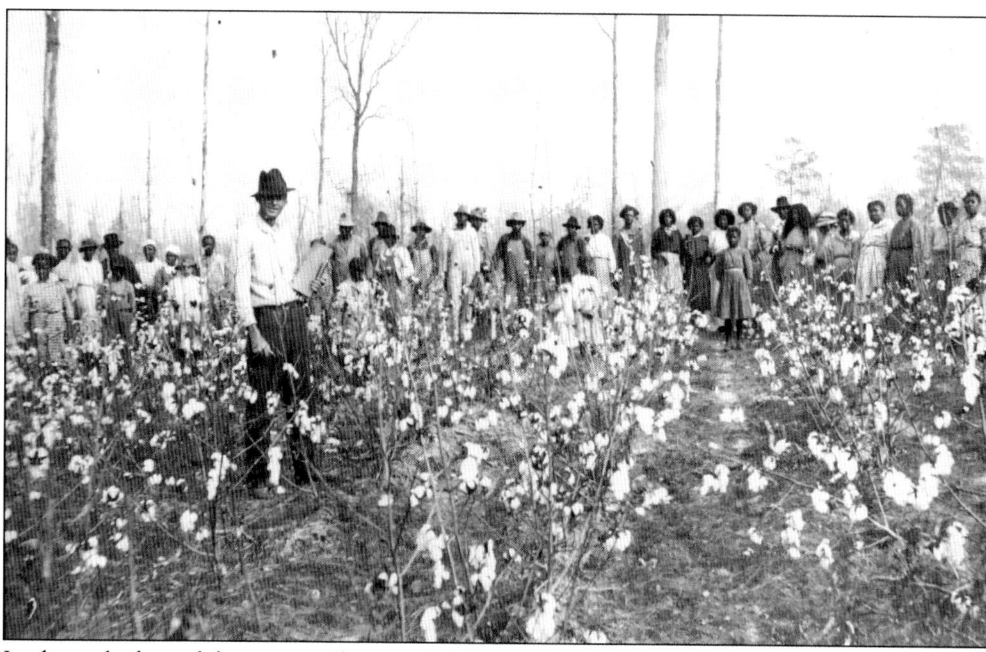

In the early days of the county, the major cash crop produced was cotton. Entire families, from the youngest to the oldest, were employed to coax the soft, white cotton from its prickly home on the cotton stalk. A group of people picking cotton is shown near Brister around 1910. John Starling, in the foreground, is checking weights. (Mrs. Margaret Burks.)

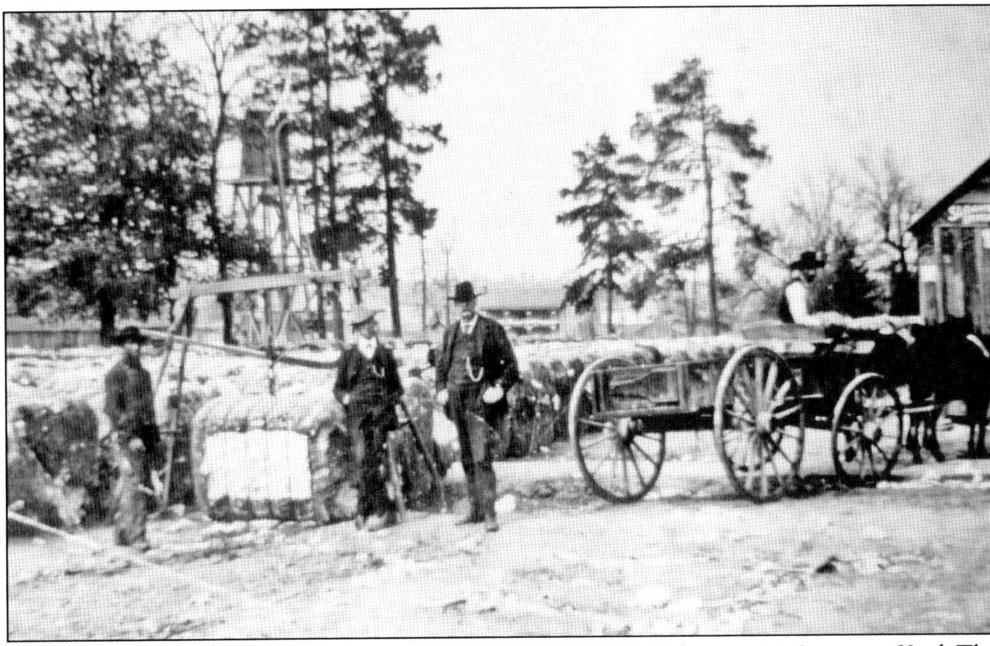

Unidentified men are working and weighing cotton at the Magnolia Cotton Compress Yard. The photograph is believed to have been taken in the late 1890s or early 1900s. (Dr. Robert Walz.)

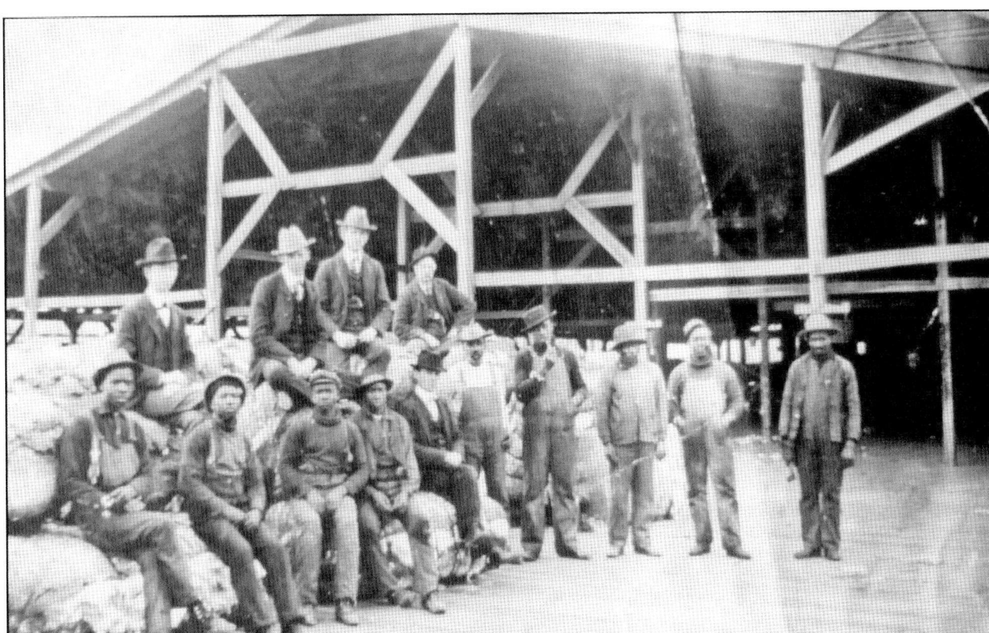

Sitting on and perched atop bales of cotton is a group of men in front of the Magnolia Cotton Compress storehouse. Judging from the type of dress, some of the men are laborers who work for cotton compress, and some of the men are supervisors. This image is believed to have been taken in the late 1890s or early 1900s. (Dr. Robert Walz.)

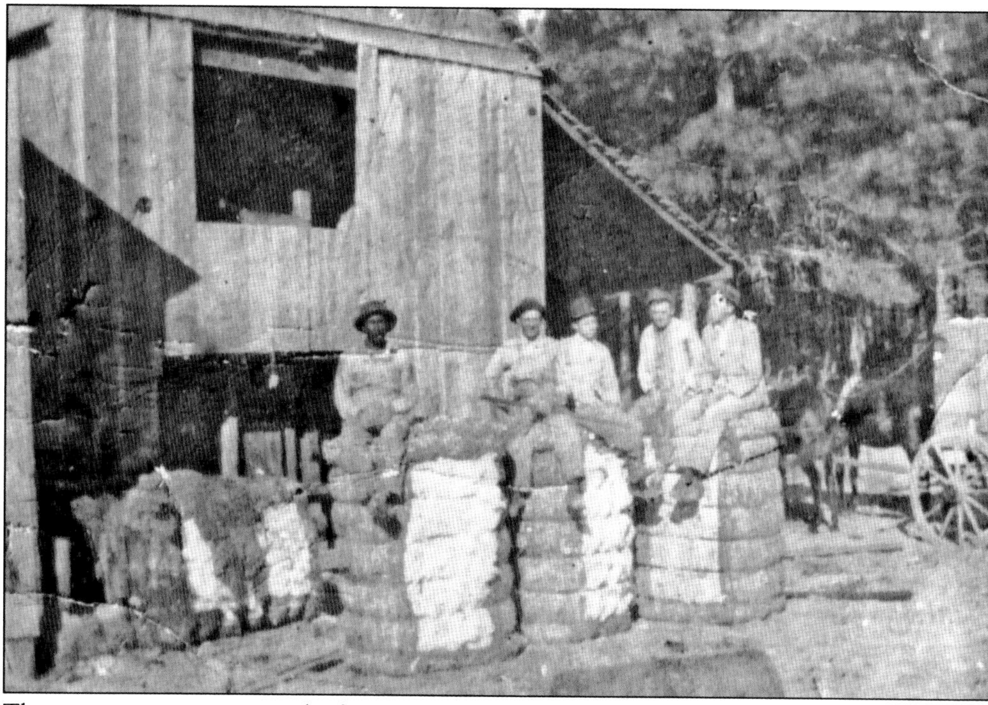

These men are resting upon the fruits of their labor at a busy Emerson, Arkansas, cotton gin. In the background, a wagonload of unprocessed cotton waits to be separated from its seed and sent on its way to the textile mills in the North. At one time, Magnolia produced the finest broadcloth west of the Mississippi. It was sent as far away as London, England, to be sewn into fine clothing. This photograph was taken in the early 1900s. (Christine Butler Snider.)

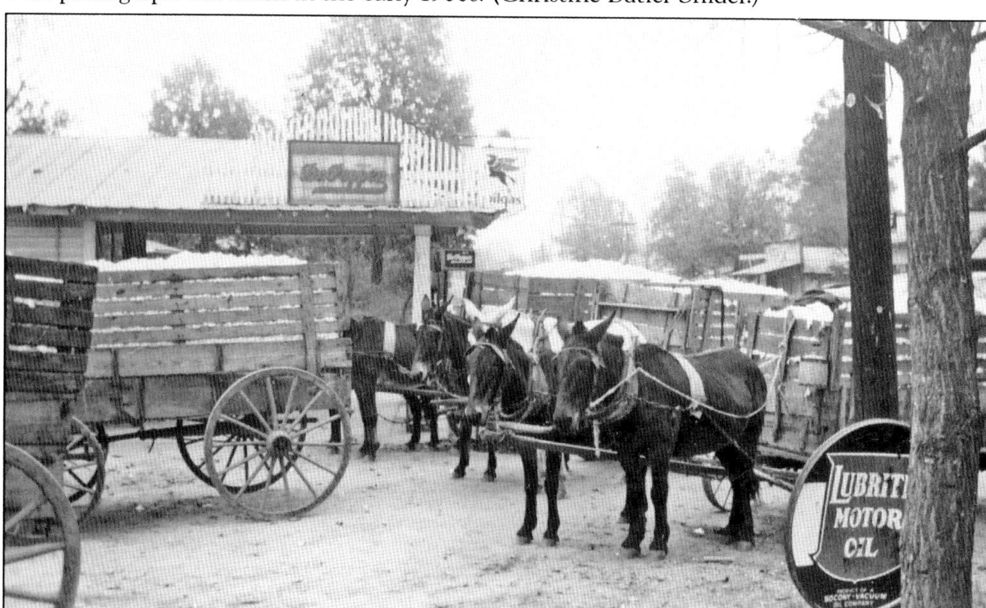

Cotton-filled, mule-drawn wagons are lined up in front of Owen's Grocery store in Emerson. Hours were spent waiting in line to deliver their load of cotton to the gin for processing. (Christine Butler Snider.)

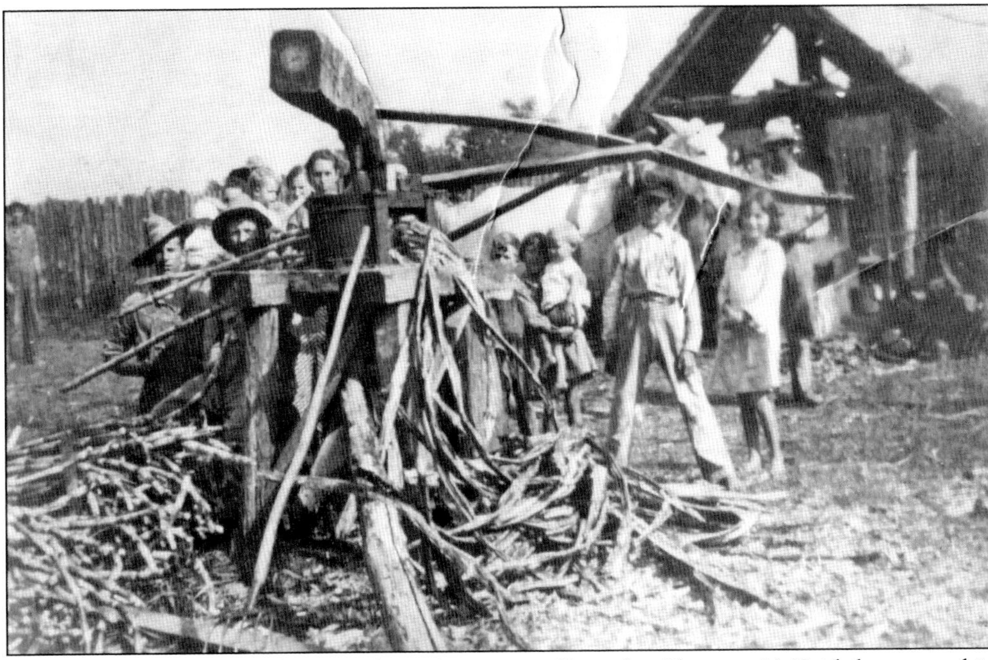

This interesting c. 1930 photograph is of a syrup mill on the Clarence V. Keith homestead in the Sharman community. The man standing at left, with his hat tilted, is David Keith. (Dr. Robert Walz.)

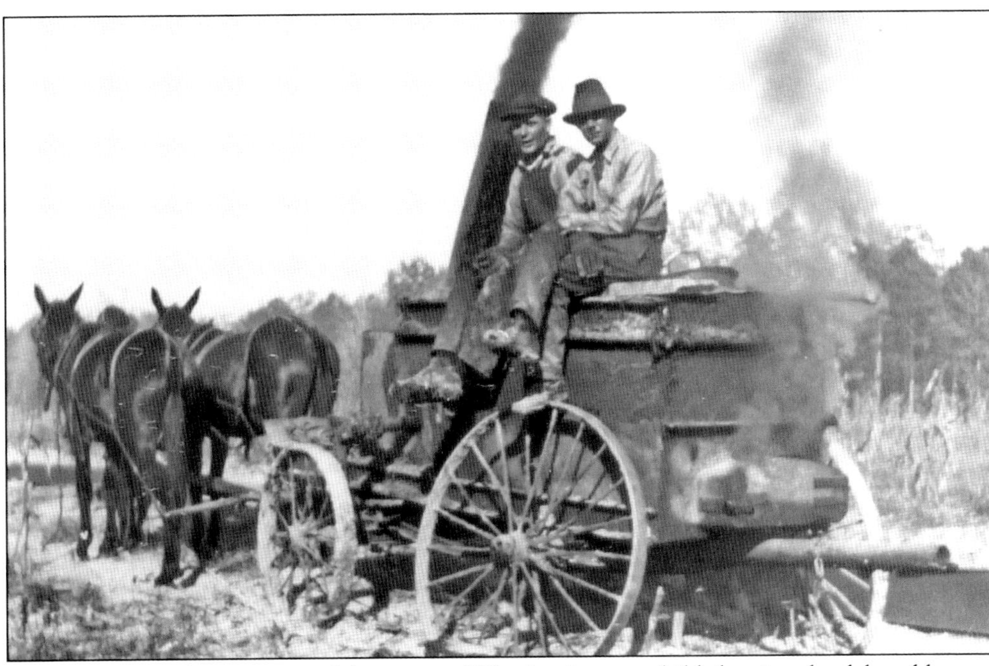

Sugarcane was a favorite crop of the county. Whether it was a child chewing the delectable cane with sticky juice running down his chin or a serious farmer bent on raising a bountiful crop to make into syrup, this crop was a benefit to all. Ed (left) and Bill Walker are resting from the milling work at the Butler/Walker Farm in Emerson in the early 1930s. (Christine Butler Snider.)

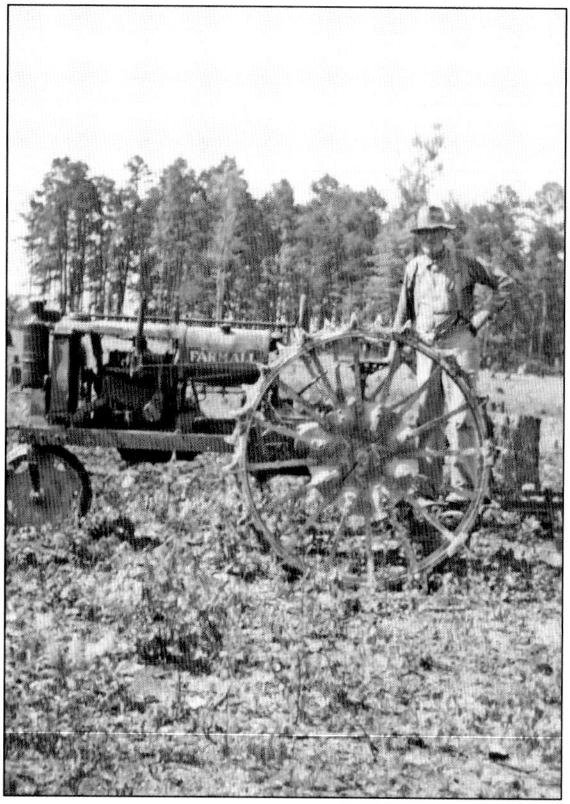

W.H. "Dock" Butler of Emerson is plowing the field with his early model Farmall tractor in 1938. With the introduction of the tractor to local agriculture, the slower, mule-drawn plow was retired when affordable. The tractor enabled forward-thinking farmers to diversify their crops and yield better quality produce for their customers and families. (Christine Butler Snider.)

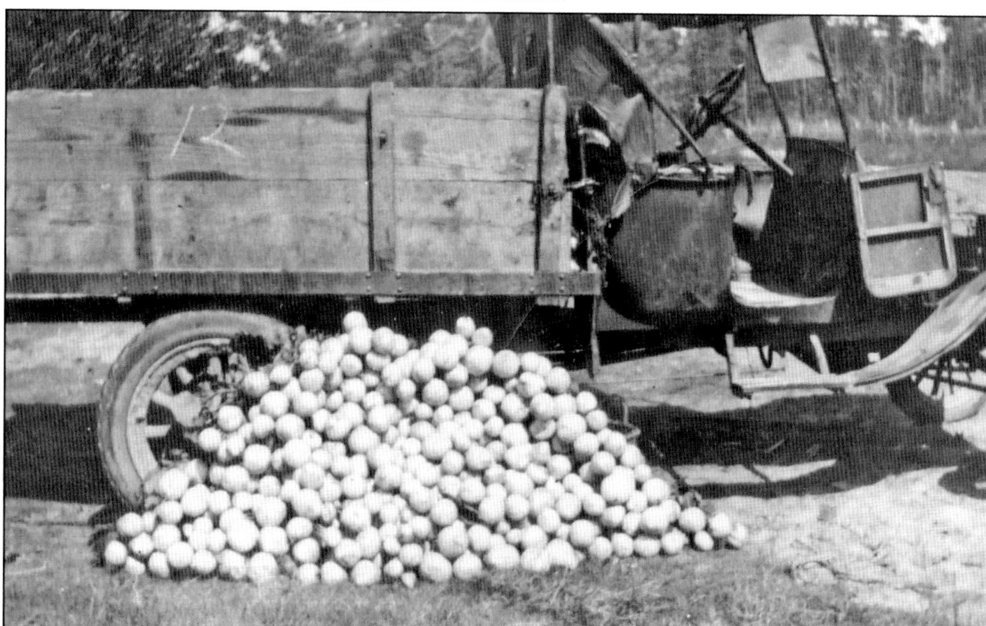

They just fell off the turnip truck! Seen in 1930, a large pile of turnips lays alongside Dock Butler's wood-slatted farm truck, another example of more modern farming enabled by the tractor. Dock Butler owned and operated a farm in the Emerson, Arkansas, area. (Christine Butler Snider.)

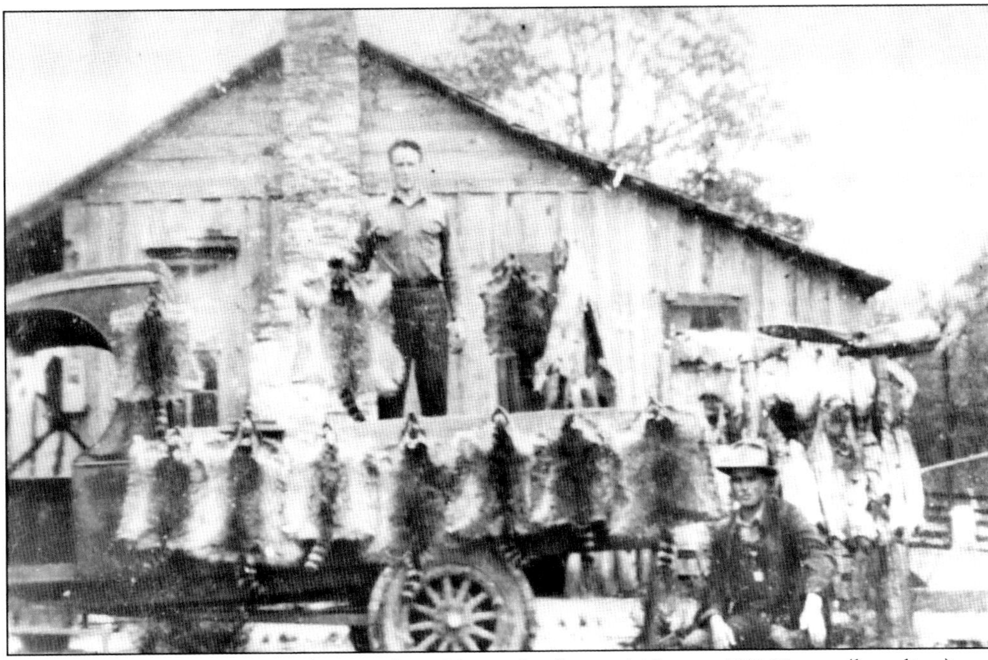

Shown in the early 1930s with a good week's catch of coon hides are E.F. Dyson (kneeling) and B.C. Dyson. This shot was taken at the Berry Dyson home, just west of Magnolia near Big Creek. Ernest Dyson recalled that the several hundred dollars the hides brought in were a welcome source of extra income during the hard times of the Great Depression. (Sammie Dyson.)

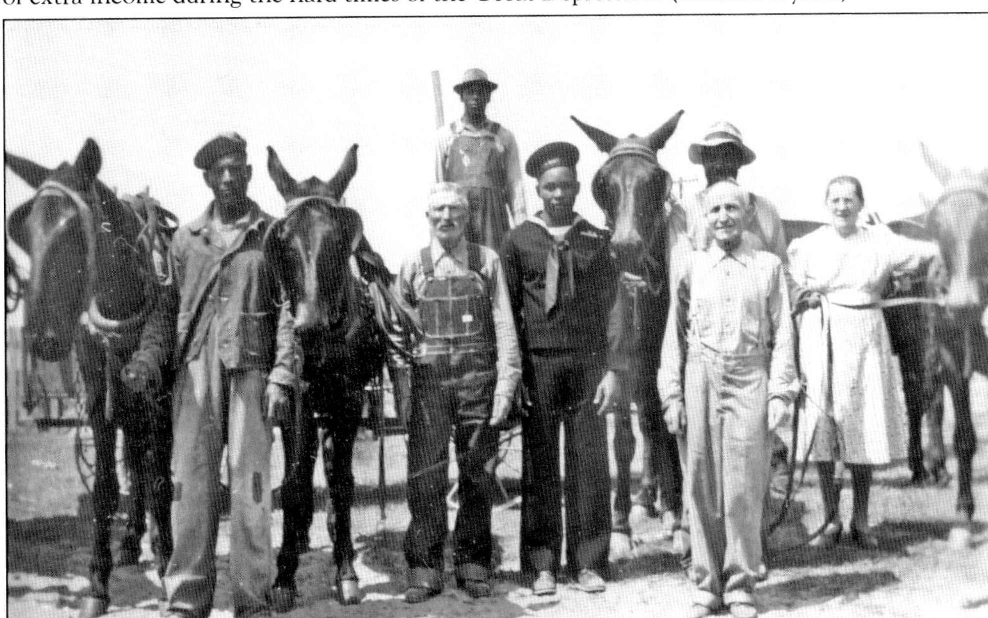

In the 1940s, the Genestet farm in Waldo made use of many mules in its farm operation. The big red barn (not pictured) held over 40 teams at one time. From left to right are (first row) Zeke Alexander, Henri Ginestet, an unidentified sailor, and Henry Genestet; (second row) James McGee, George Rhone, and Emilie Genestet. The different spelling of the Genestet name for Henri was on the back of the original image. (Bob Genestet.)

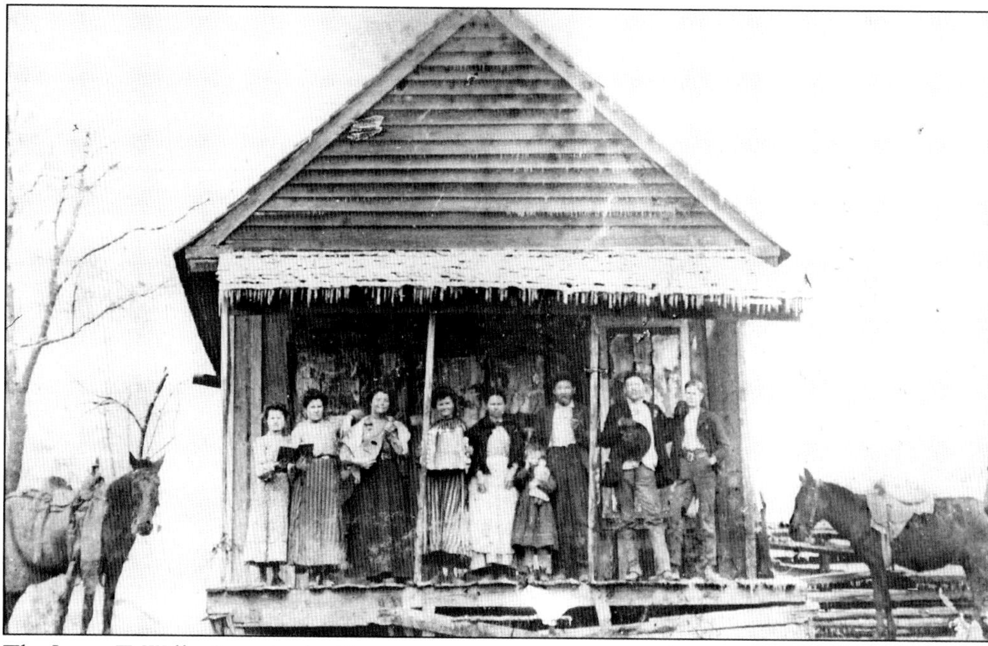

The James T. Willis Store in the Sharman community is pictured around 1905. From left to right are Lucina Dodson Willis, Clara Willis Caswell, Eutoga Willis Helms, Mary Francis Dodson Smith, Josephine Burrow Dodson-Willis (mother), Ella Willis McKinley Null, James T. Willis (father), Lee Willis, and Tom Burrow (nephew of Josephine). Note the musical instruments and songbooks they hold. (Dr. Robert Walz.)

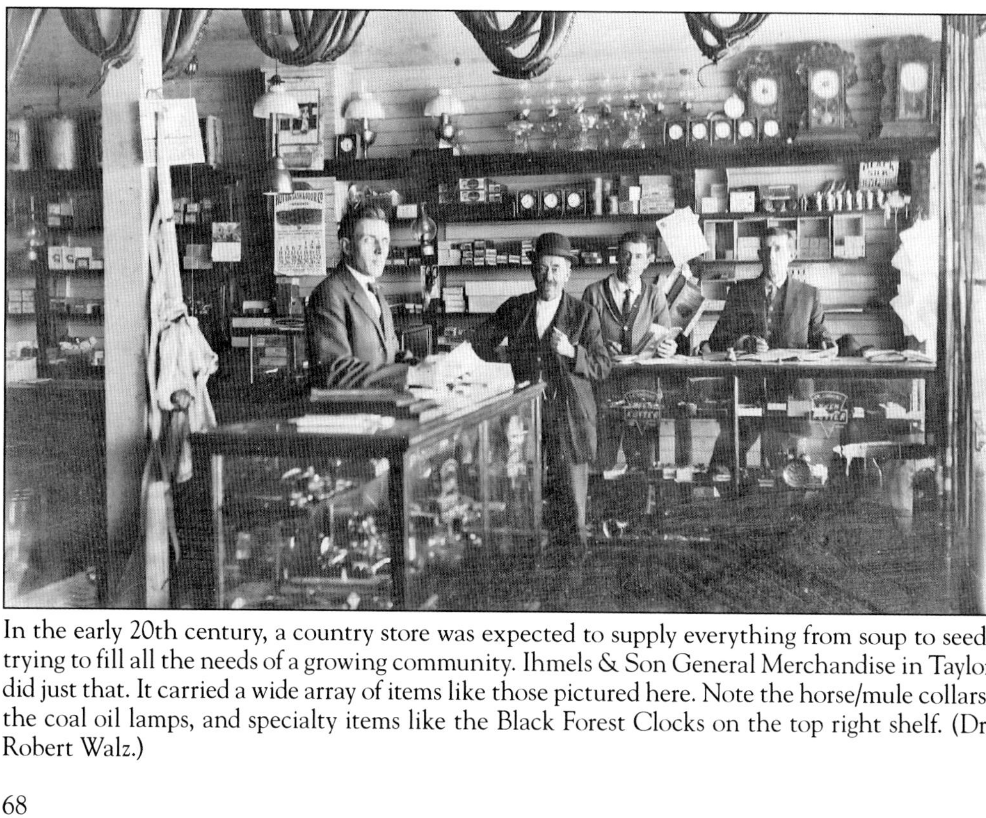

In the early 20th century, a country store was expected to supply everything from soup to seed, trying to fill all the needs of a growing community. Ihmels & Son General Merchandise in Taylor did just that. It carried a wide array of items like those pictured here. Note the horse/mule collars, the coal oil lamps, and specialty items like the Black Forest Clocks on the top right shelf. (Dr. Robert Walz.)

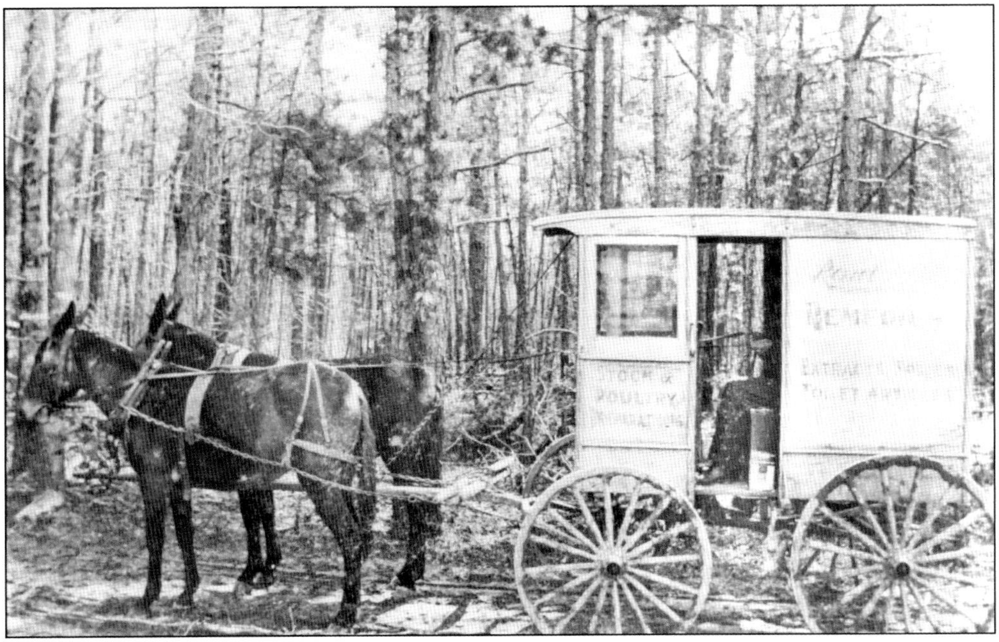

This Rawleigh Remedies wagon was photographed about 1920 and belonged to Frank Lowrance Hodge of McNeil, Arkansas. The owner sold extracts, spices, and toiletry articles and also did stock and poultry preparations. (Kathryn Jean Cashion.)

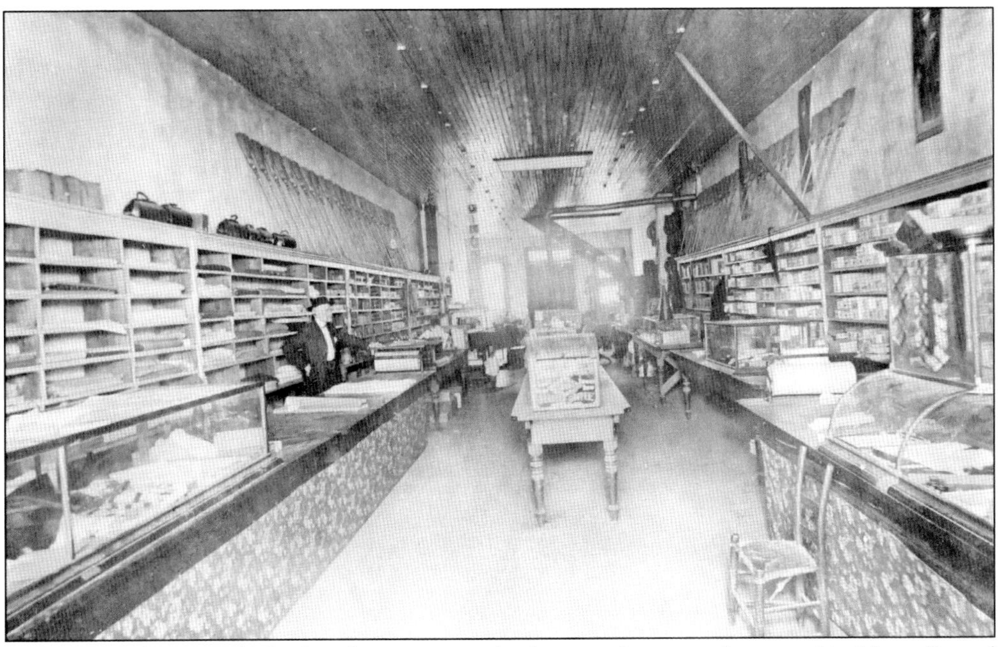

The J.E. Smith General Merchandise store was the first retail mercantile opened in Magnolia and the first two-story brick building. This photograph was taken in 1909, the last year (of 34) that Smith was in the retail business. Due to the panic of 1907, he sold the store to pay off creditors. This photograph was sent to his eight-year-old son L.B., telling him that he was sending him a pair of overalls and an Easter suit. (Belva Smith.)

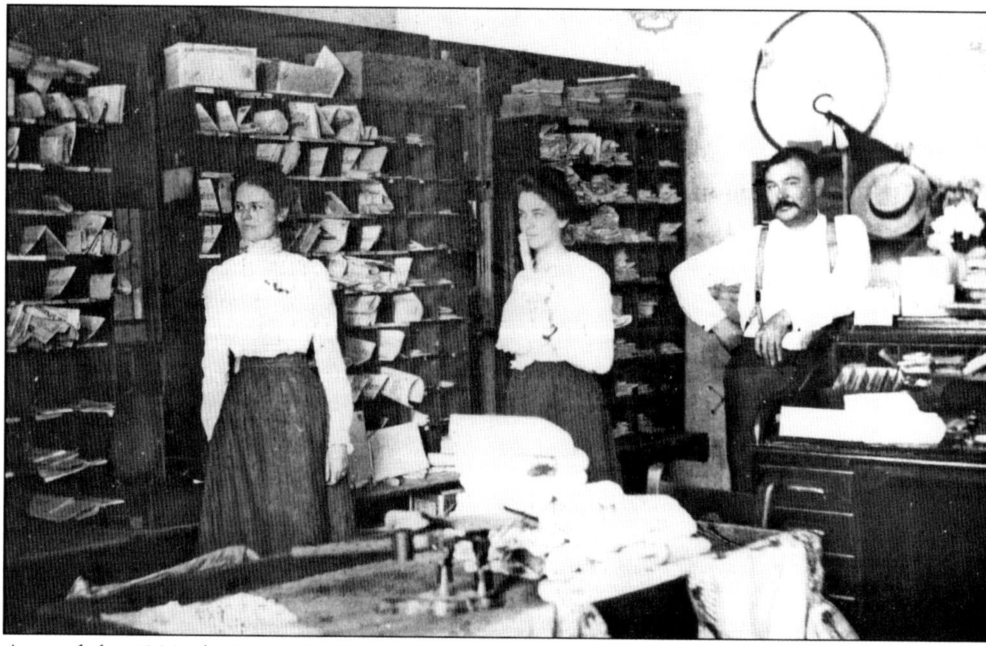

Around the 1900, the Magnolia Post Office was located in the northwest corner of the wooden courthouse. Pictured from left to right are Ophelia Brown, an unidentified woman, and James G. Brown Sr. James was postmaster from 1897 to 1911 and from 1922 to 1934. (Jim Brown Jr.)

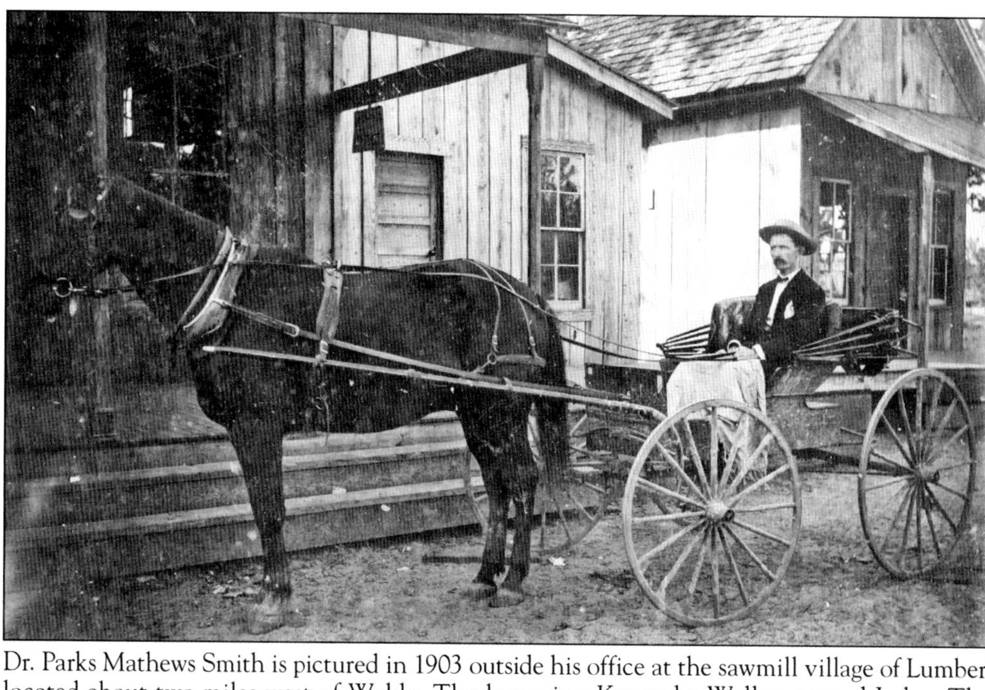

Dr. Parks Mathews Smith is pictured in 1903 outside his office at the sawmill village of Lumber, located about two miles west of Waldo. The horse is a Kentucky Walker named Judge. The doctor also doubled for a time as sawmill superintendent, according to son Don Ross Smith. (Belva Smith.)

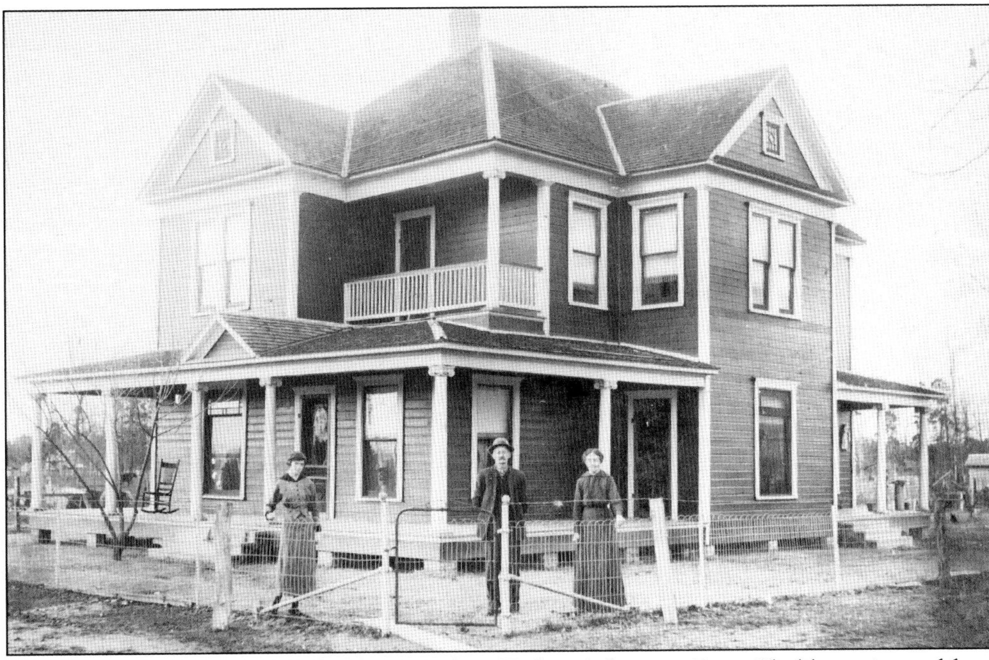

This stately building is the Sheldon Hotel in Taylor, Arkansas. Dave Sheldon, pictured here with his wife, Mary, and daughter Alma, was the owner. The photograph was taken in the early 1900s. (Ronald Orrick.)

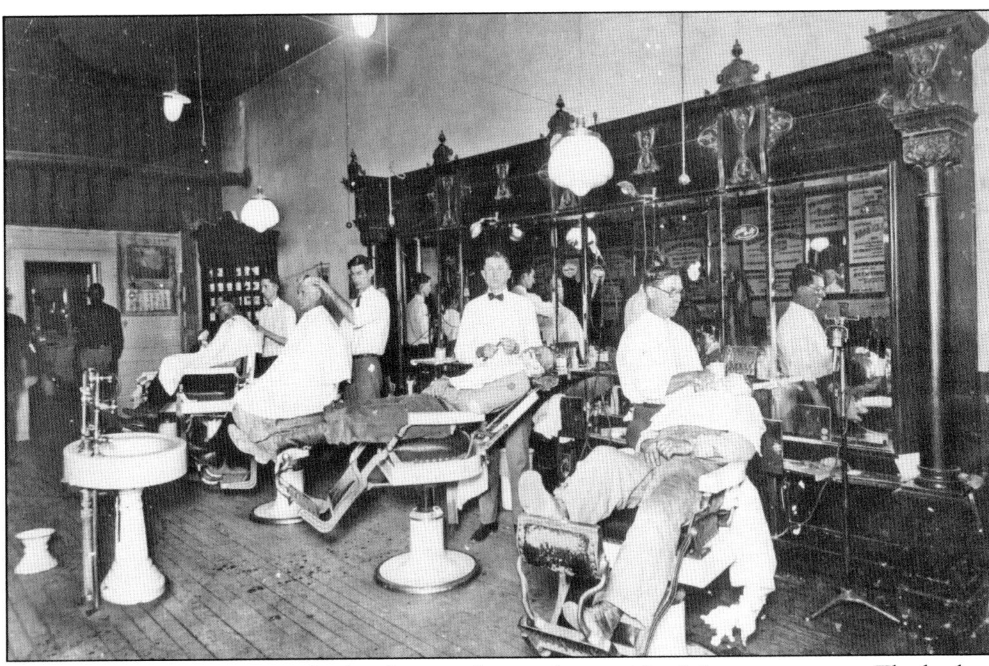

It is December 1925 in Dee's Barbershop on the northwest side of the court square. The barbers are, from left to right starting in back, Johnny Sumner, Clarence Duhon, Walter Dees, and J.E. Atkins; the shoe-shine man is Ben Scott. Female customers had to walk through the men's shop to reach Cecil Dee's new beauty parlor. (Frances Hall.)

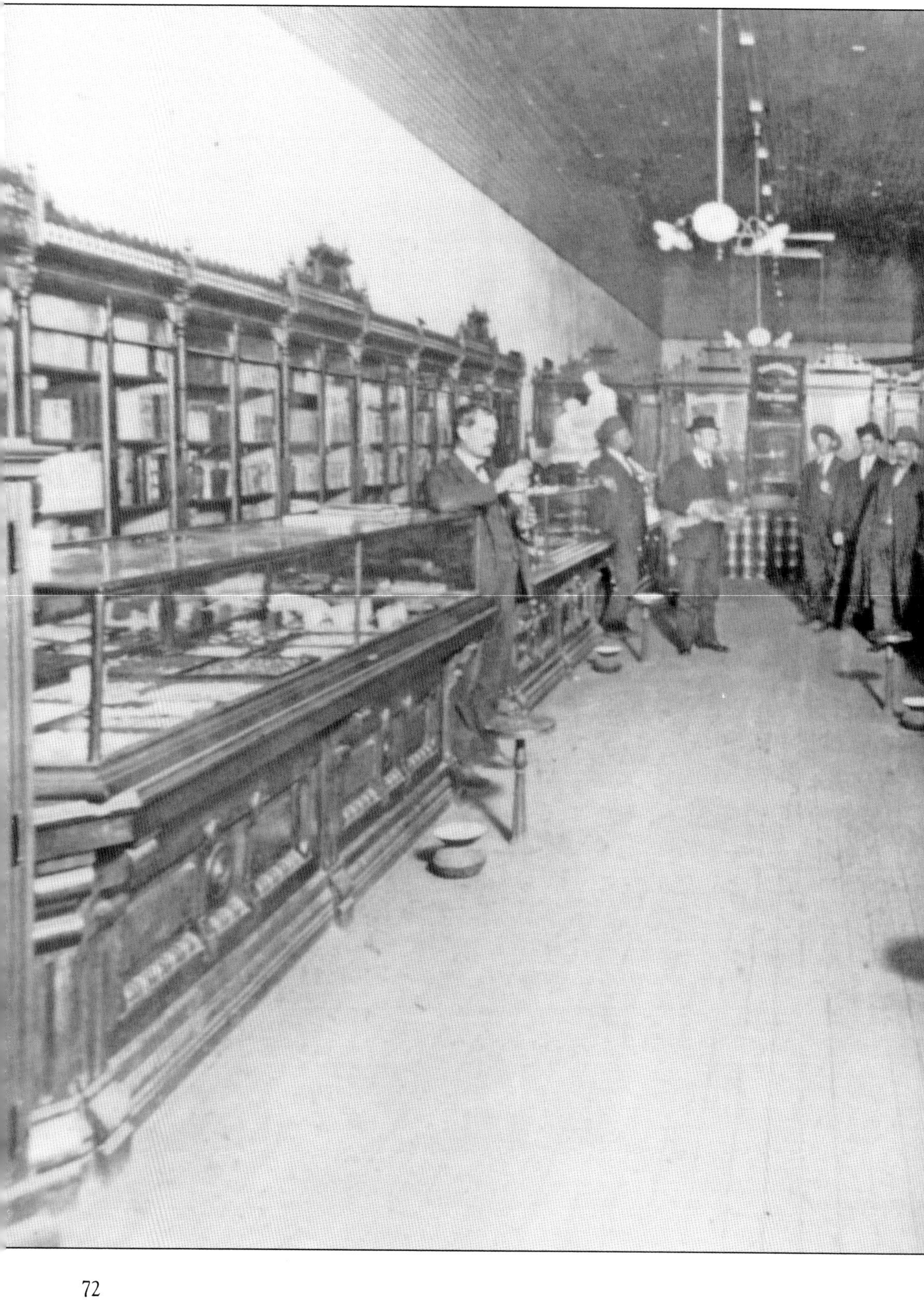

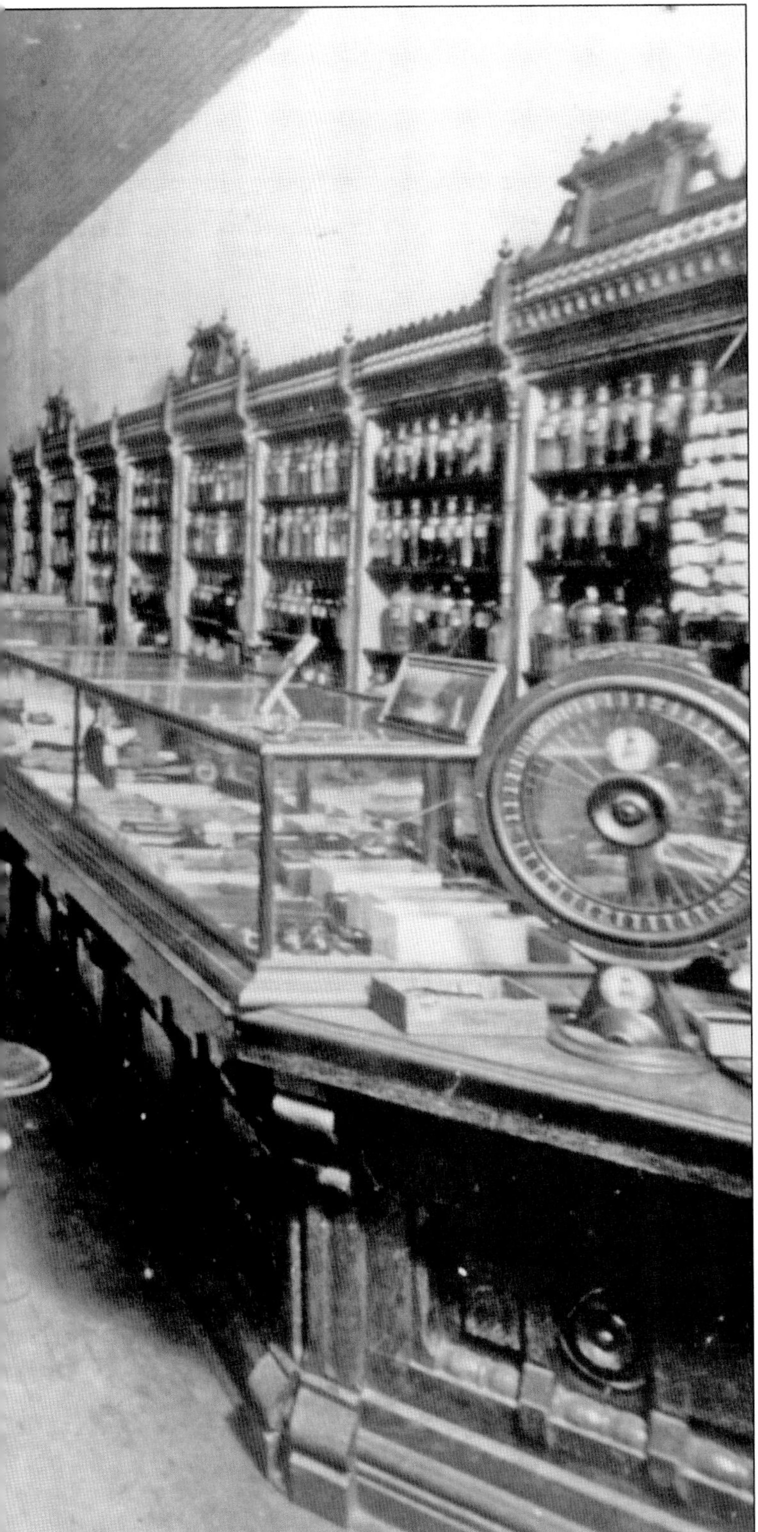

E.T. Hutcheson & Sons Drugstore was open in Magnolia from 1877 to 1973. This picture was taken around 1900 after electricity had been installed. Established by E.T. and A.G. Hutcheson as Hutcheson Brothers, the firm on south court square was in the same family for 96 years. On the far left is J.O. Hutcheson, the store owner from 1923 until his death in 1947. He was the father of Fred A. Hutcheson, who joined him at the drugstore business in 1933. Fred sold the firm to Bascom Jones in 1973. Every child loved a trip to the drugstore to sample the penny candy. (Dr. Robert Walz.)

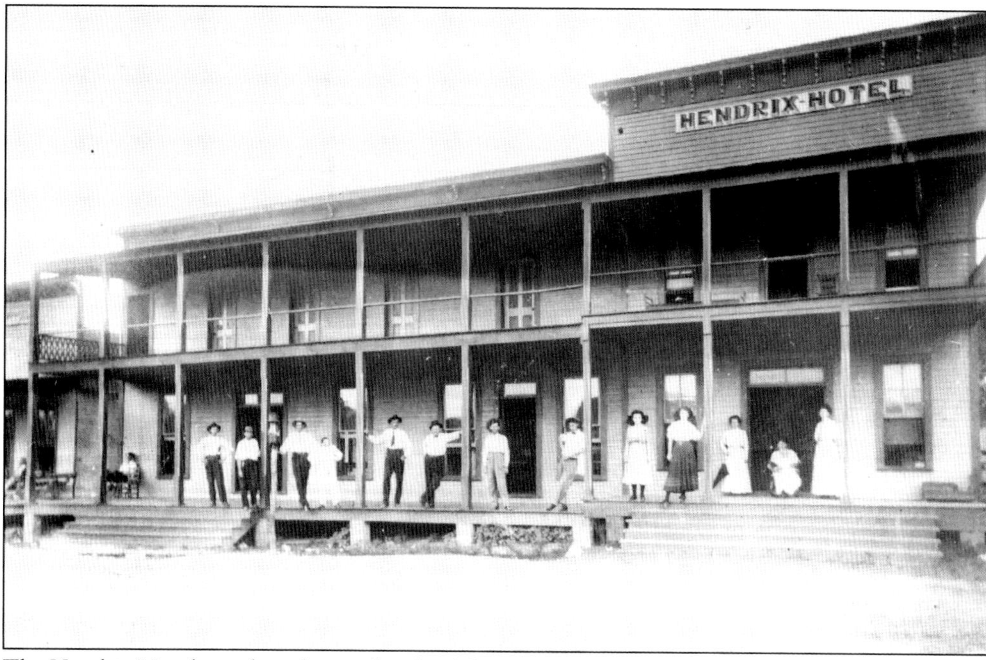

The Hendrix Hotel stood on the south side of the Cotton Belt Railroad tracks, facing north toward the depot in Waldo. This photograph was taken around 1908. Johnny Tidwell is the fourth man standing from the left; at the top of the steps on the right are Ruby Hendrix McElroy (left) and Willie Mae Hendrix Wright. (James Askew.)

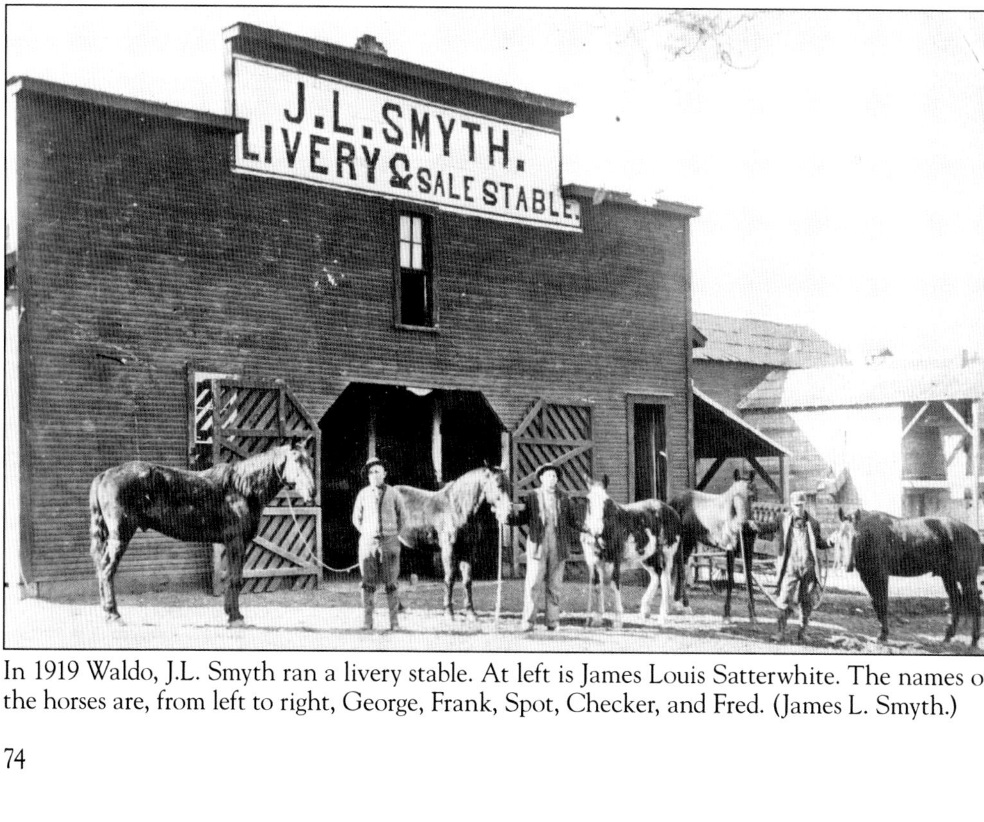

In 1919 Waldo, J.L. Smyth ran a livery stable. At left is James Louis Satterwhite. The names of the horses are, from left to right, George, Frank, Spot, Checker, and Fred. (James L. Smyth.)

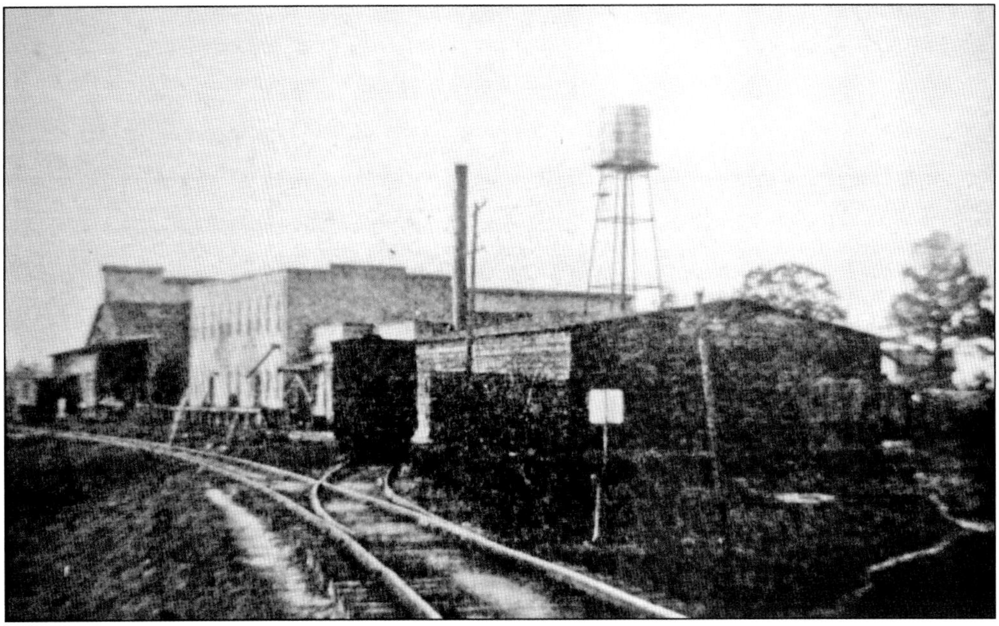

The west side of Magnolia, Arkansas, was the site of many industries. The Columbia Cotton Oil Mill was located on this side of town between the railroad tracks and the city water tower. Here, cottonseeds were received and put through a process that separated the hull and seed to get to the protein and oil-rich kernel. This photograph was most likely taken in 1916. (Columbia County Library.)

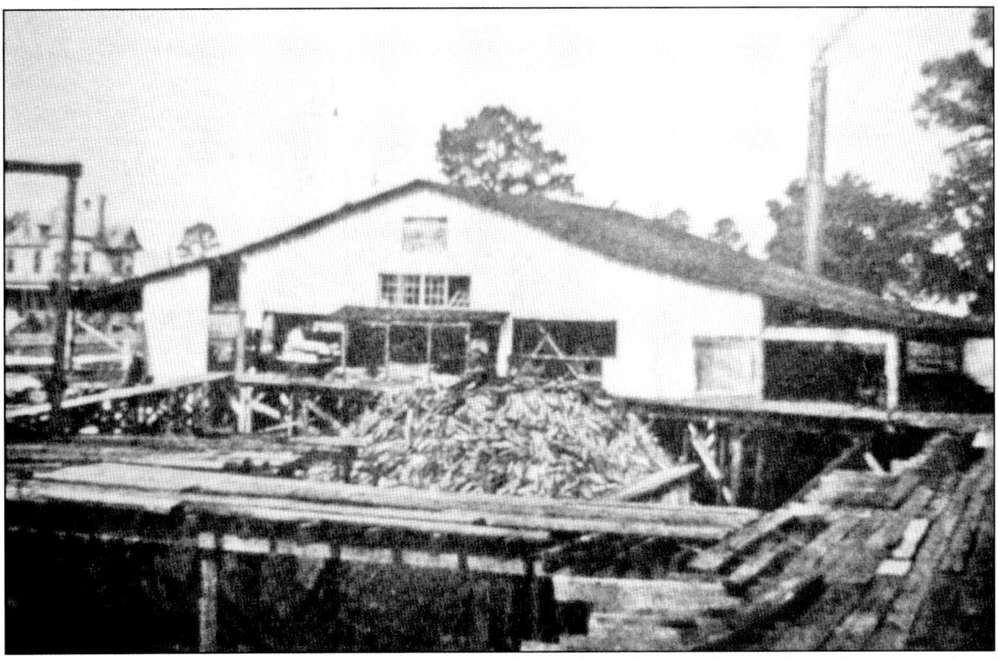

The Magnolia Hardwood Mill was also one of the early industries located on the west side of Magnolia. The mill supplied finished hardwood needed to build the many new businesses and fine homes that were being constructed by the founding families of the city and county. (Columbia County Library.)

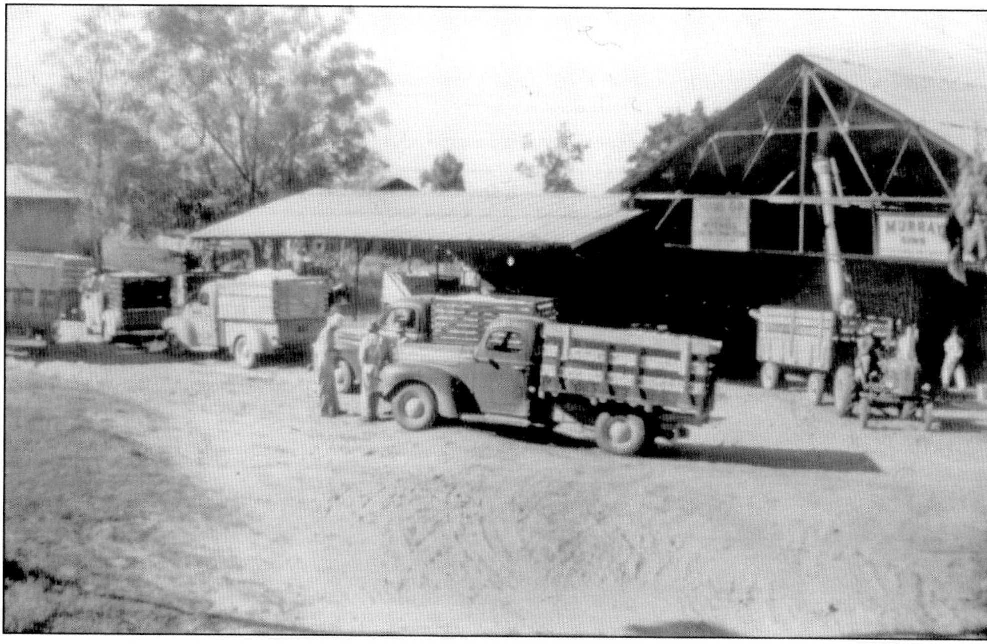

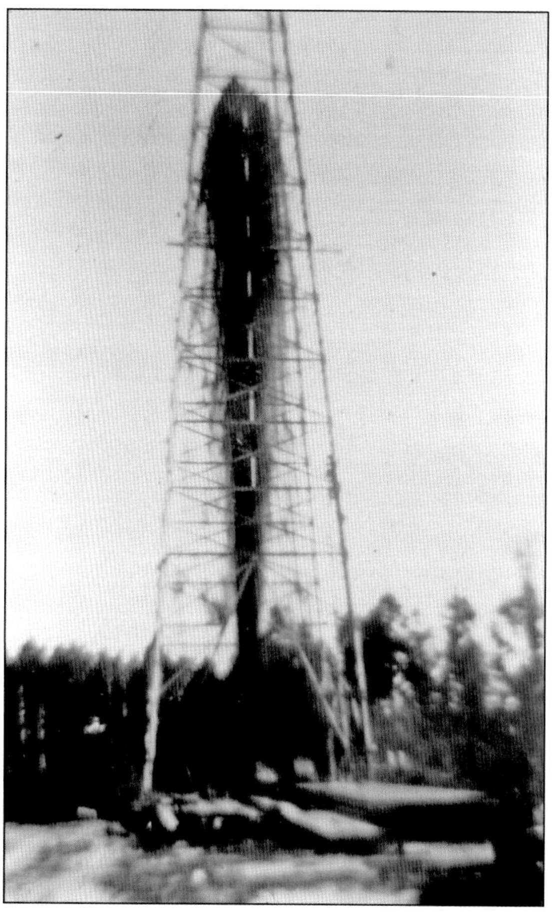

The Thomas Cotton Gin in Magnolia is pictured here. There were four other cotton gins in Columbia County in 1947: the Hicks Gin, J.K. Zachry Gin, Jean Gin Company, and J.A.W. Souter and Son. During the late 1930s and early 1940s, automation came to the local cotton industry with the use of Murray Gin equipment. (Columbia County Library.)

Oil, black gold, and Texas tea are various names used to refer to a substance known as crude oil. A fossil fuel is formed when large quantities of dead organisms are buried underneath layered rock that undergo intense heat and pressure over thousands of years. This photograph, taken in 1937 or 1938, is just one of the many gushers that introduced Columbia County to petroleum. This introduction would catapult the county into a realm of oil fields, roughnecks, and rigs. This rich heritage is still evident from the many oil wells in production here today. (Columbia County Library.)

Five

County Seat and Court Square

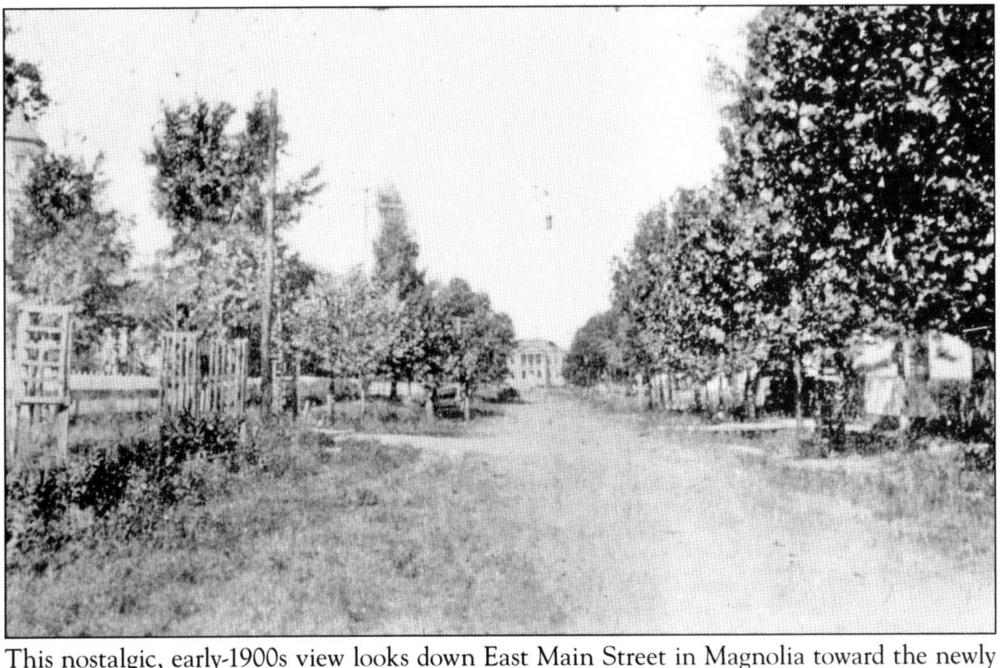

This nostalgic, early-1900s view looks down East Main Street in Magnolia toward the newly constructed brick courthouse. The street is unpaved, and the trees have wooden framework around the trunks to protect them from harm. (Columbia County Library.)

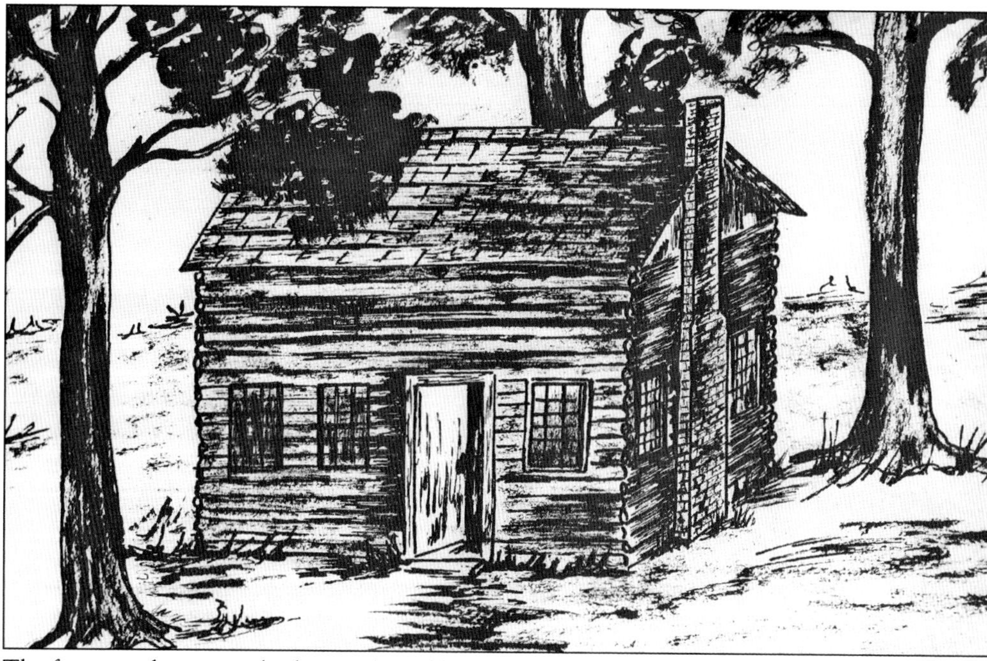

The first courthouse was built in 1853 and located at the corner of East Main and South Jackson Streets in Magnolia. Plans for a temporary courthouse were submitted in October 1853 with the stipulation that the cost could not exceed $450. It was to be built of hewn logs measuring 24 feet by 36 feet. (Glenn Martell.)

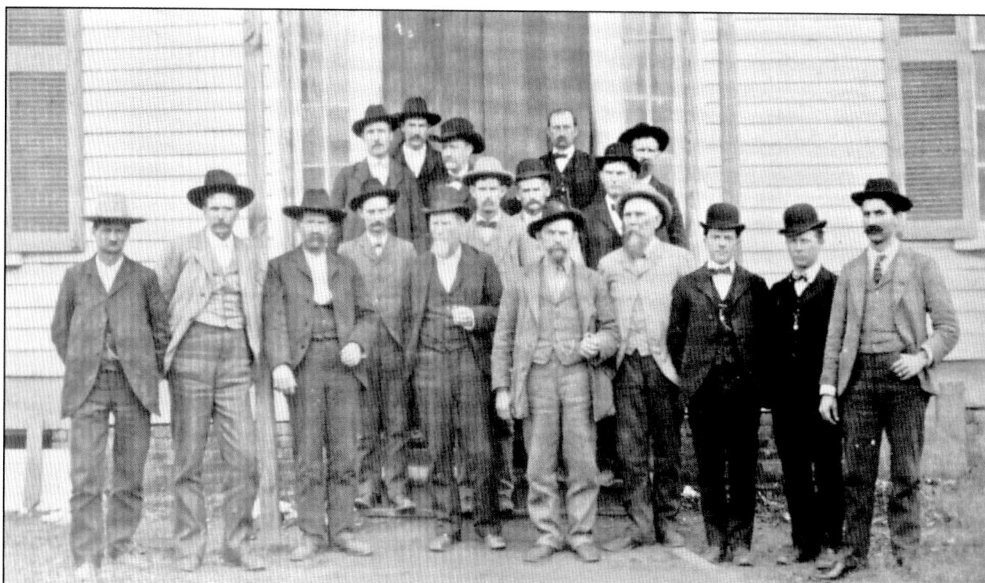

A Columbia County, Arkansas, grand jury in 1902 stands outside the two-story wooden courthouse, which stood in Magnolia from 1856 to 1904. Members of that jury are, from left to right, (first row) E.W. Warren (sheriff), John Dennis (special sheriff), Mathew Hayes, John Bates, Charles Lewis, A.B. Henderson, Charles Gordon, A.J. Trammell, Walter Hudson, and J.D. Threilkill; (second row) J.E. McAlister, Watson Keith, James Craig, W.B. Atkinson, John Alexander, Litt Wilson, Tom Souter, and M.J. Talley. (Dr. Robert Walz.)

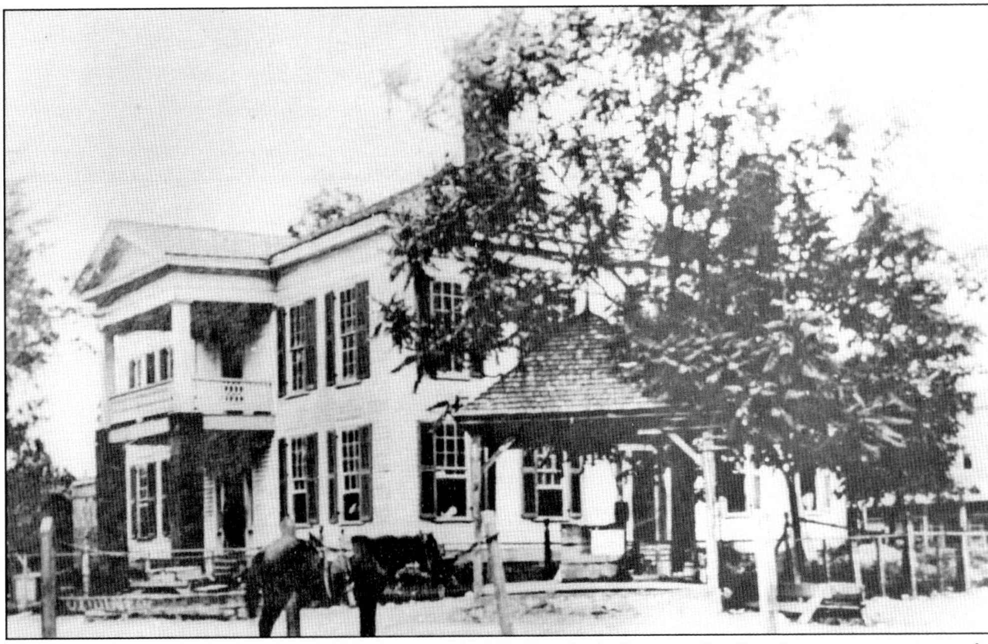

On January 10, 1855, the county court ordered that bids be sought for the construction of a permanent courthouse to be built on the public square. An advertisement was published in the *Ouachita Herald* at Camden, and $6,000 was appropriated for the erection of the building. (R.S. "Bob" Warnock.)

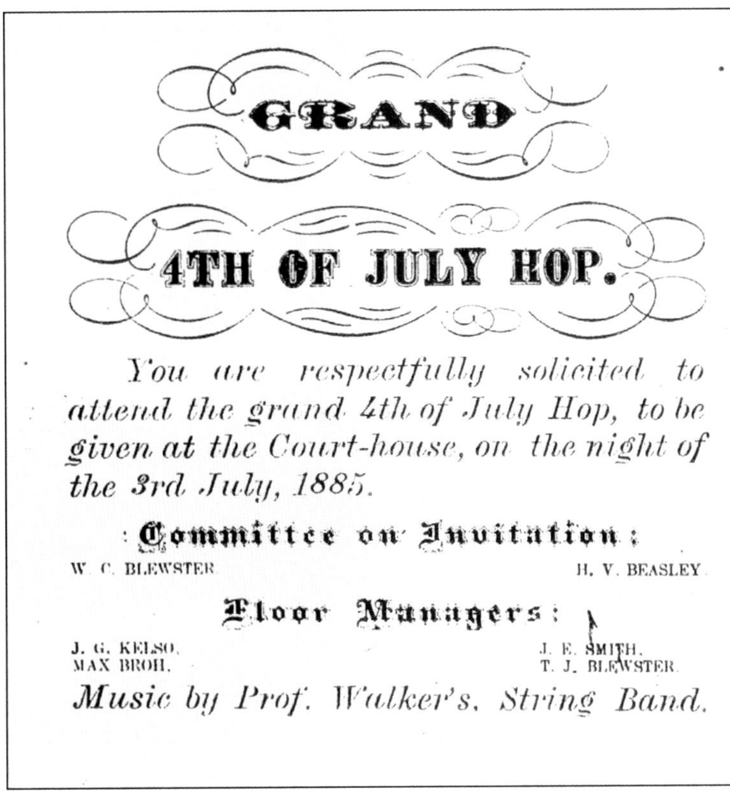

GRAND

4TH OF JULY HOP.

You are respectfully solicited to attend the grand 4th of July Hop, to be given at the Court-house, on the night of the 3rd July, 1885.

Committee on Invitation:

W. C. BLEWSTER H. V. BEASLEY

Floor Managers:

J. G. KELSO, J. E. SMITH,
MAX BROH, T. J. BLEWSTER.

Music by Prof. Walker's, String Band.

This invitation, extended by the Knights of Pythias, was to a "Grand Hop" held on Friday night, July 3, 1885. The hop would be held at the wooden Columbia County Courthouse. The local lodge practiced the tenets of Damon and Pythias but was, at times, socially inclined, as can be seen on the invitation. (Wilbur A. Smith of Texarkana.)

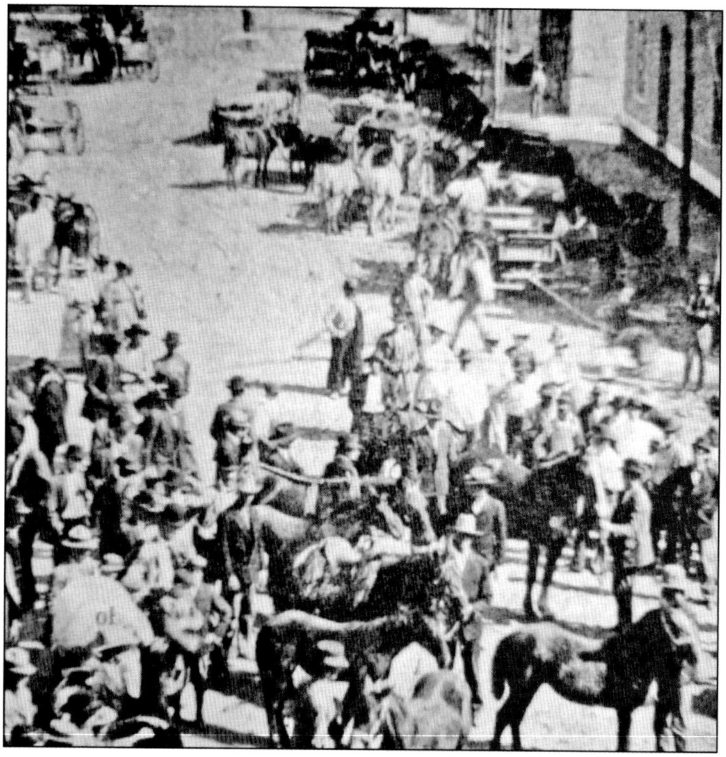

An example of commerce conducted on the courthouse square is this Colt Show and Sale that occurred in either 1915 or 1916. Stockmen came from far and wide to buy, sell, and trade horses. Animal husbandry arrangements were also likely made. (Columbia County Library.)

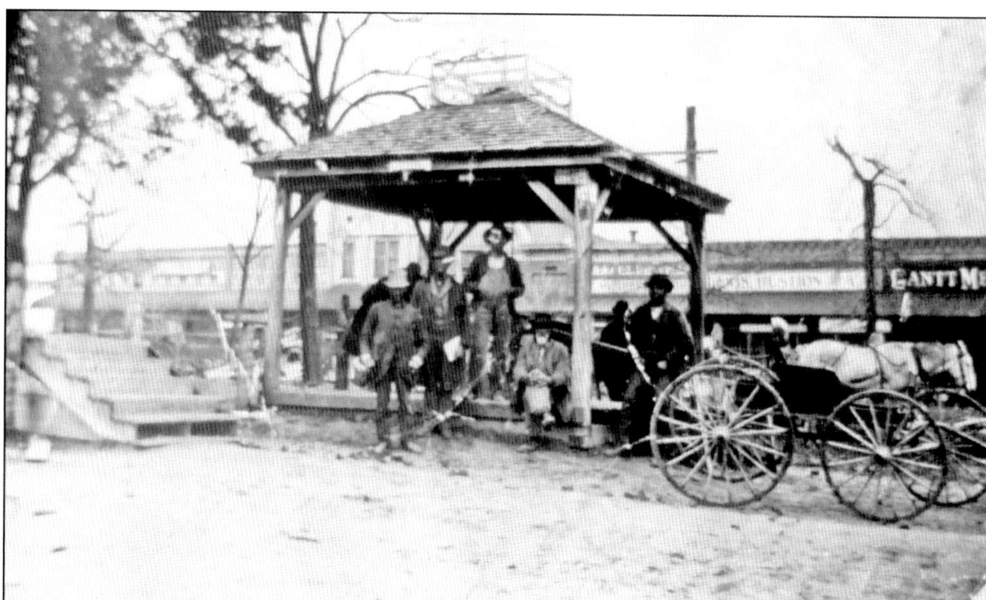

This is a rare, c. 1902 photograph of the courthouse well on the southwest corner of the square in Magnolia. (Alice Monroe.)

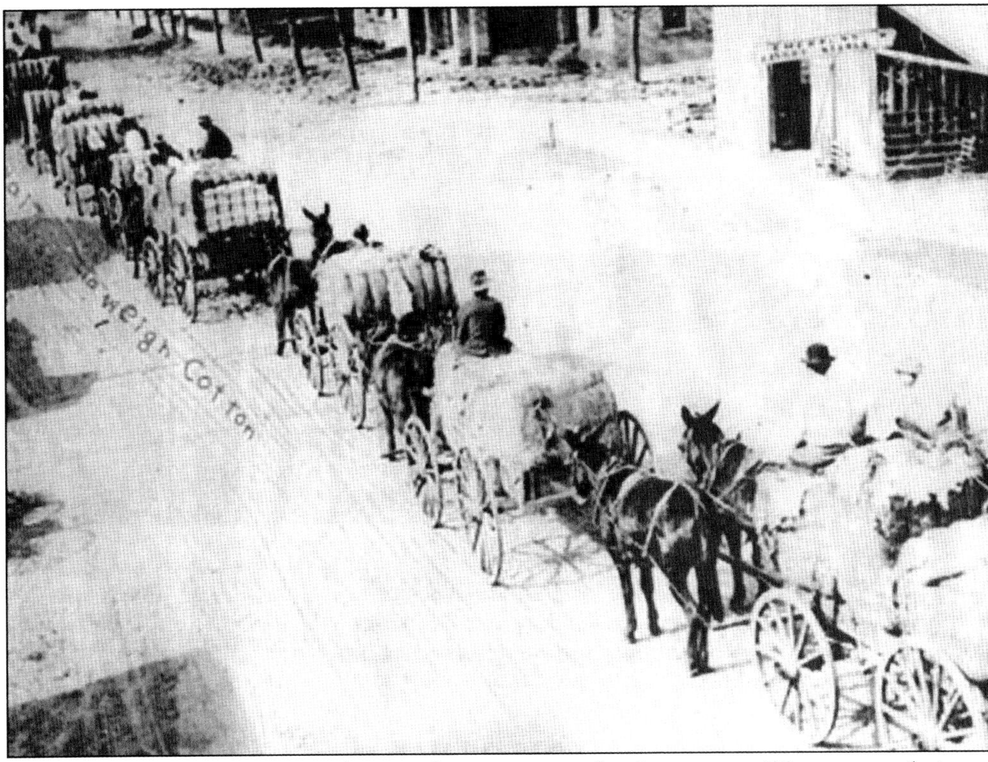

A mule-drawn wagon train on the courthouse square is hauling cotton. They are on their way to the compress to have the cotton weighed. In 1913, cotton sold for 12.47¢ per pound; the price would fall the following year. (O.A. "Buddy" Franks.)

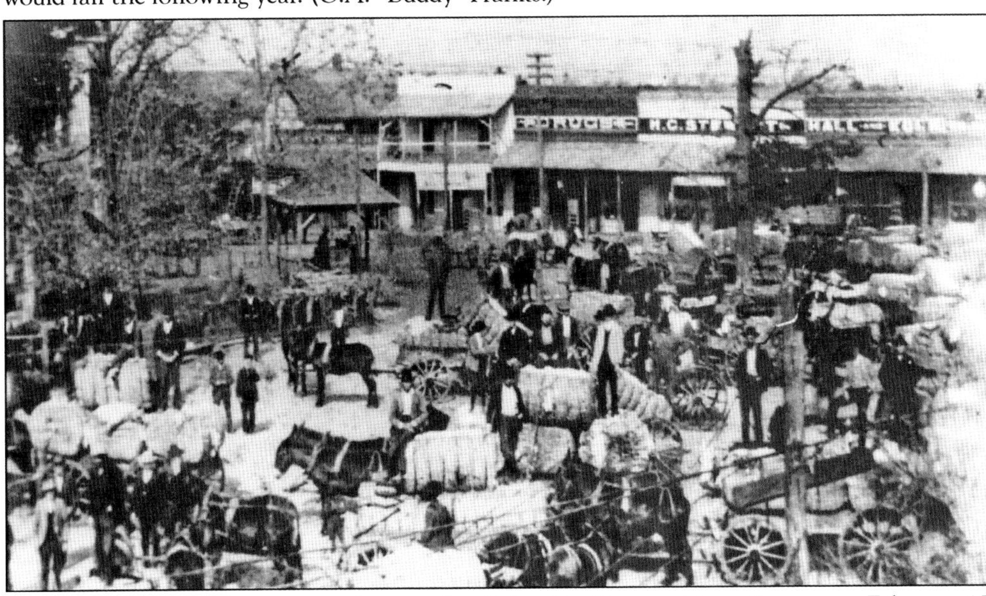

A very busy group of citizens gathers at the Columbia County Court Square on February 15, 1904. It is nearing the end of the season, as evidenced by the few remaining leaves on the trees. The cotton has been picked, cleaned, baled, weighed, and brought to market. Written on this photograph is the price of cotton at the time in Magnolia—15¢ per pound. (Dr. Robert Walz.)

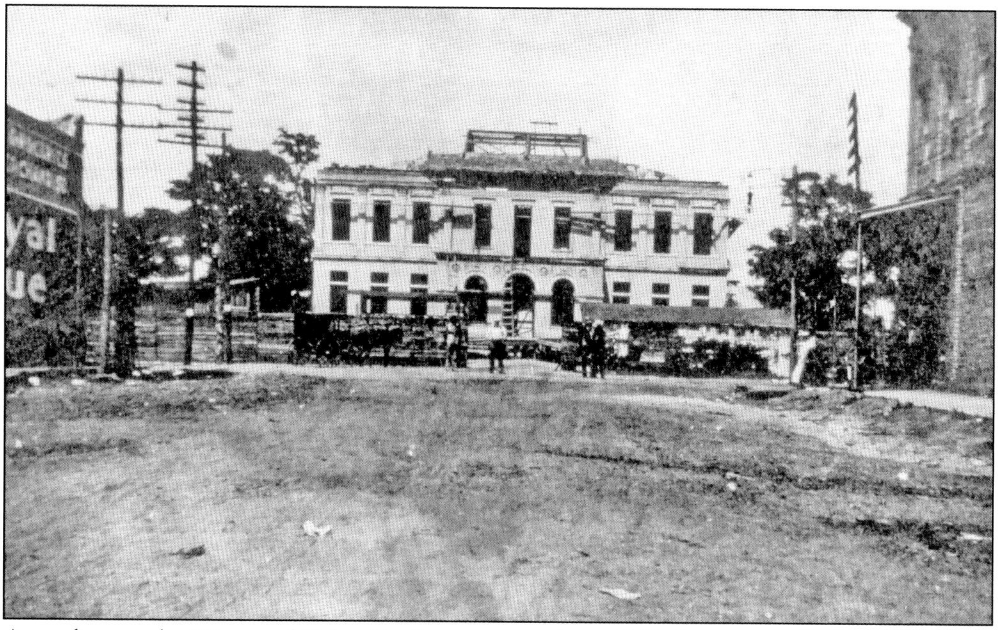

According to the *History of Columbia County*, as early as 1902 there was talk around town of building a new courthouse. A two-mill levy was voted on by the quorum court of Columbia County in 1903, and plans for the new courthouse were submitted in December 1904. (Sybil Jones.)

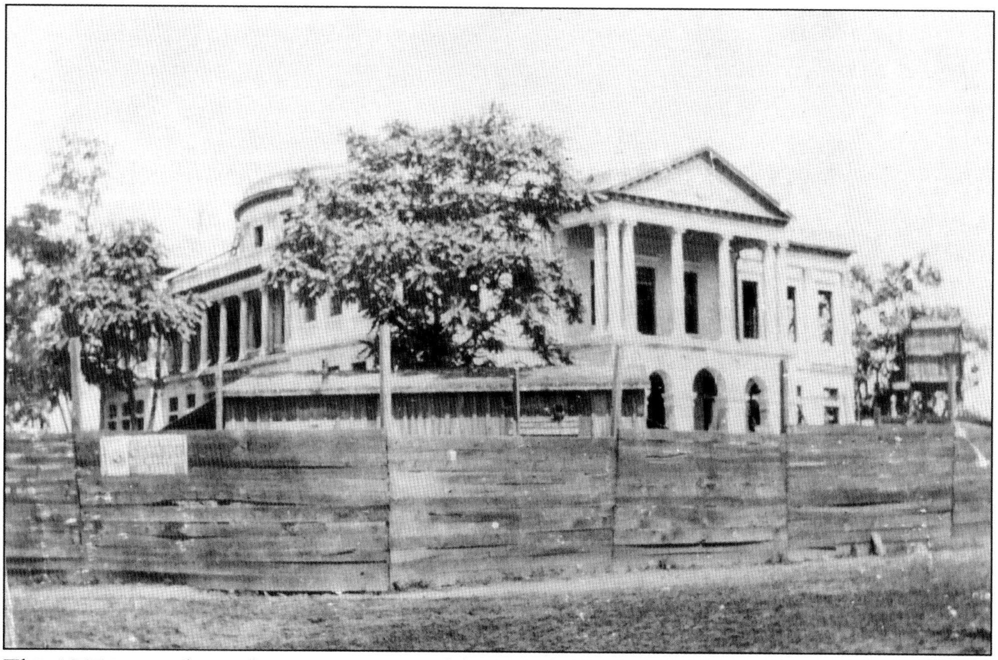

This 1906 image shows that construction of the courthouse is nearing completion. Note that the roof is incomplete, and no windows are yet installed. Magnolia trees did not yet grace the square, for the hardwoods shown in this picture shaded the frame courthouse. The structure was moved in 1905 to clear the site for the new brick building. (Dr. Hugh Longino.)

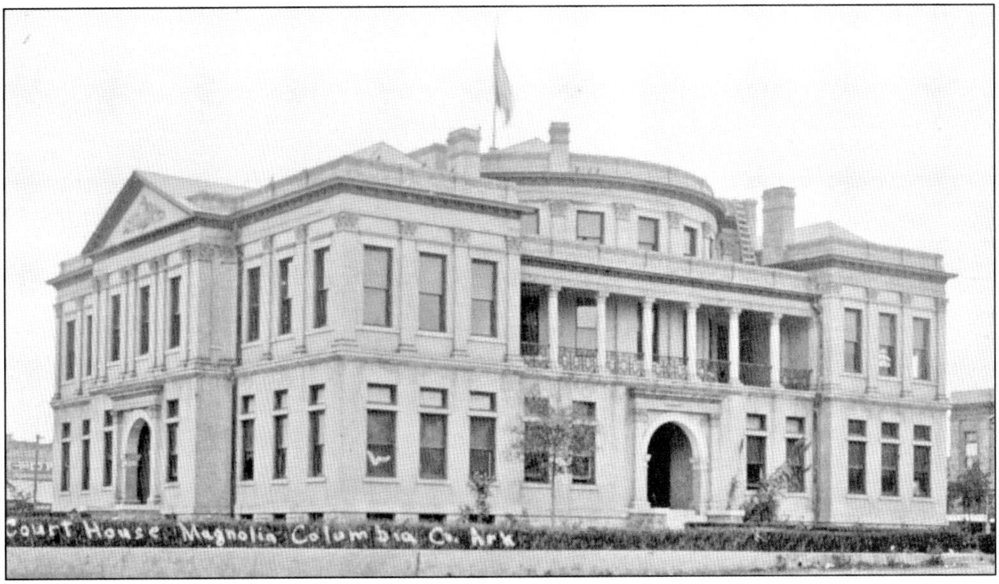

This view of the north facade of the Columbia County Courthouse, in its completed splendor, was taken in 1908. Take note of the tiny oaks planted on both of sides of the right-hand entry. Today, many mature and majestic magnolia trees grace the courthouse lawn. (Ellen G. Lewis.)

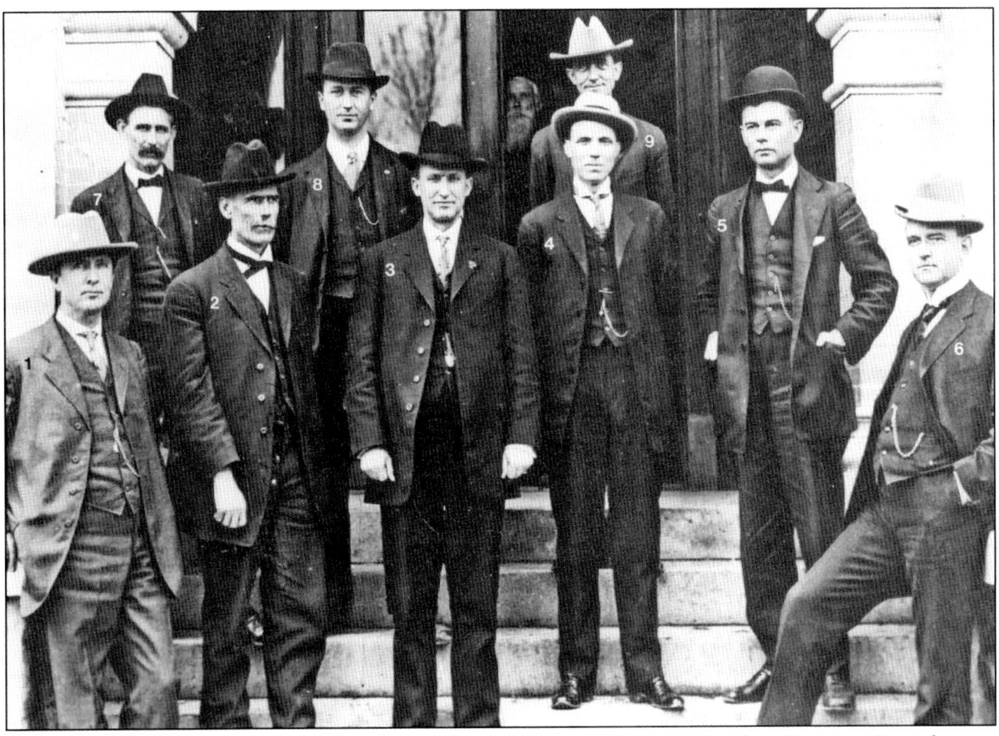

A group of lawyers is pictured congregated on the steps of the Columbia County Courthouse, which was completed in 1906. In numerical order, they are Col. Charles W. McKay, Henry Stevens, unidentified, Edgar Hawkins, J.G. Lile, Hamp Smead of Camden, J.Y. Stevens, George LeCroy, and Will Askew. (Allie Wallis Souter.)

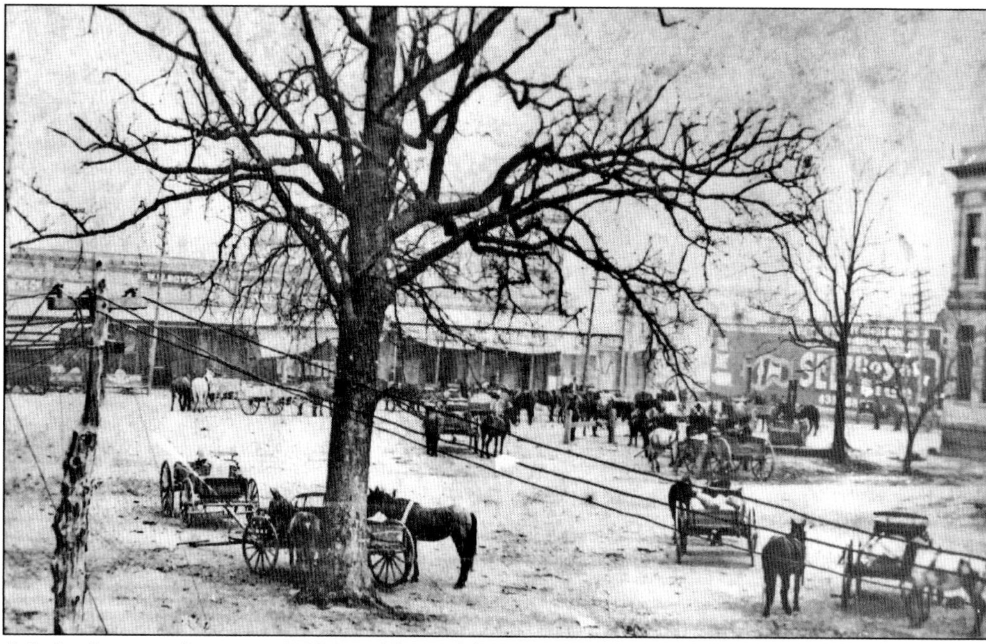

A light dusting of snow in 1907 heralds a cold winter day on the north side of the court square. Note the thickness of the telephone lines attached to the rough-hewn pole on the left. The first telephones in Magnolia were installed in 1885 between the Louisiana and North West Railroad depot and the clerk's office at the courthouse. (Dr. Robert Walz.)

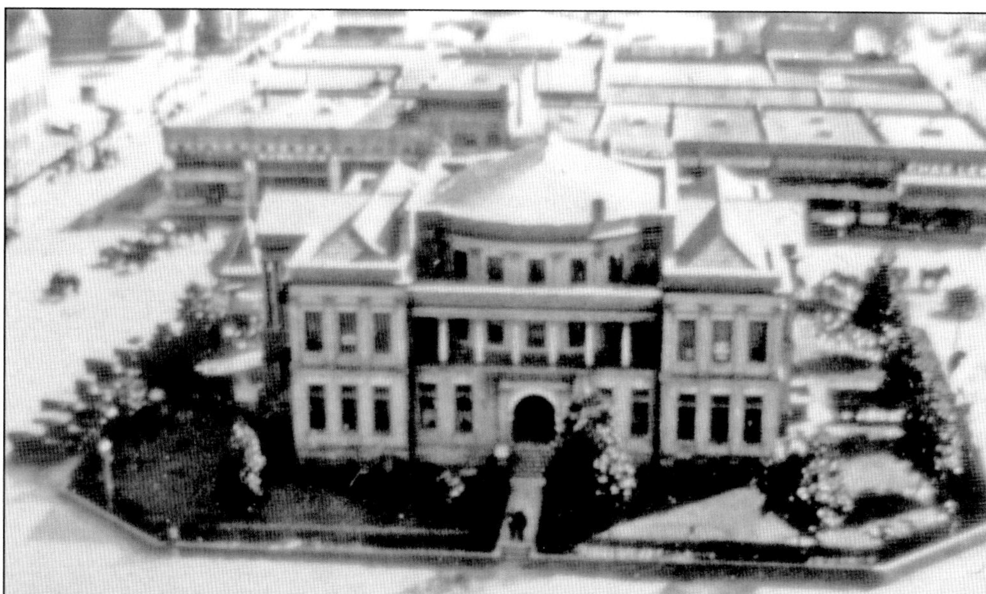

This is an aerial view of the Columbia County Courthouse taken in 1920. The courthouse has stood the test of time and has served its citizens for more than 100 years. A restoration committee oversees the building and keeps the property in good repair for daily use by elected officials and the citizens of the county. (Dr. Robert Walz.)

Six

EARLY TRANSPORTATION

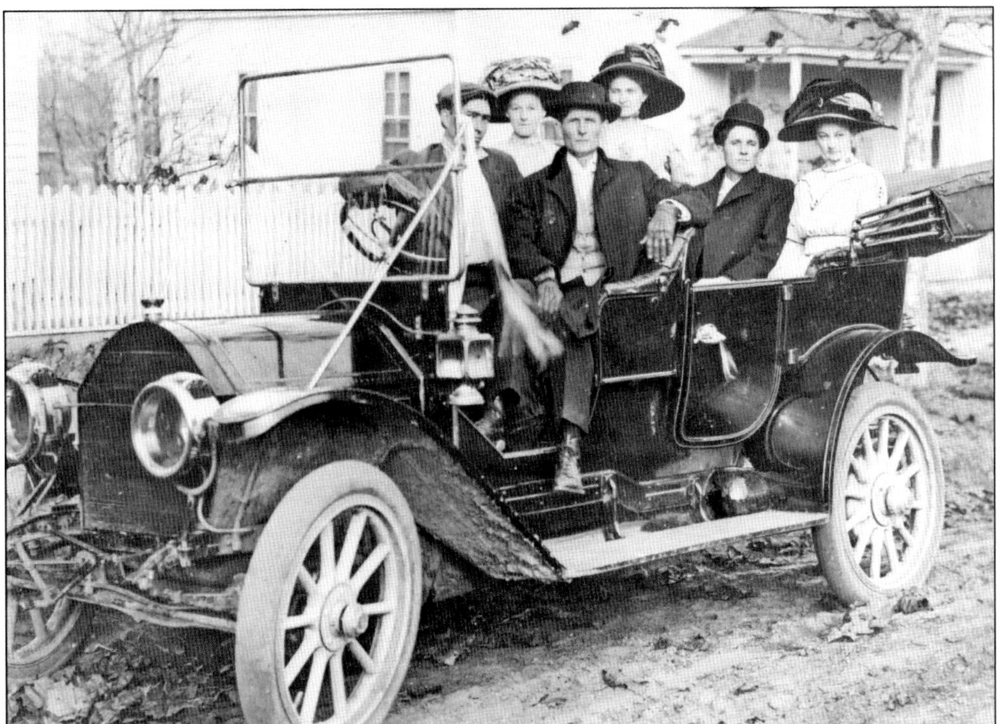

The introduction of the automobile to Columbia County as a new and distinct curiosity was welcomed into the lives of the citizenry. Many couples chose to have their marriage ceremonies performed in a car, and this practice continued into the late 1920s. This is a photograph of the first couple married in the first automobile in Magnolia, Arkansas, on November 20, 1910. The groom and the bride, Burkett Daniels and Lessie Henry, are seated in the back seat; In the front of the car are, owner of the 1910 Cadillac Duke Emerson (left) and Buck McKissick; standing behind the car are Floy Warren (left) and Callye Daniels. In the background is the First Baptist parsonage, home of Reverend Scarbrough, the minister who performed the marriage ceremony. (Lessie Daniels.)

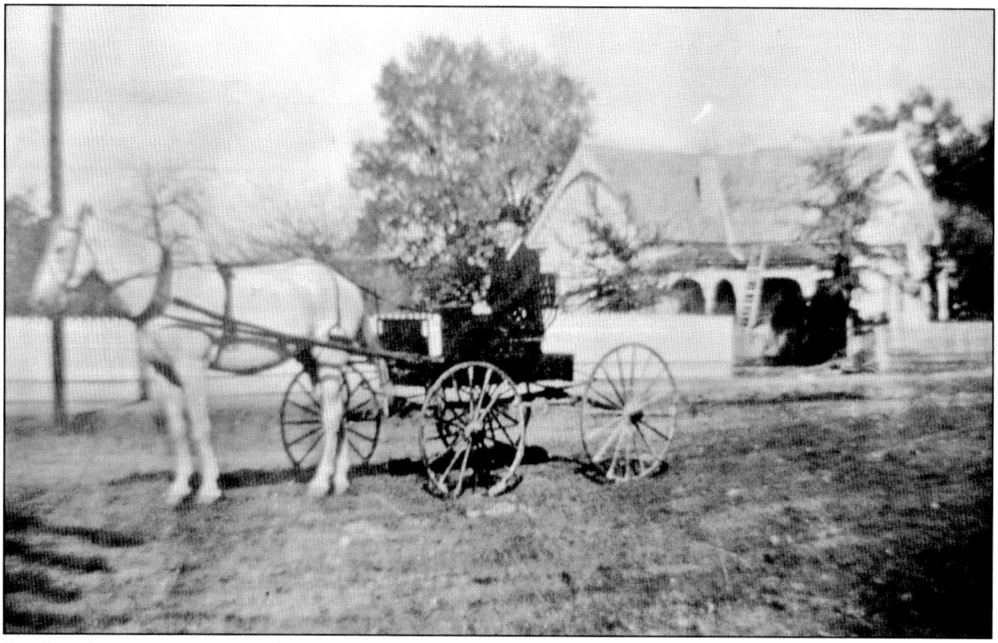

Dr. Hugh Longino, one of Columbia County's earliest doctors, is pictured in his horse-drawn buggy while on a house call in the early 1900s. The days of a country doctor were often long and arduous. They were general practitioners whose abilities ran the gamut from removing splinters to delivering babies. (Dr. Robert Walz.)

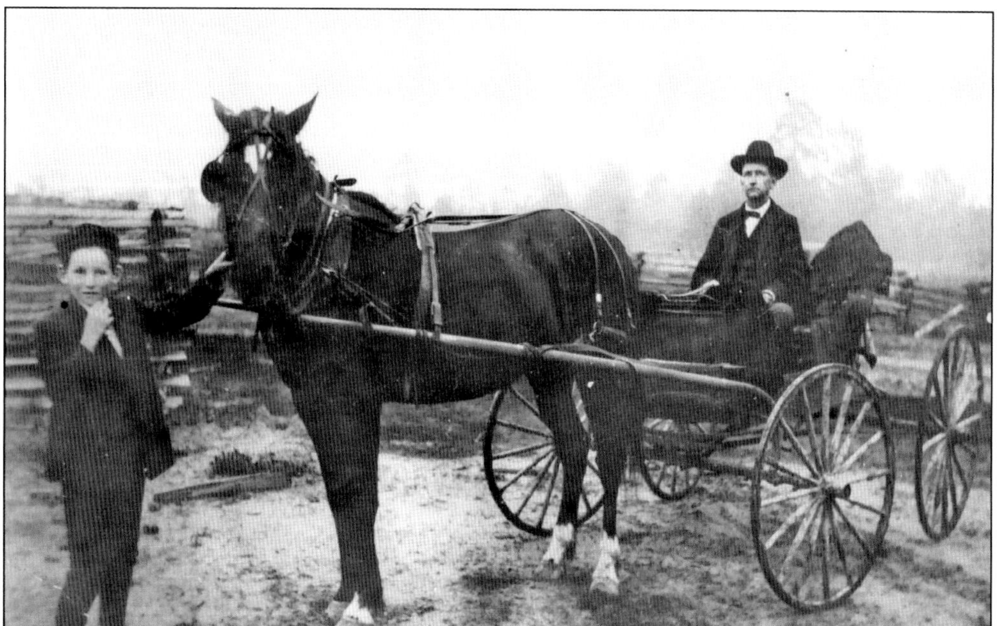

Seated in his buggy in 1906 is W.S. Pace, and holding the horse is Pace's nephew Isaac T. Hudgens. The photograph was taken near the old brick kiln, two miles north of Waldo. Pace was one of two bachelor uncles who helped raise Hudgens, whose mother had died when he was quite young. (I.T. Hudgens.)

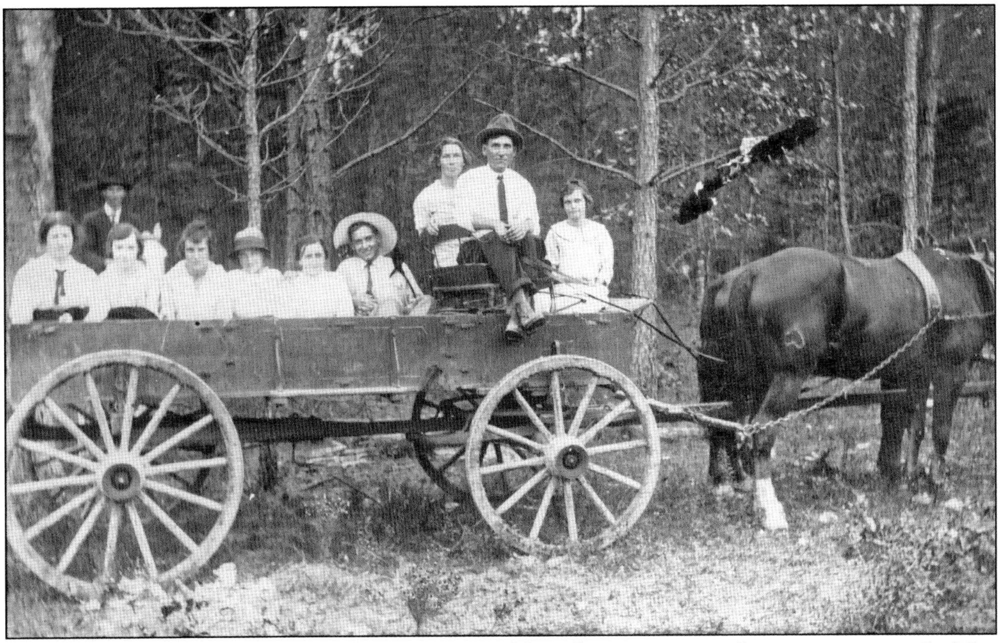

The smiles in this photograph indicate a group of friends enjoying an afternoon wagon ride. The group was on a Sunday school picnic in the Taylor area. Somewhere in this wagon, there is likely a basket containing tasty fried chicken, scrumptious potato salad, and lovingly prepared apple pies. (Ronald Orrick.)

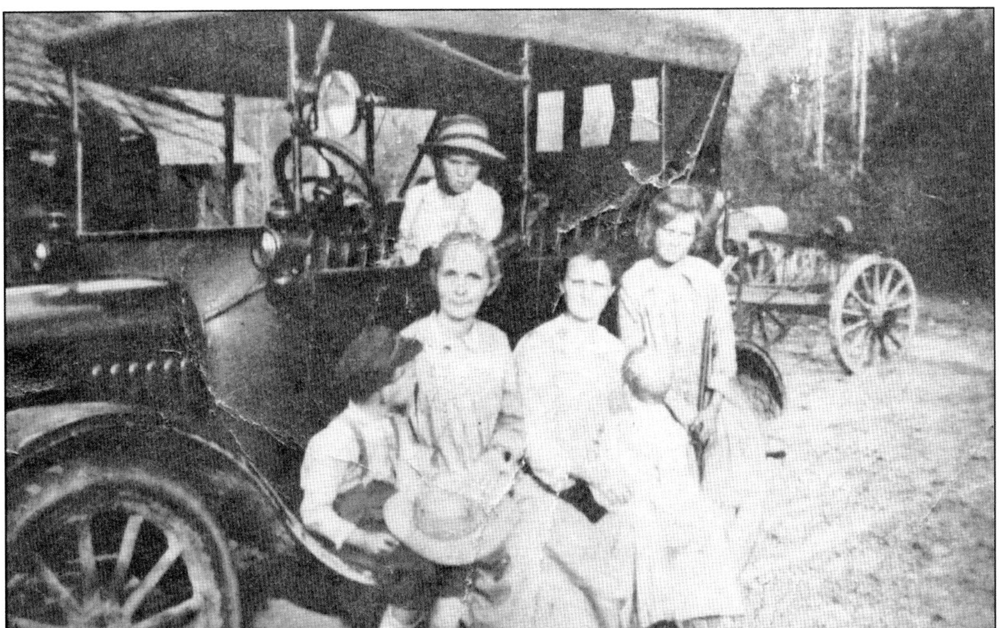

Enjoying their new car, Shepherd family members in Atlanta pose for the camera. From left to right in front are (first row) unidentified, Bell Jean Shepherd, Clara Shepherd Peace, Mary Shepherd, and Shepherd Adkins; behind the wheel is Roger Shepherd. (Marie Shepherd.)

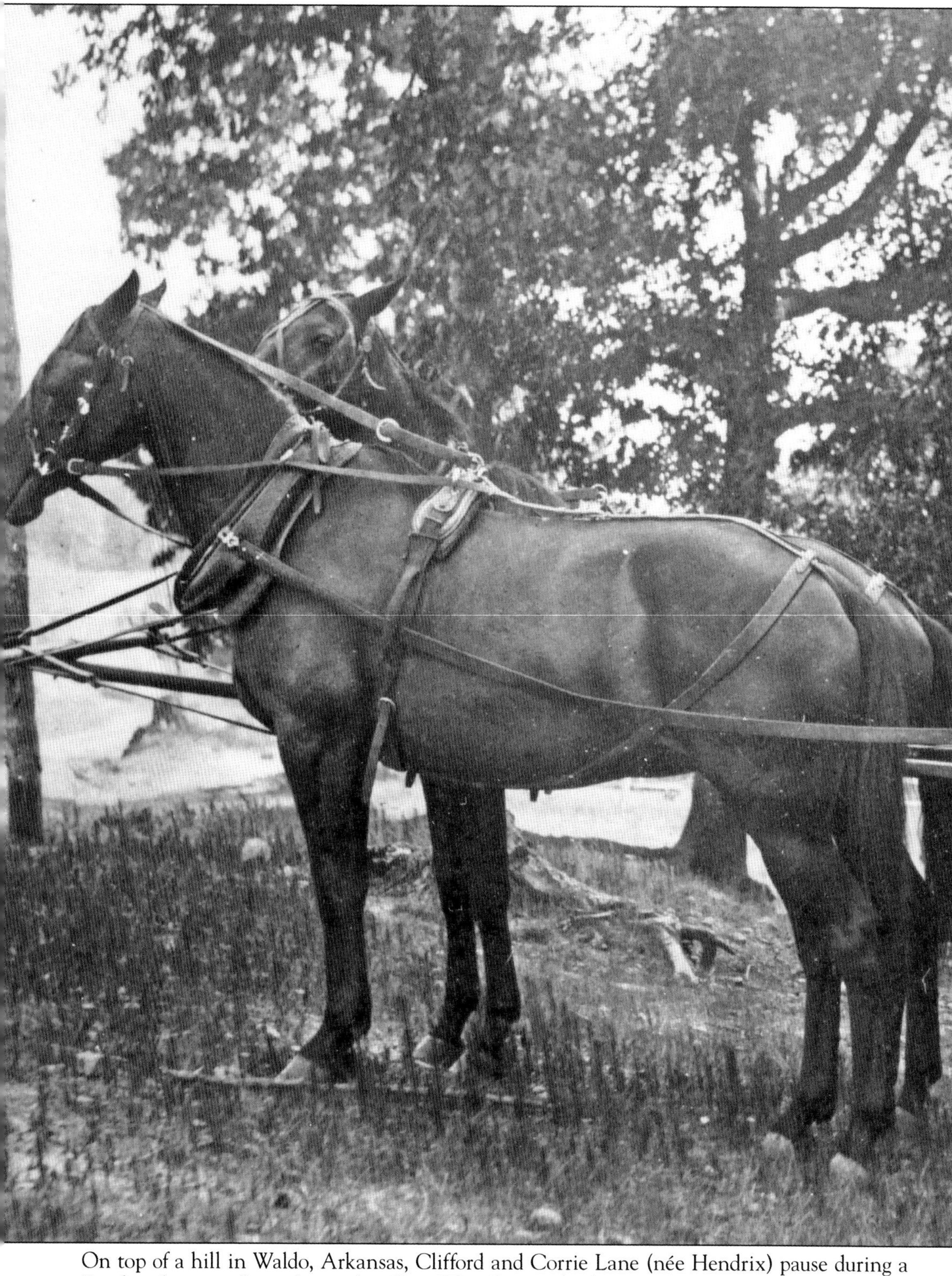

On top of a hill in Waldo, Arkansas, Clifford and Corrie Lane (née Hendrix) pause during a Sunday afternoon drive; the rig chauffer is Wirt Sheppard. The 1910 photograph of this handsome

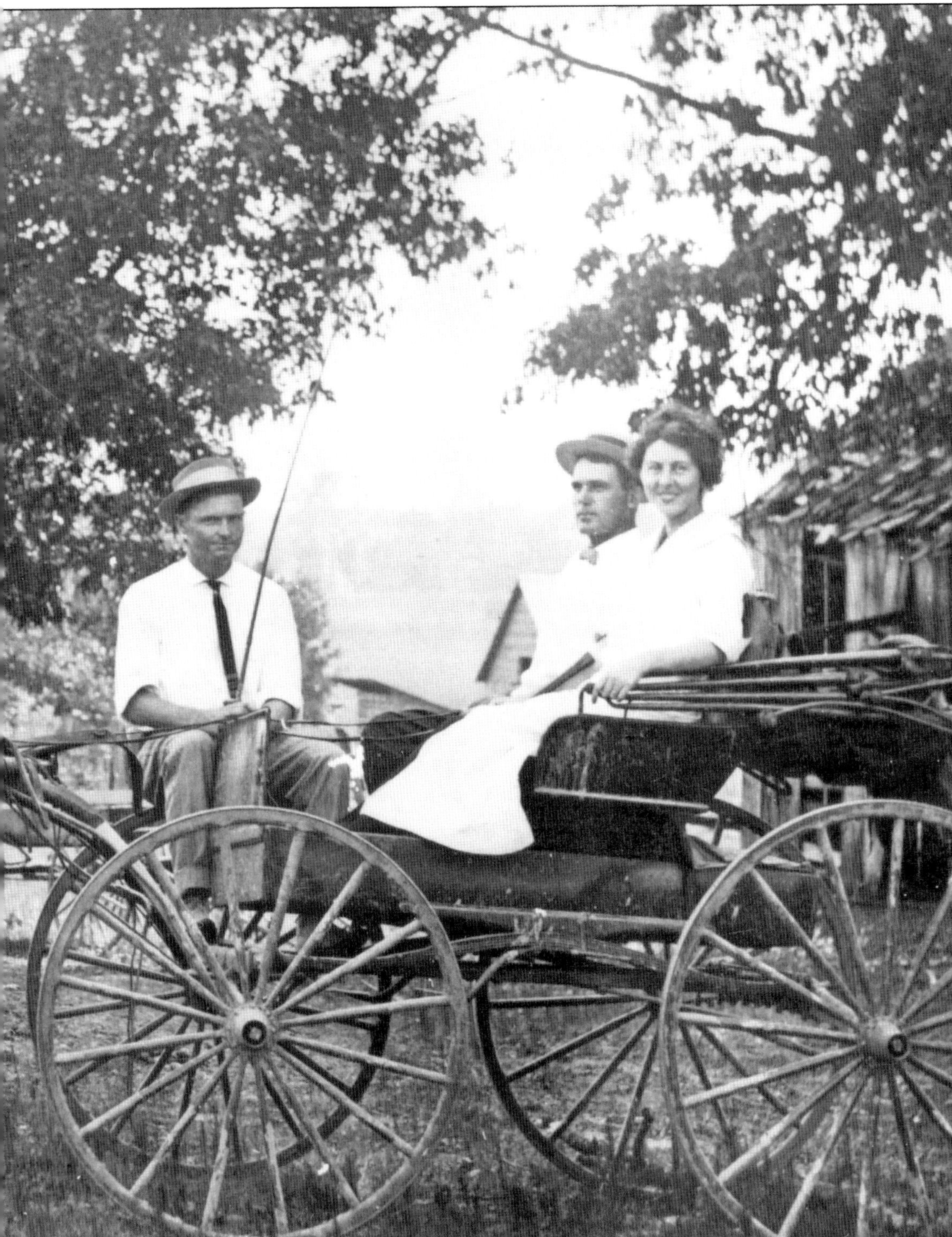

couple in a beautiful pastoral setting is reminiscent of an age when life was languid and genteel. (Betty Askew Genestet.)

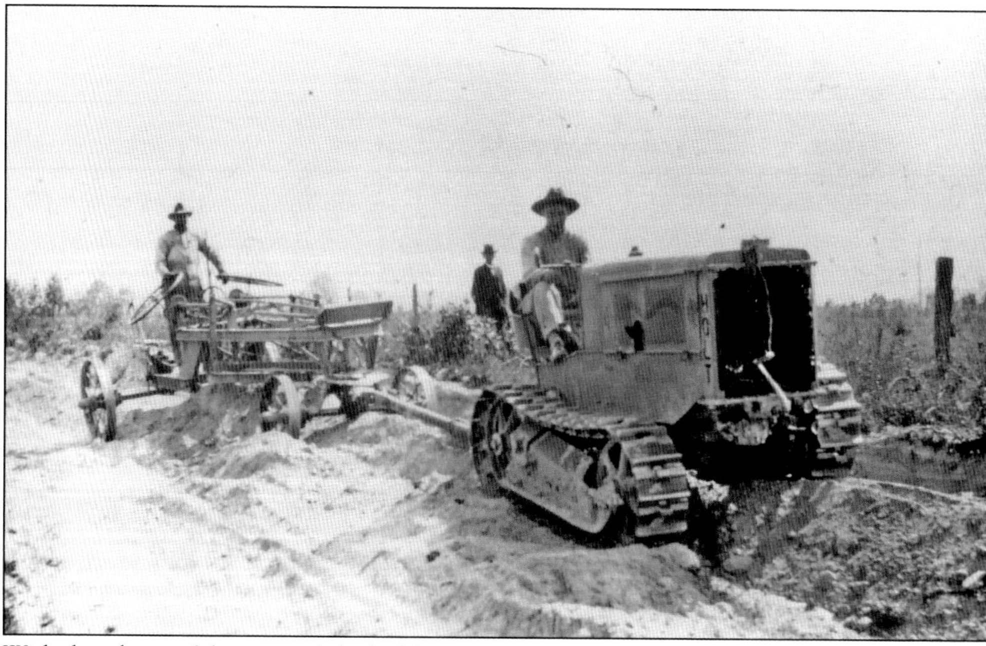

With the advent of the automobile, building better roads in the county became a necessity. Here, the county judge supervises the building of Calhoun Road in 1925. From left to right, Howard King is on the "blade," county judge W.J. Reid is in the background, and W.W. Reid is driving the hand-cranked "Holt Crawler." (Patsy McKinney.)

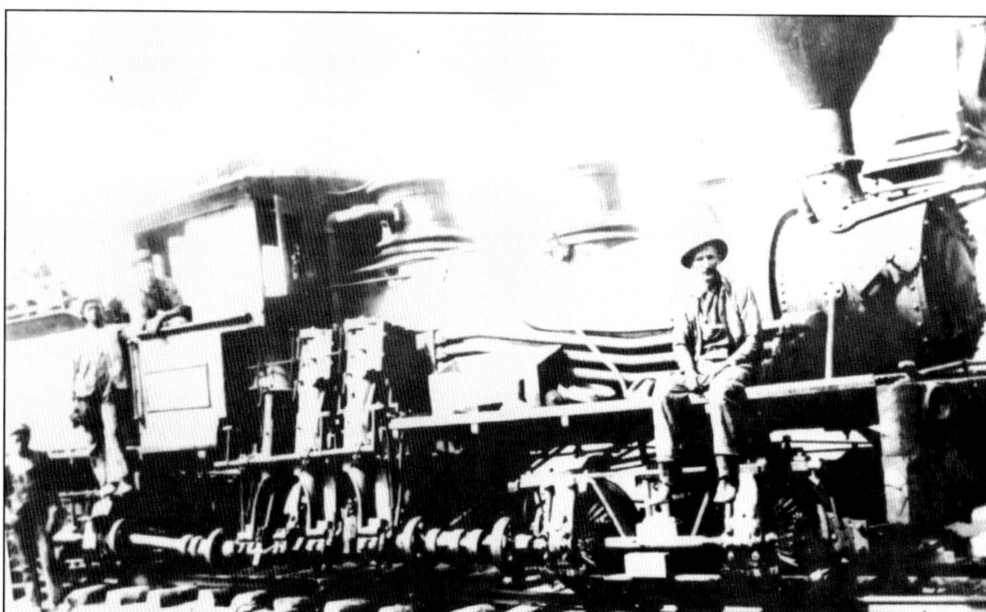

Pictured around 1900 is a Shay locomotive at Lumber, two miles west of Waldo. The Shay steam engine was specially geared to pull heavy loads but at slower speeds. It was frequently used in the logging industry. Dan Hays is on the far right. (Don Ross Smith.)

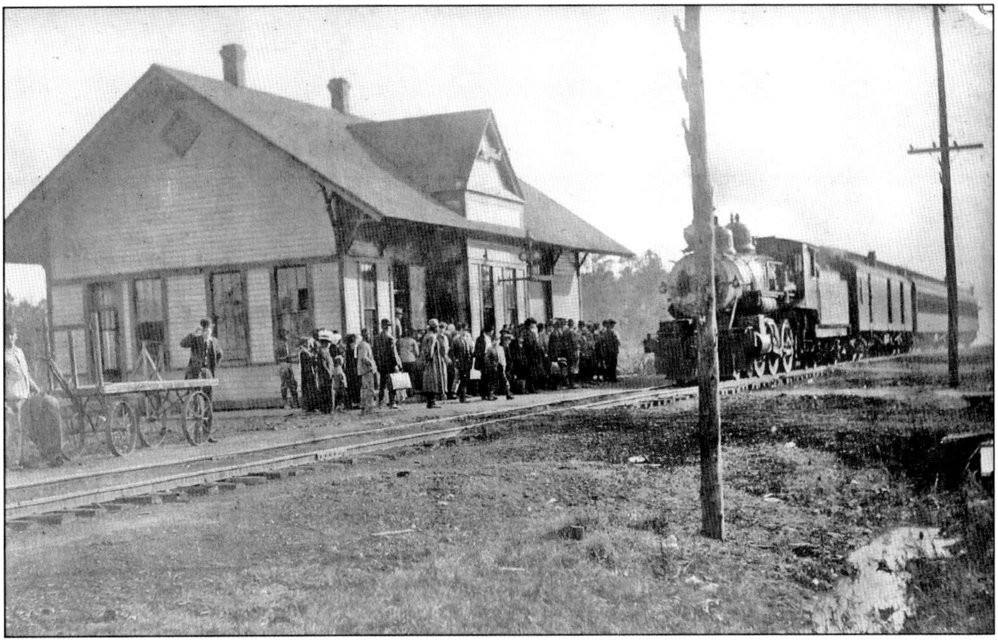

A group of people waits to board the approaching train at the Taylor, Arkansas, depot. At the time this photograph was taken, most people did not have an automobile and depended upon the train for extended travel. In these times as well, everyone wore their Sunday best when on excursion. (Ronald Orrick.)

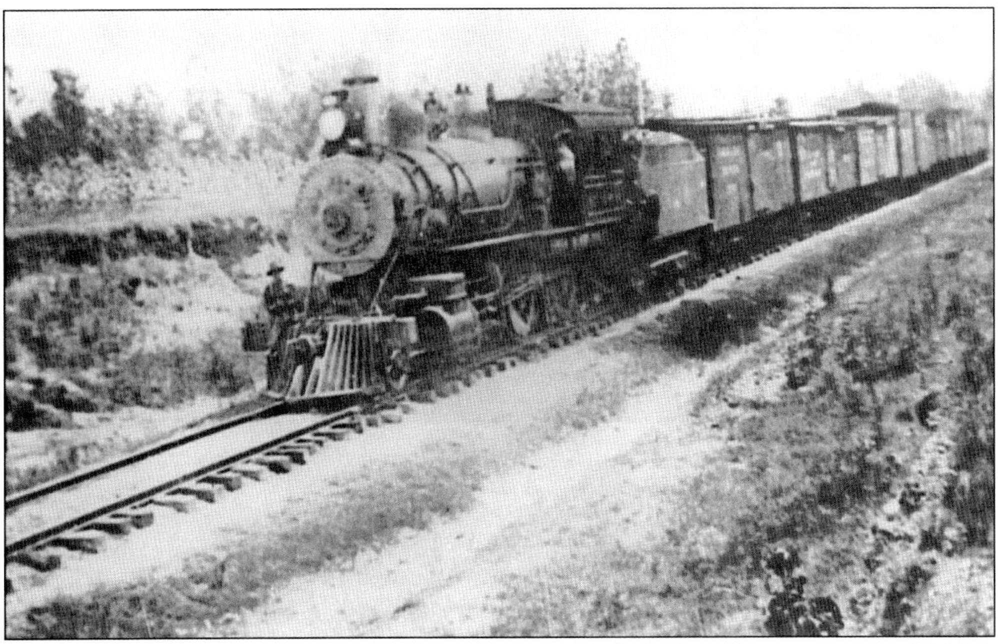

An engineer is perched on the cowcatcher of a Cotton Belt Railroad locomotive near McNeil, Arkansas. Originally, rivers were used to carry natural resources to market; however, the railroad created an improved transportation source for commerce, industry, farmers, and the common man. It also brought affluence and outside influence into Columbia County. (Dr. Robert Walz.)

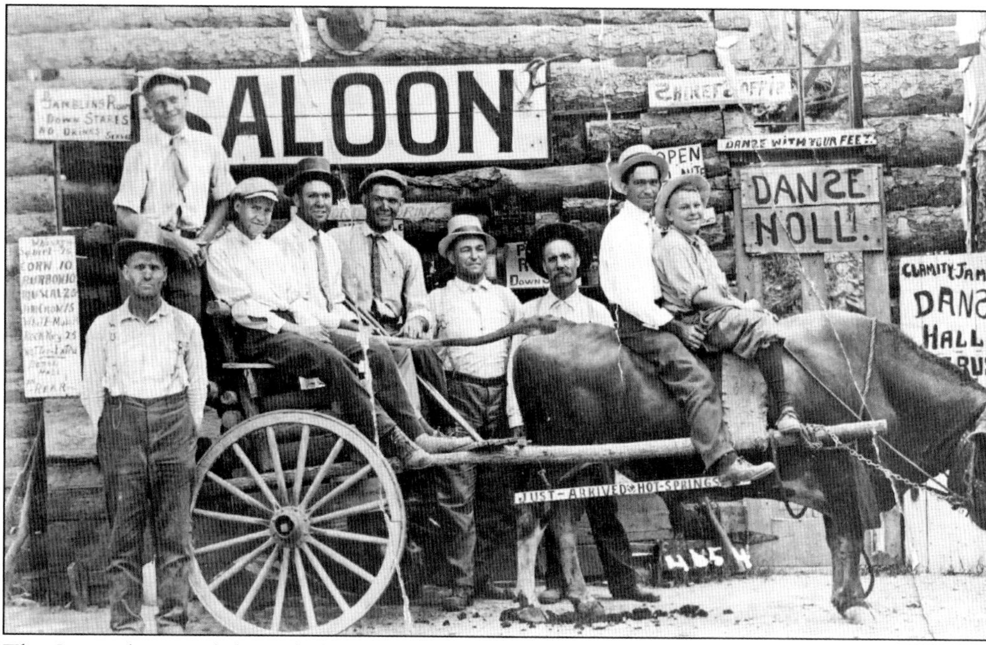

The Souter boys and the Whaley boys are having fun in Hot Springs in the early 1900s. They are, from left to right, Walter Souter, Ellis Souter, Glen Souter, Hilliard Whaley, Opie Souter, Gus Souter, Fletcher Souter, Charley Whaley, and Avery Souter. (Dorothy Whaley.)

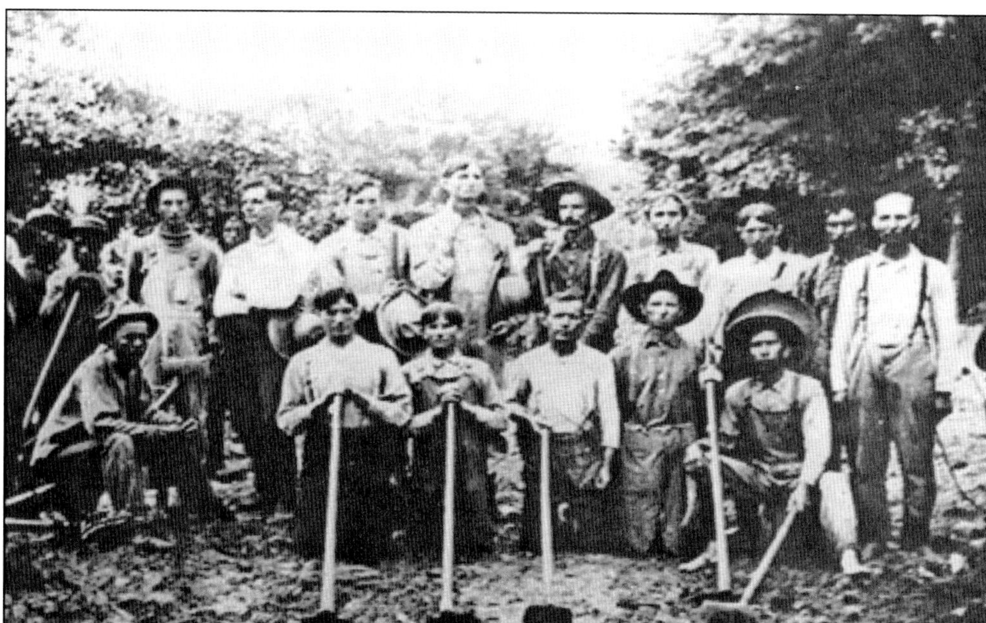

In 1914, each adult male in the county was taxed for road upkeep. At one period, this head-tax was $4 a year, payable in cash or worked out at $1 a day or $2 for a man with a mule. Substitutions, like the older boys in this image of a citizen's work crew on Burnt Bridge Road, were allowed. (Vernon Elmore.)

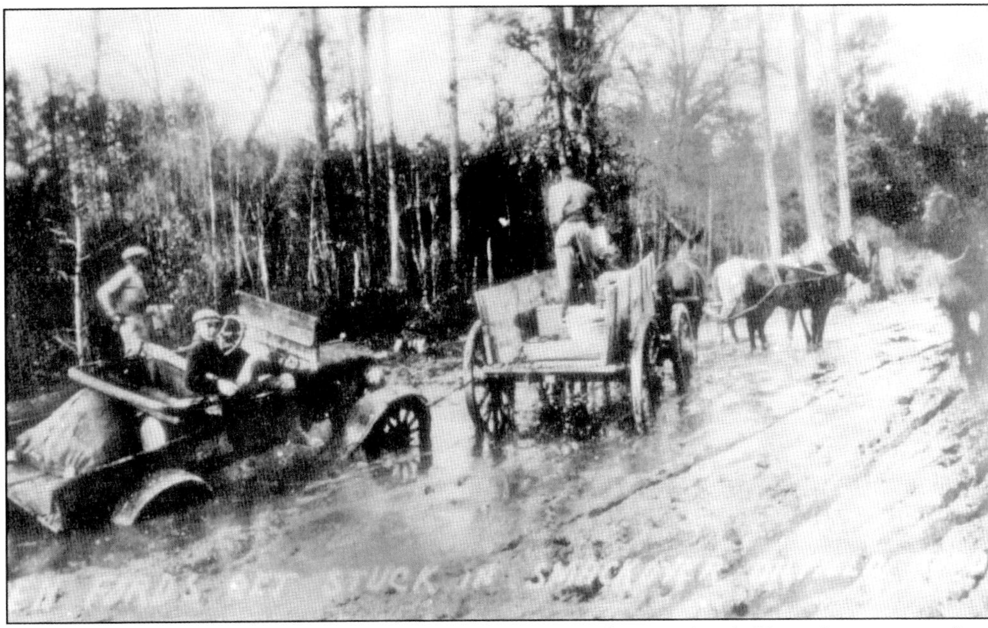

An unidentified driver of a horse-and-wagon team rescues the new-fangled horseless carriage from a muddy demise. These men were on their way to the Smackover oil field when a sudden downpour turned the roadbed into a mud hole. The four four-footed team members harnessed affront the wagon are more suited to this type of treacherous terrain. (Columbia County Library.)

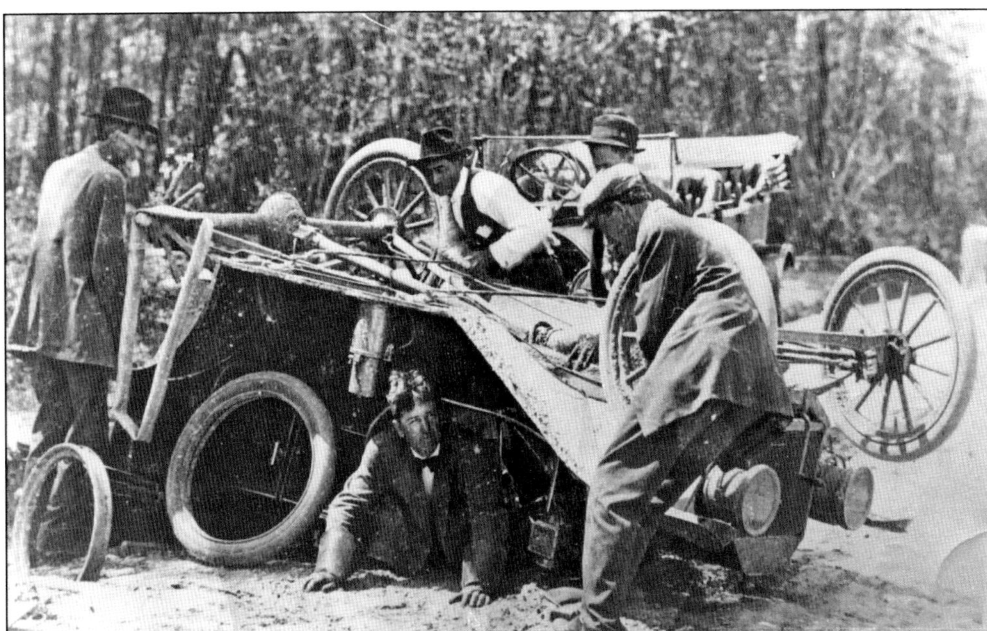

The first car wreck in Columbia County occurred about 1911 or 1912 on the then dirt road between Magnolia and McNeil. Willie Carraway was the owner of the overturned Ford roadster. According to the late Ester Emerson, "Duke Emerson and Willie Carraway were drag racing, and Willie, in his Ford, hit a rut and flipped over. Duke Emerson's 1910 Cadillac was not damaged, nor was Willie Carraway hurt." (Dr. Robert Walz.)

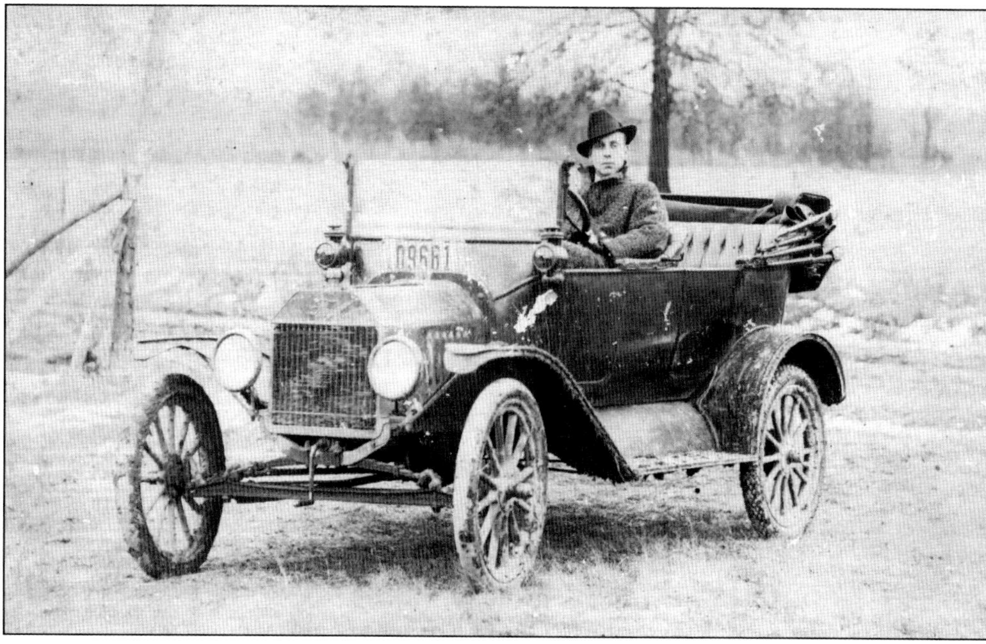

An unidentified debonair man is taking his roadster for a spin in Taylor in the early 1900s. The jaunty angle of this man's hat indicates the confidence needed to drive a ragtop car in a day when few people owned automobiles. (Ronald Orrick.)

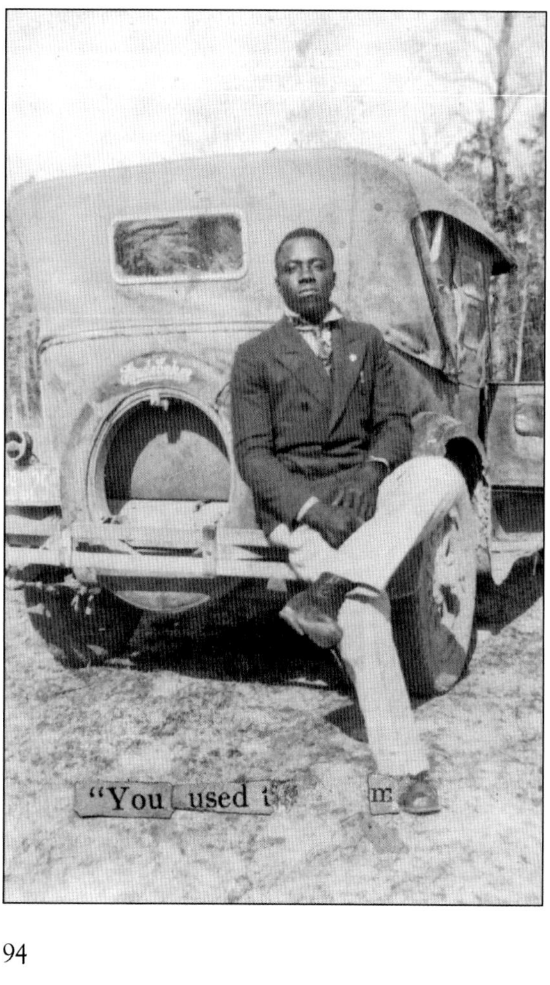

Booker Webb sits on the back bumper of his 1920 Studebaker convertible in Magnolia, Arkansas. Across the bottom of the photograph, one will see a partial line of text. It was a fad of the time to cut and paste sentimental sayings on the bottom of gift photographs. (Peggy Goode Rudd.)

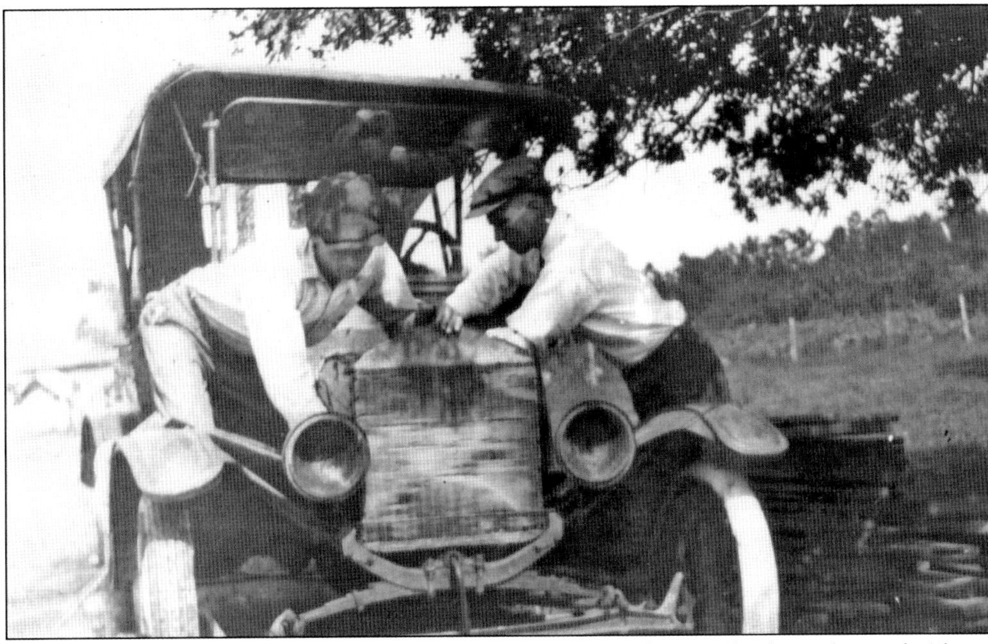

Bill (left) and Floyd Butler of Emerson work together to get their car back on the road. Almost every automobile owner of the time was forced to become a "shade-tree mechanic." Wise owners carried both tools and extra gasoline with them for such roadside emergencies. (Christine Butler Snider.)

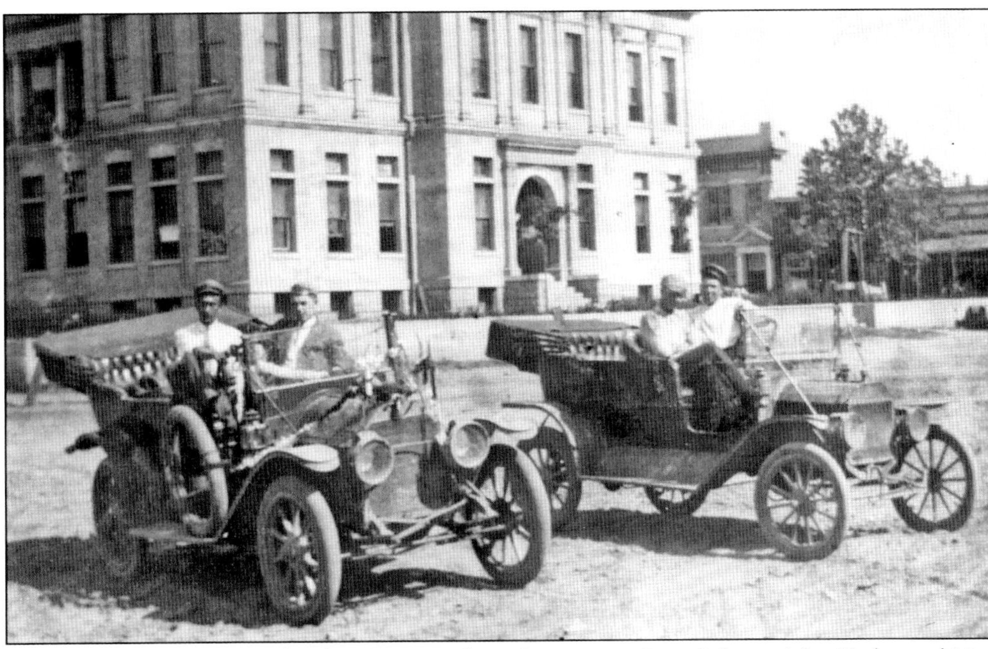

Parked in front of the Columbia County Courthouse are, from left to right, Duke and Van Emerson in the 1910 Cadillac, and next to them in a Ford roadster unidentified and Willie Carraway. Duke would later be involved in the first automobile accident in Columbia County. (Dr. Robert Walz.)

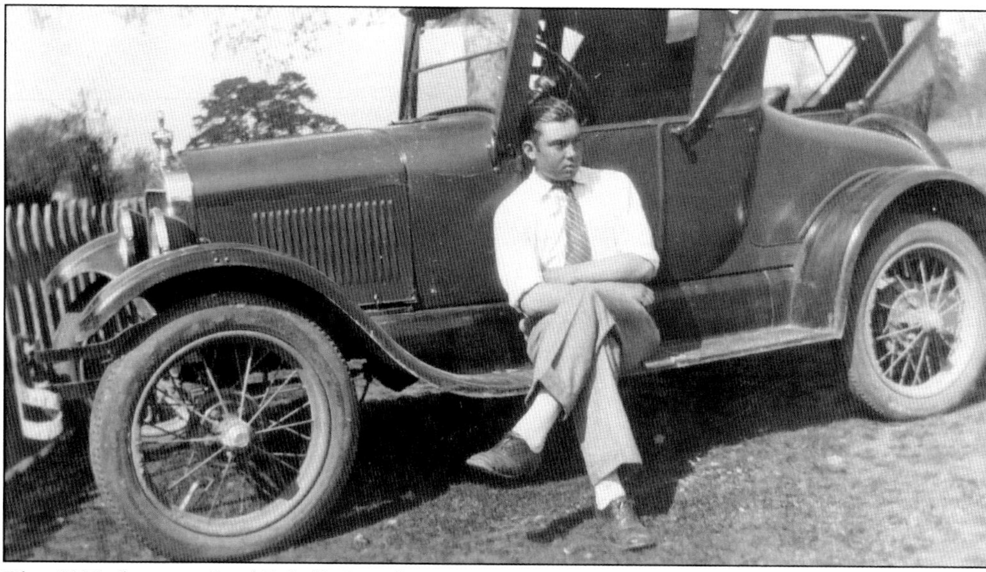

This 1925 photograph of Othell "Punch" Burnett sitting on the running board of his early model roadster was taken in the Sharman community. Judging by his burly appearance, one wonders if the nickname "Punch" was derived from his pugilistic tendencies. (Authors.)

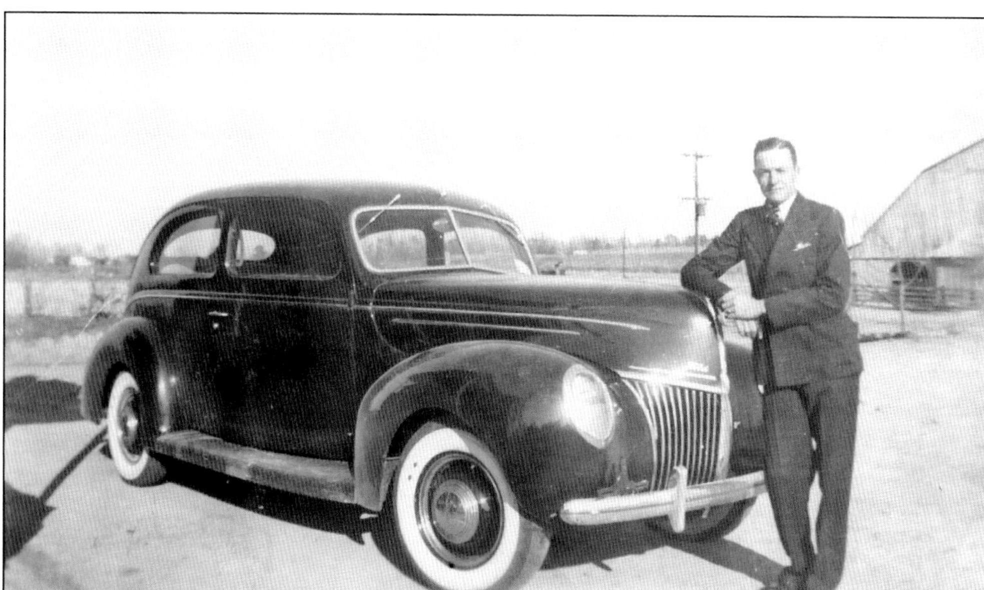

Robert Genestet of Waldo is pictured in front of his 1939 Ford sedan. Genestet was a landowner, cotton farmer, and later a cattleman. He was more often seen in his working Western wear than this handsome suit. His descendants have continued his legacy by caring for the land. (Bob Genestet.)

Seven

PUBLIC SERVICE AND MILITARY SERVICE

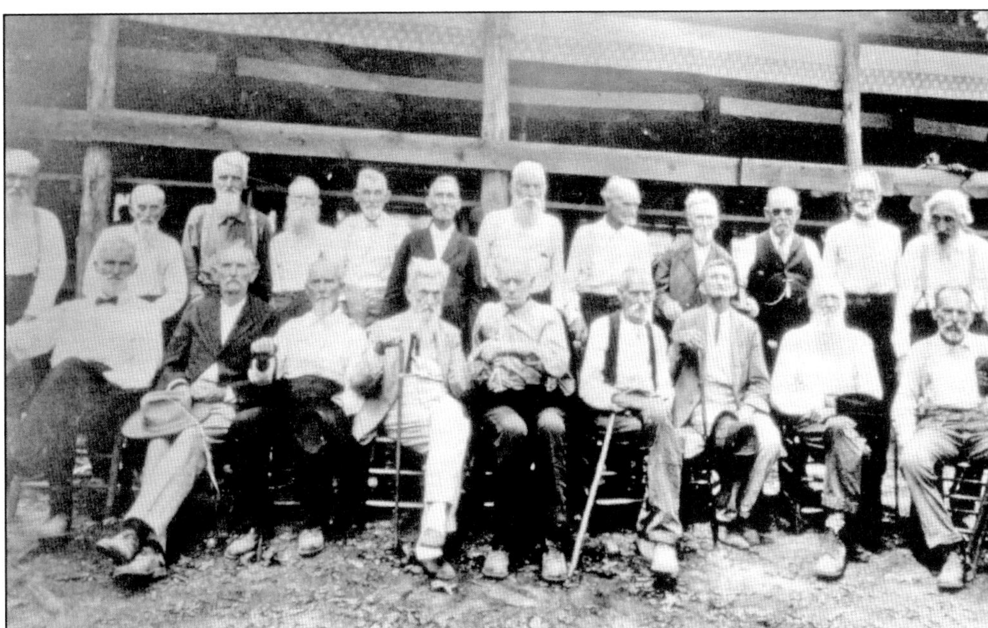

A 1903 reunion of Confederate veterans was held at the Old Soldiers Reunion Ground in McNeil. From left to right are (first row) James F. Renfroe, ? Bustion, Thomas B. William (or Williamson), ? Boggs, Pat Casidey, unidentified, T.R. Norman, ? McGloten, and unidentified; (second row) John Baker, Ezie (or Exie) Ansley, ? Wilson, John Warnock, unidentified, ? Wynn, Tom McGloton, ? Wilson, ? Burton, two unidentified, and Dan Triplett. (Ed Dees.)

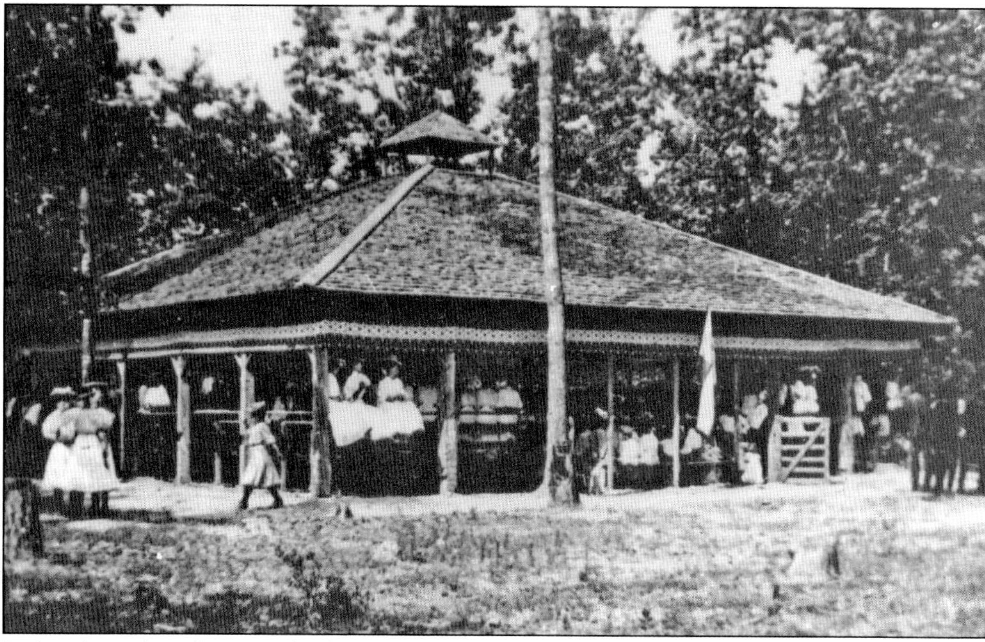

Ladies dressed in their Sunday best enjoy a community gathering at the Old Soldiers Reunion Shed in McNeil. The structure was built for the gathering and veneration of returning Confederate veterans. It was most often used on Memorial Day, which used to be known as Decoration Day. No commemorative assembly would be complete without the traditional "dinner on the grounds." (Dr. Robert Walz.)

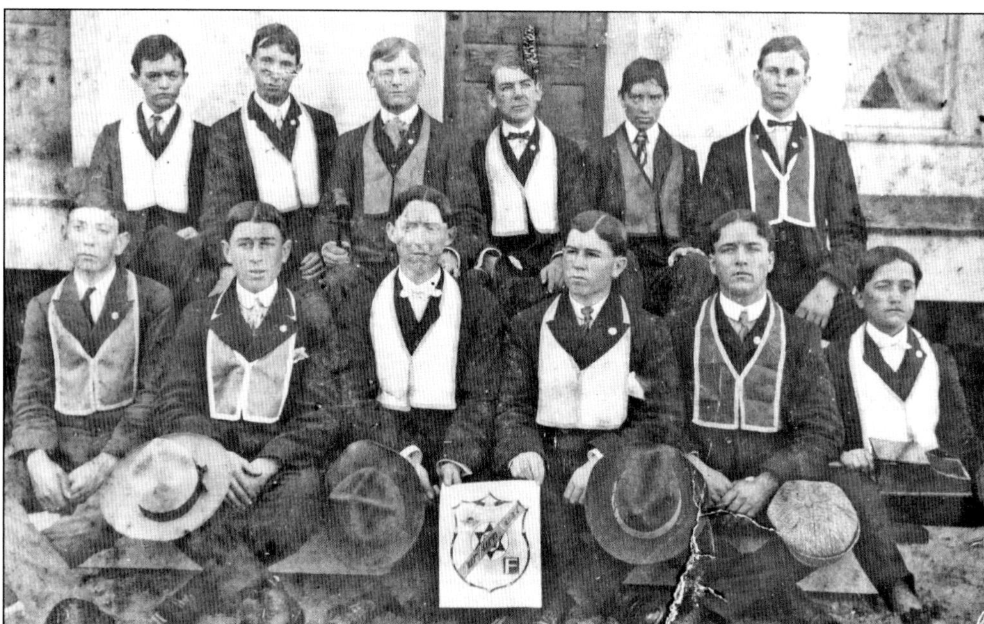

This 1904 photograph is of the members of the Coming Men of America Lodge of McNeil, Arkansas. From left to right they are (first row) Frank Key, Floyd Carraway, Claude Runyan, Will Carraway, Winfrey Smith, and Clyde Smith; (second row) Eddy Gordon, Lovette Horton, Arthur Hunt, Edgar Davis, Ben Horton, and Pete Bustion. (Frank Key.)

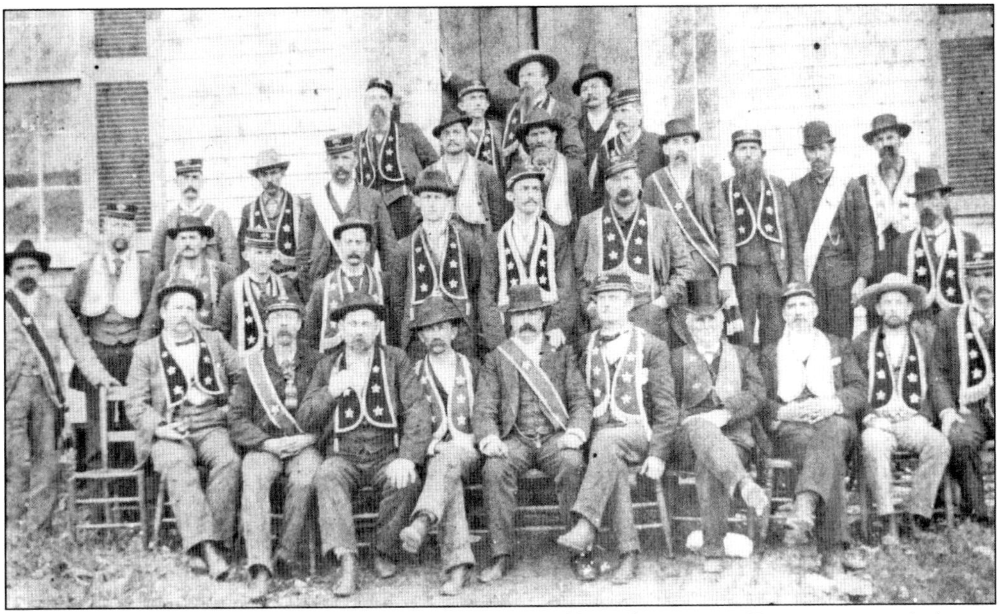

The Odd Fellows of Magnolia pictured here were held to this tenet: "To improve and elevate the character of mankind by promoting the principles of friendship, love, truth, faith, hope, charity and universal justice." There were also Odd Fellow lodges at Waldo and Lone Beech. (Dr. Robert Walz.)

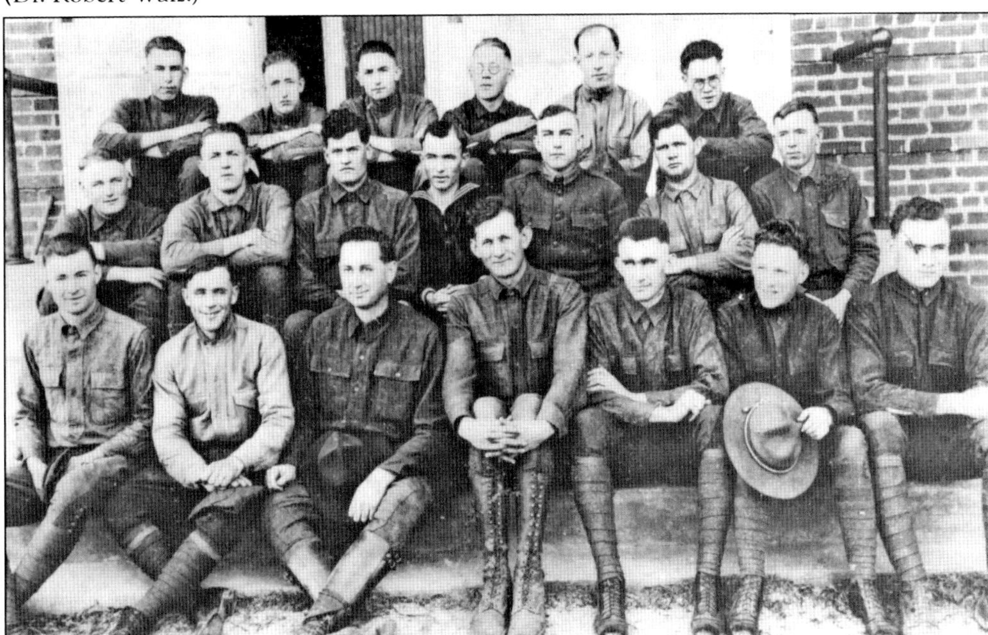

Pictured is the 1919–1920 Fate Camp, Post No. 108, American Legion, Third District Agricultural School. From left to right are (first row) Hilliard Crain, Shorty ?, N.O. Taff (English teacher), E.E. Graham (agronomy teacher), Ben Green, Robert "Red" Taylor, and unidentified; (second row) H.T. Nesbit, F.O. Middlebrooks, Ira Garner, Hosie Camp, two unidentified, and Thurman Chisholm; (third row) Neal Wood, John Graham, "Corporal" Orndoff, two unidentified, and Victor Wilson. (Harper Nesbit.)

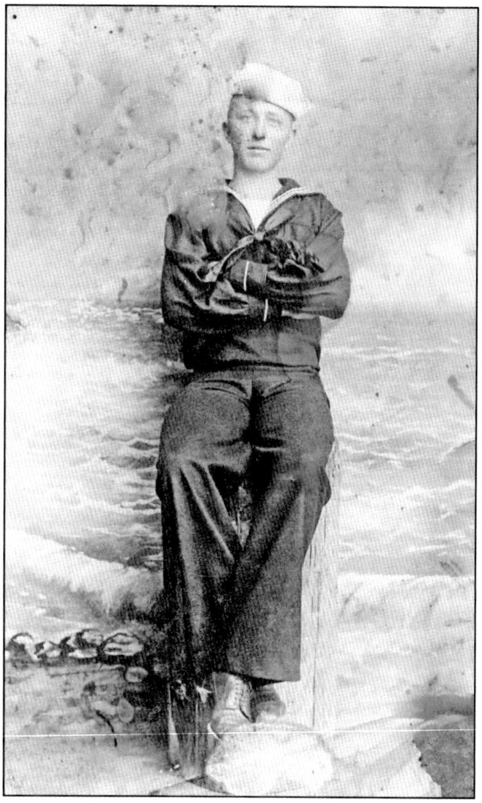

Ambros Christie was a World War I sailor from the Emerson area. His relaxed pose suggests that he is on leave. America entered World War I in April 1917 when it was found out that Germany was attempting to have Mexico join them as an ally against the United States. Submarine warfare would be used on a wide scale for the first time in naval engagements. (Christine Butler Snider.)

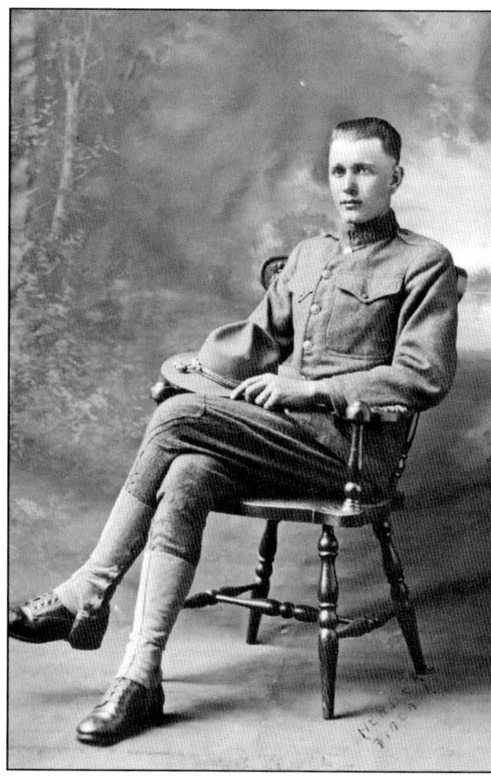

Herbert Fincher is photographed in his World War I uniform. After the war, he returned to south Arkansas and resumed his entrepreneurial efforts. He married Edna Clark, and they had two children. He was a pioneer in the banking industry and a lifelong resident of Waldo. His descendants run Peoples Bank today. (D.J. Fincher.)

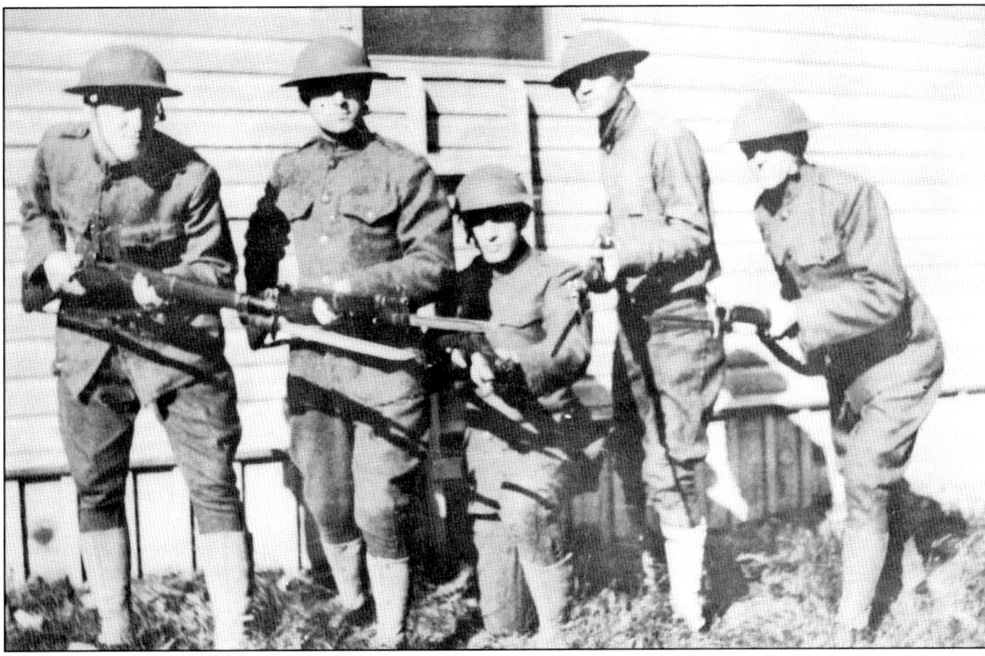

World War I soldiers pictured here are, from left to right, James K. McKee of Pennsylvania, Ronald G. Harton of West Virginia, Herbert Fincher of Arkansas, Huey G. Kraus of Louisiana, and Elmer Rowe of New York. (D.J. Fincher.)

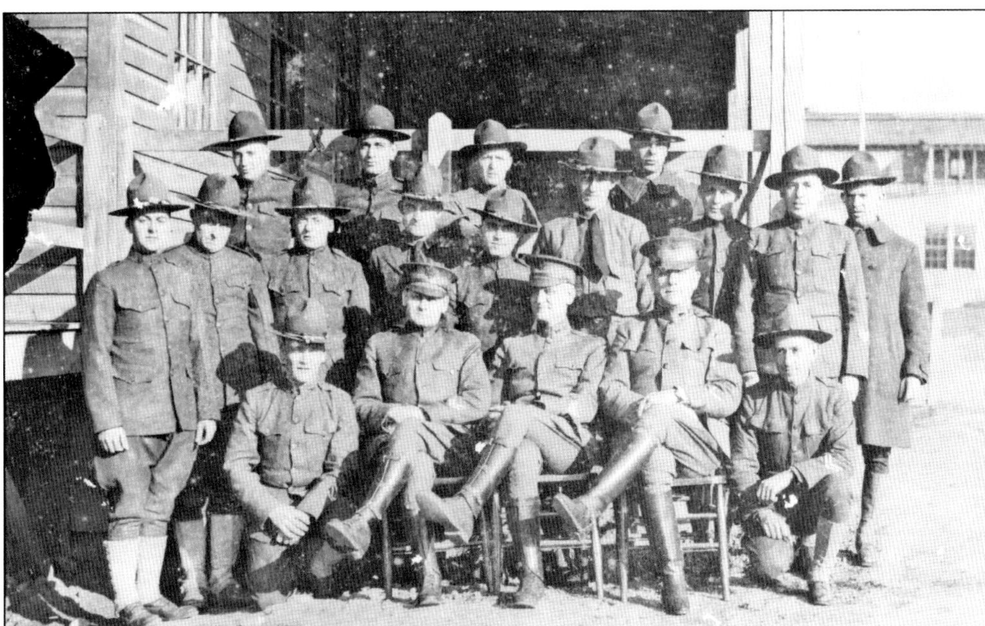

This is a group of World War I soldiers who served with Herbert Fincher of Waldo. The image was taken in 1917 or 1918. After the war's end, some of these men would continue to meet on a regular basis for many years. (D.J. Fincher.)

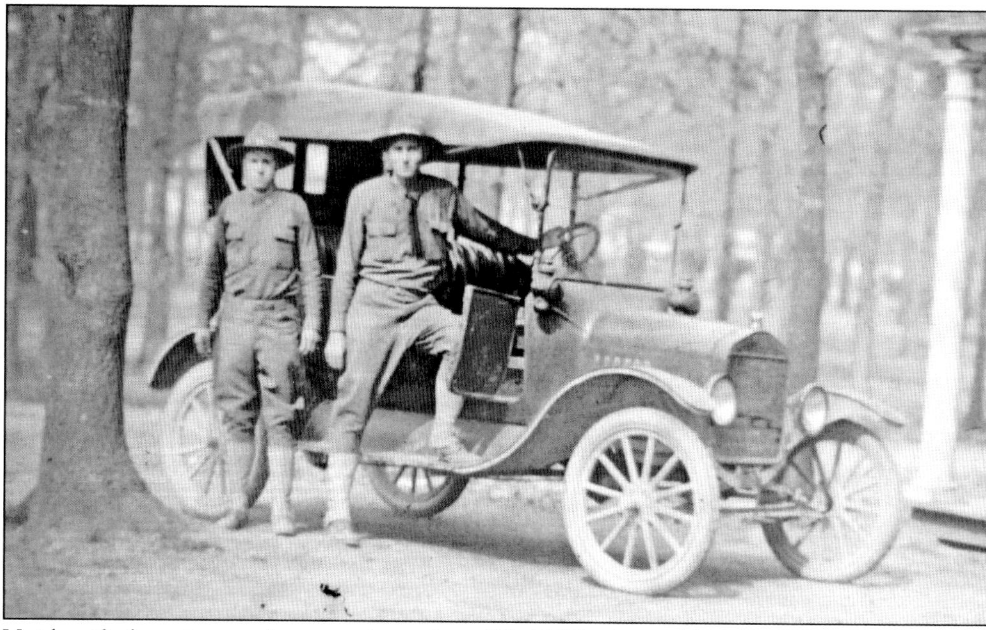

Unidentified servicemen home on leave from World War I stand beside a Model T Ford. This photograph was taken in the Philadelphia community around 1918. Many soldiers who were fortunate enough to return at the war's end would suffer the effects of the first use of chemical warfare. (Jo Key.)

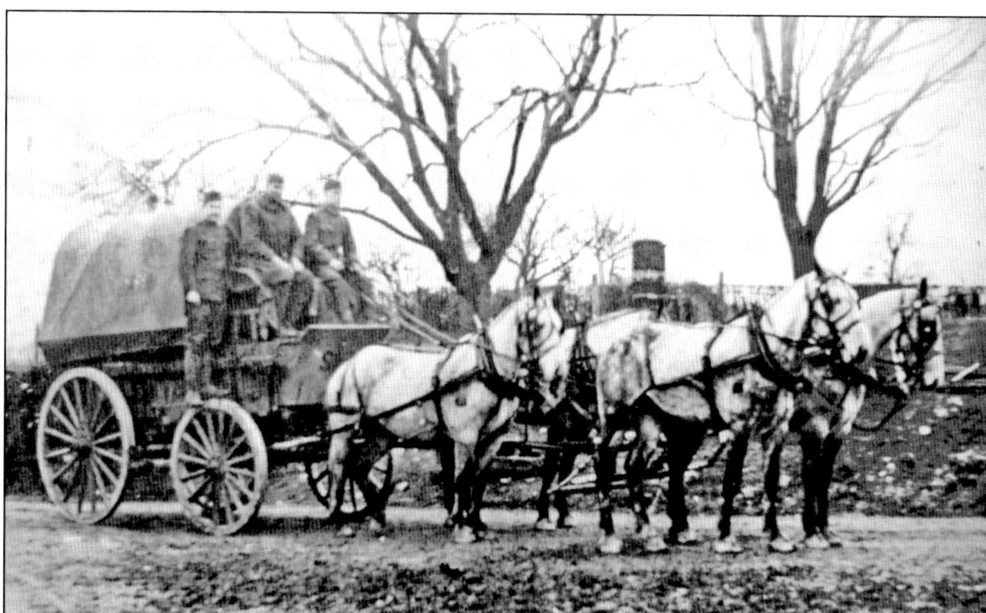

Unidentified soldiers sit aboard a World War I supply wagon being pulled by a team of white mules. The logistics of transporting supplies put these men in harm's way, at the mercy of their suppliers, and leave them subject to the instability of weather. (Dr. Robert Walz.)

This photograph of Milton Talley, Company B, 153rd Infantry, American National Guard, was taken in front of the old armory at State A&M College in 1926 or 1927. The National Guard was using surplus World War I uniforms and weapons. (Alice Wallace Talley.)

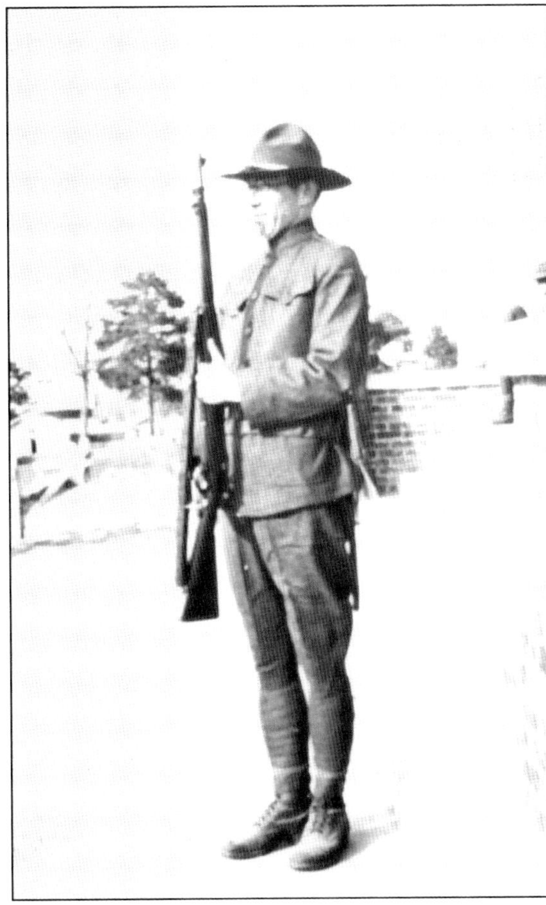

This photograph of the A&M Armory at Magnolia was taken in 1912. Dr. Robert Walz served in this armory as a private first class in 1939. The building was used for many years. (Dr. Robert Walz.)

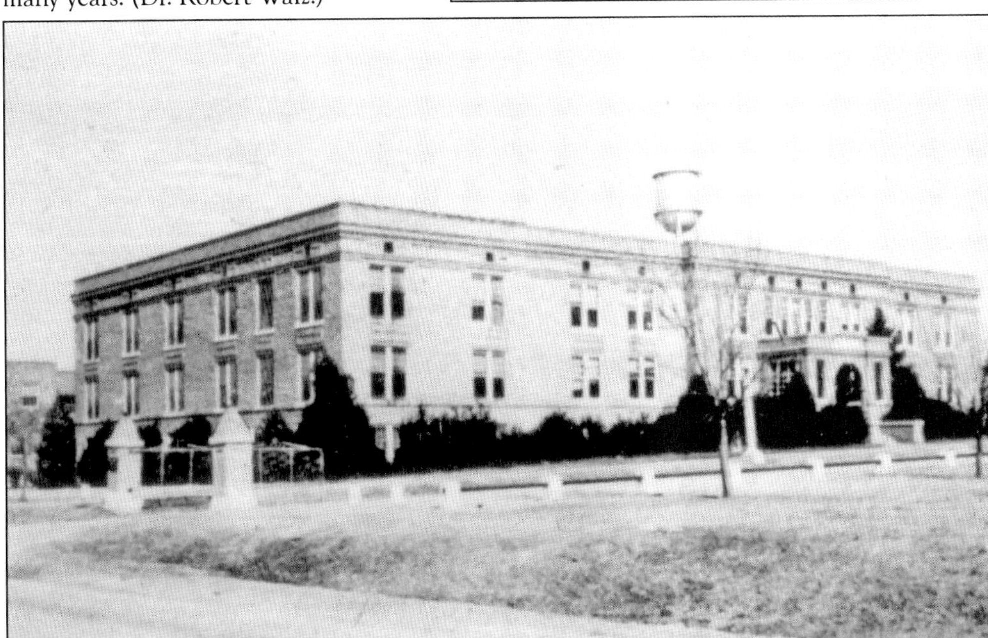

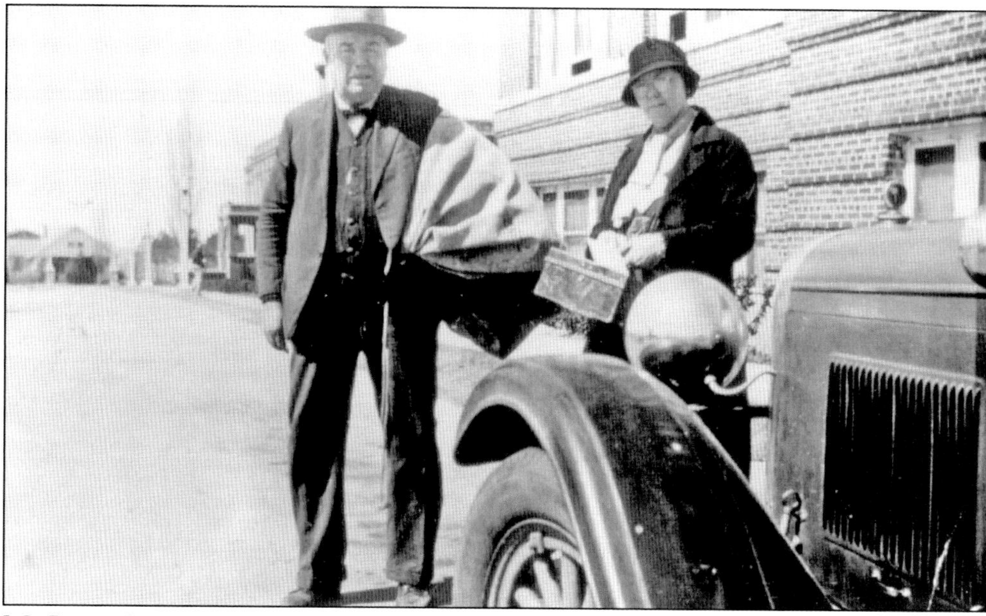

J.G. Brown Sr., city postmaster, and his wife, Capitola B. Brown, are seen delivering the mail to Old Main on the campus of A&M. Capitola was the first campus postmistress, and she served from 1925 to 1933. The first mail room was on the second floor of Old Main. (Jim Brown.)

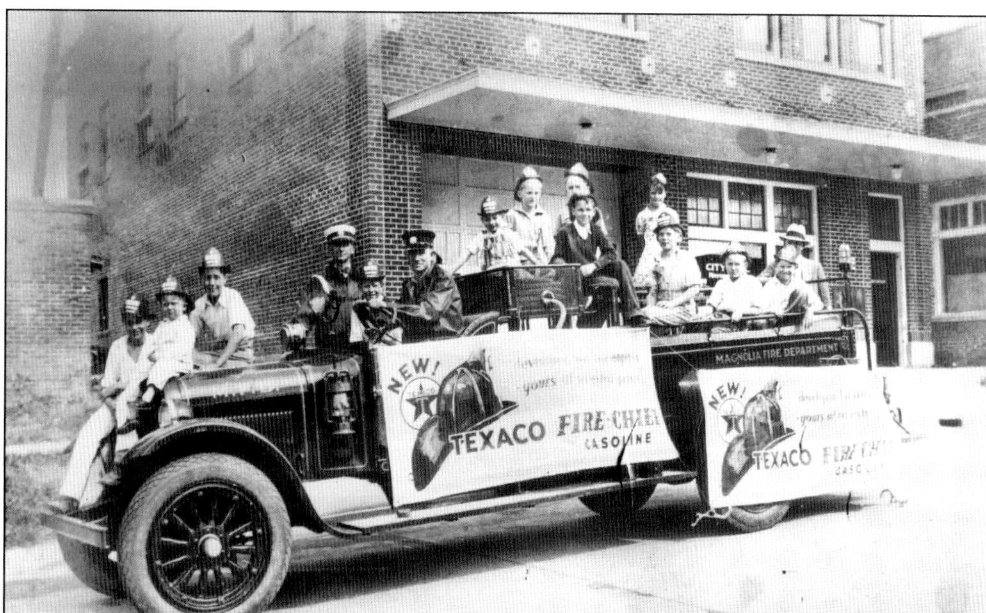

This is a early-1930s scene in front of the old city hall and fire station on North Jefferson Street in Magnolia. The fire truck is decorated for a promotion of Texaco's Fire Chief gasoline. The Texaco agent was R.S. Warnock Jr. (Dr. Robert Walz.)

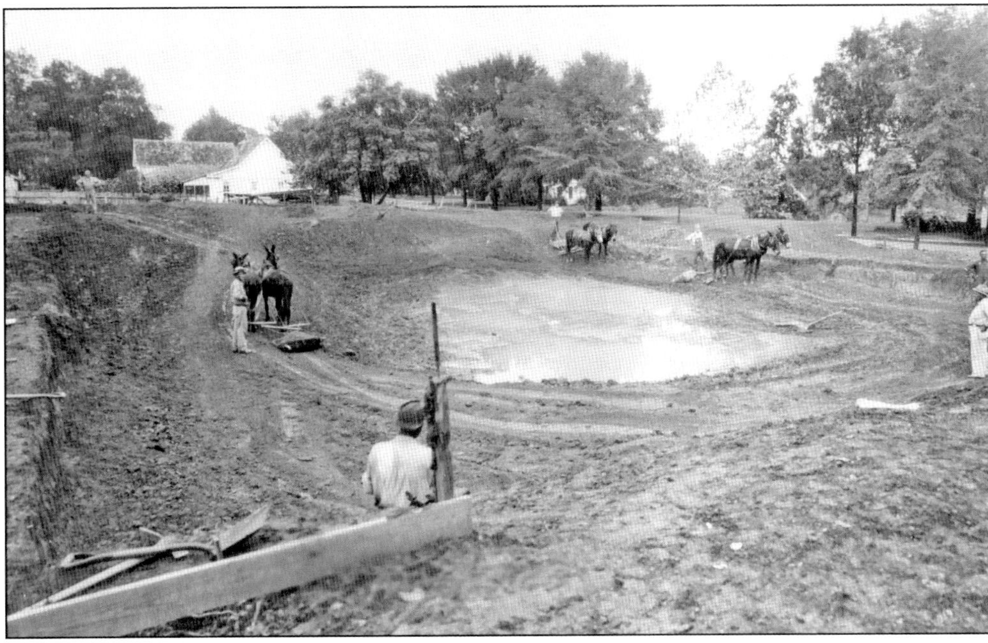

This is an image of the groundwork construction for the Magnolia, Arkansas, Federal Post Office at 220 East Main Street. Mules are being used to dig the foundation of the brick building. The original October 6, 1936, photograph is from a pictorial record kept by the builder, William Peterson General Construction of Little Rock, Arkansas. (Columbia County Library.)

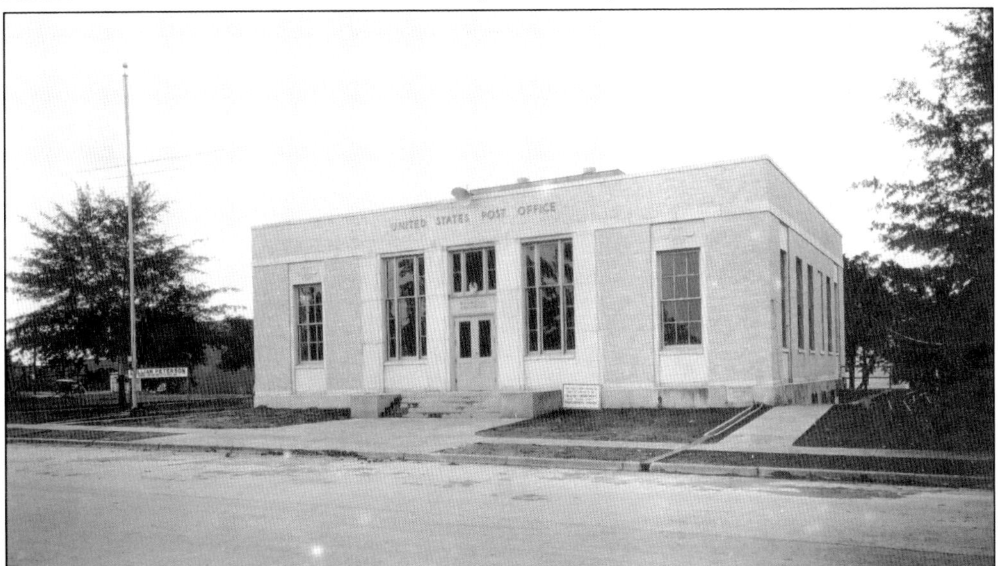

The Magnolia, Arkansas, Federal Post Office was completed on July 1, 1937. In 1938, artist Joe Jones created a mural on the wall, entitled *Threshing*, which remains the property of the federal government. Pres. Franklin D. Roosevelt created the Federal Art Project as one of the divisions of the Works Progress Administration (WPA) during the Great Depression. Historian Glenn G. Martel became postmaster in 1940 and worked here until his retirement in 1966. The building served as a post office until it was purchased by the Columbia County Library Board and converted into a modern library facility. (Columbia County Library.)

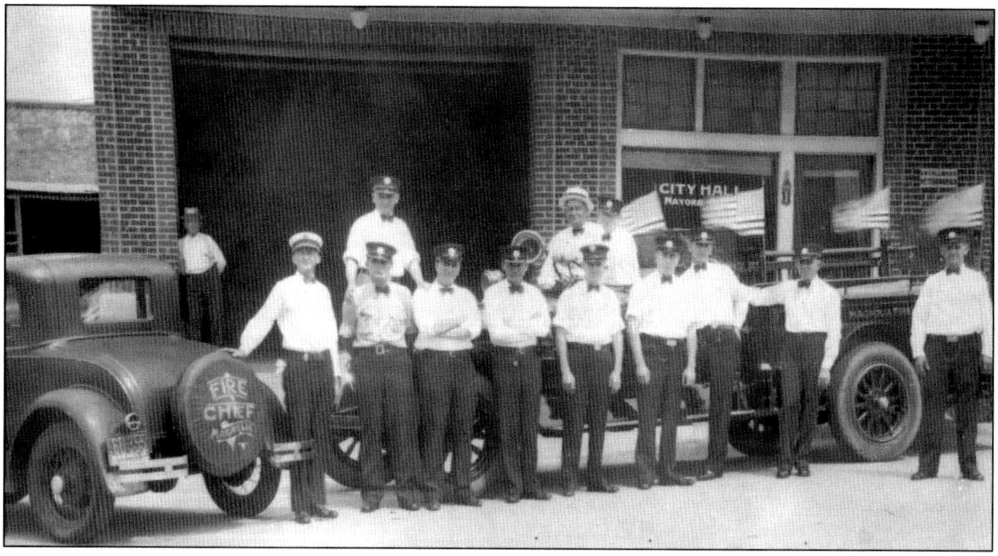

Here, the Magnolia Fire Department is pictured in 1933. From left to right are (first row) Chief Harry Baker, Ed Couch, Cecil Thorne, O.A. Reid, Marcus Justice, W.M. "Casey" Jones, Carl Wallace, Robert Henderson, and Ollie Ware; (second row) Glen "Mollie" Rountree, Claude Crumpler, and Louie Marshal. Firemen not pictured include Philip Carpenter, Grady Malone, and Charlie Ingravalia. (Dr. Robert Walz.)

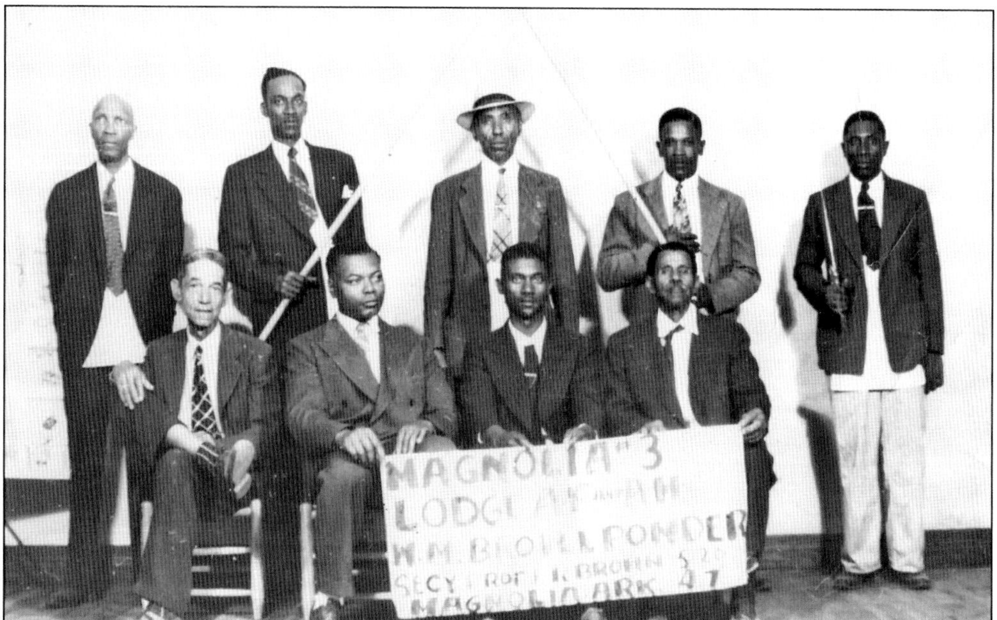

Here is the Magnolia No. 3 Lodge of Ancient Free and Accepted Masons (AF and AM). From left to right are (first row) Jim Frazier, Calvin Shepherd Sr., and two unidentified; (second row) Frank Williams and four unidentified men. (Helen Hildreth.)

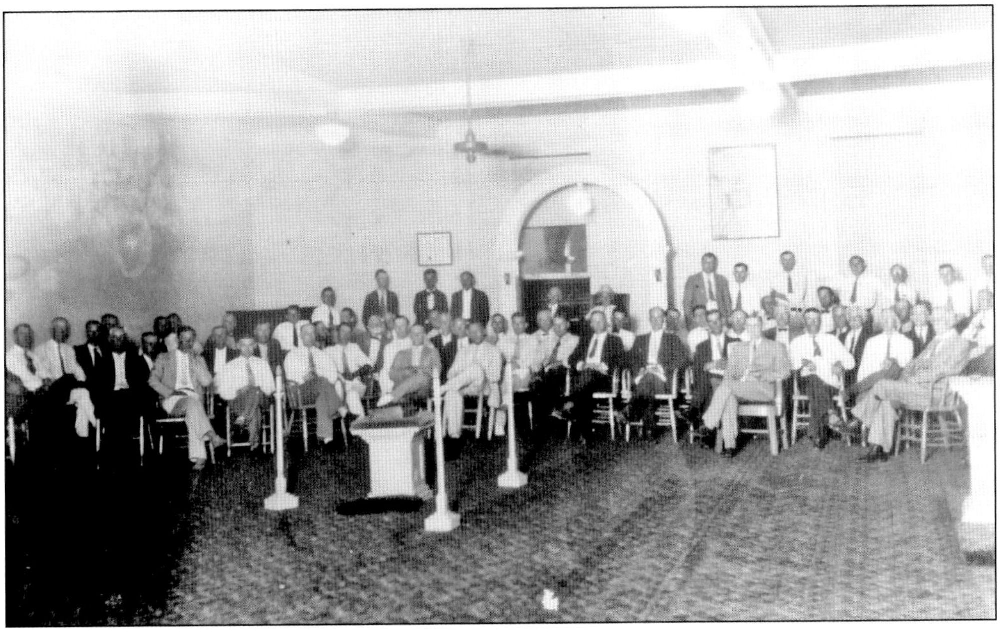

This is a 1925 photograph of the Magnolia Masonic Lodge during a meeting. The lodge was located on the east side of the square, which was lost to fire in 1944. The group continued to meet despite the loss of their downtown location. The Masonic emblem can still be seen on the south side of the brick building. (Jim Baron.)

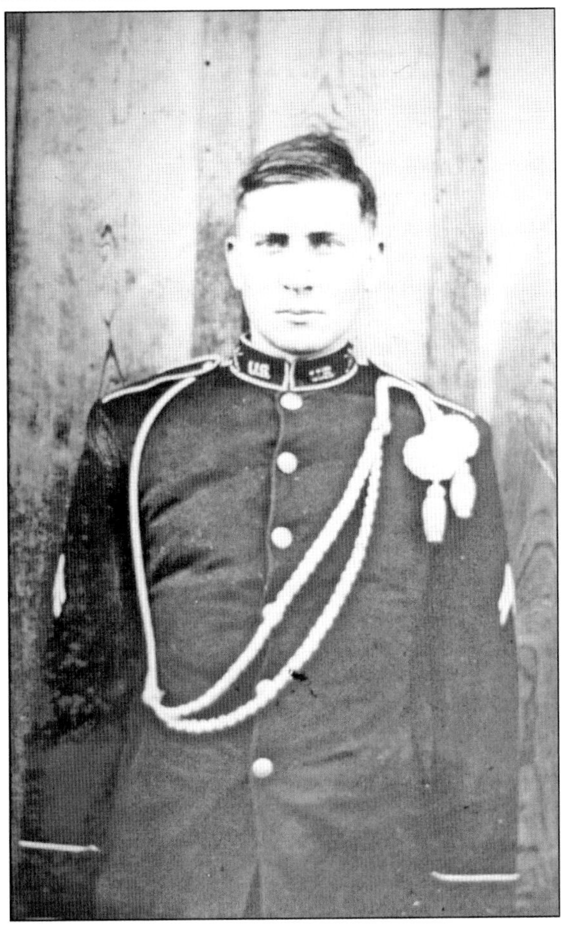

Pictured around 1918 is an unidentified War World I corporal is in his dress blouse. Note the handsome epaulets, cording, and pins embellishing his collar. Nothing is known about this soldier except that he served his country. (Bill Elmore.)

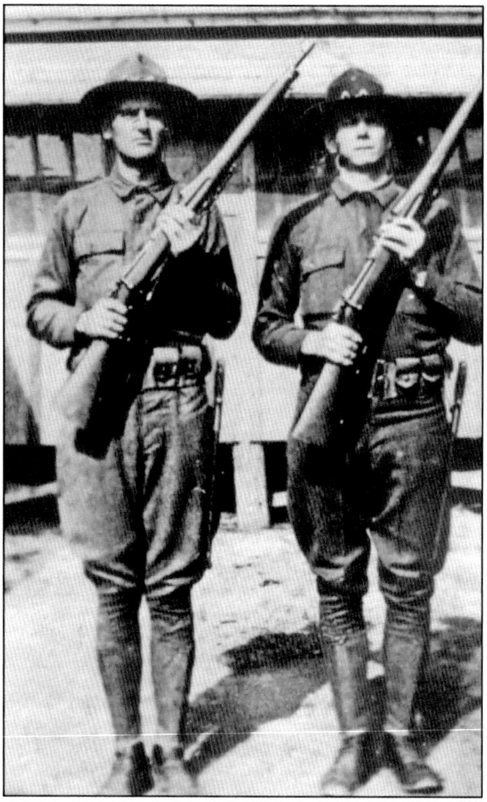

This photograph is of World War I doughboys standing sentinel. The soldier at right is W.O. "Wordie" Elmore of the Philadelphia community. (Bill Elmore.)

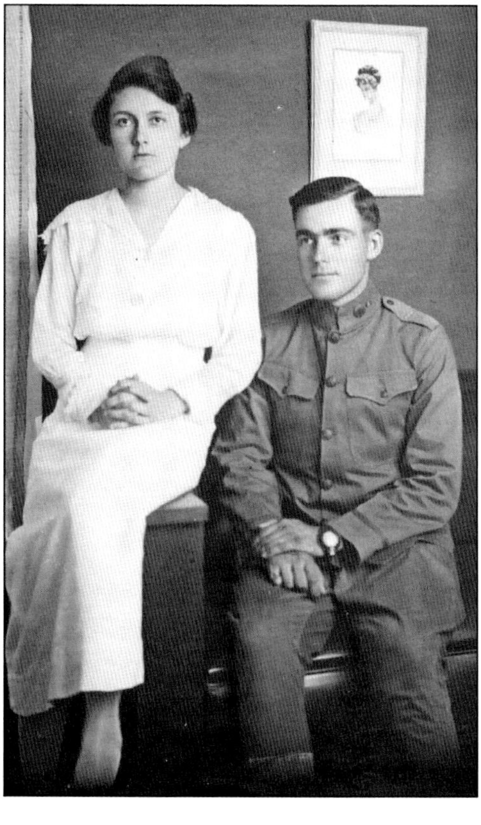

Verna Williamson Nipper and Roy Nipper of the Rocky Mound/Harmony area pose before they were married. Roy served in World War I, while Verna waited for his return: "They also serve who only stand and wait." (Christine Butler Snider.)

Eight

Outdoor Columbia County and Disasters

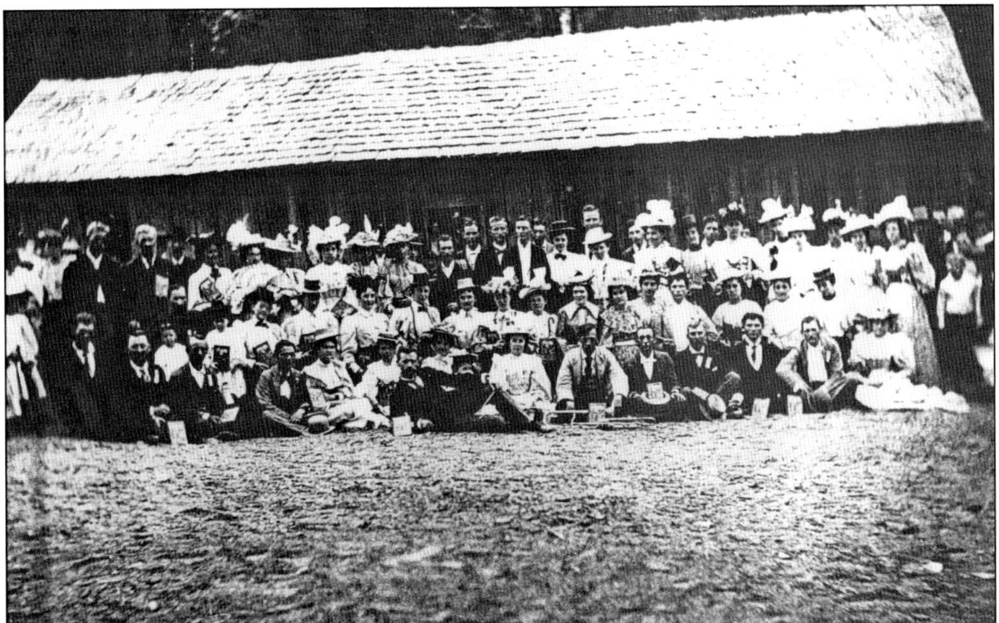

This large group was attending an old-time camp meeting believed to be near Magnesia Springs. Tellena Lyle, who attended the event, wrote down the subject and the exact date of Friday, September 4, 1896, on the back of the original picture. (T.H. Maloch.)

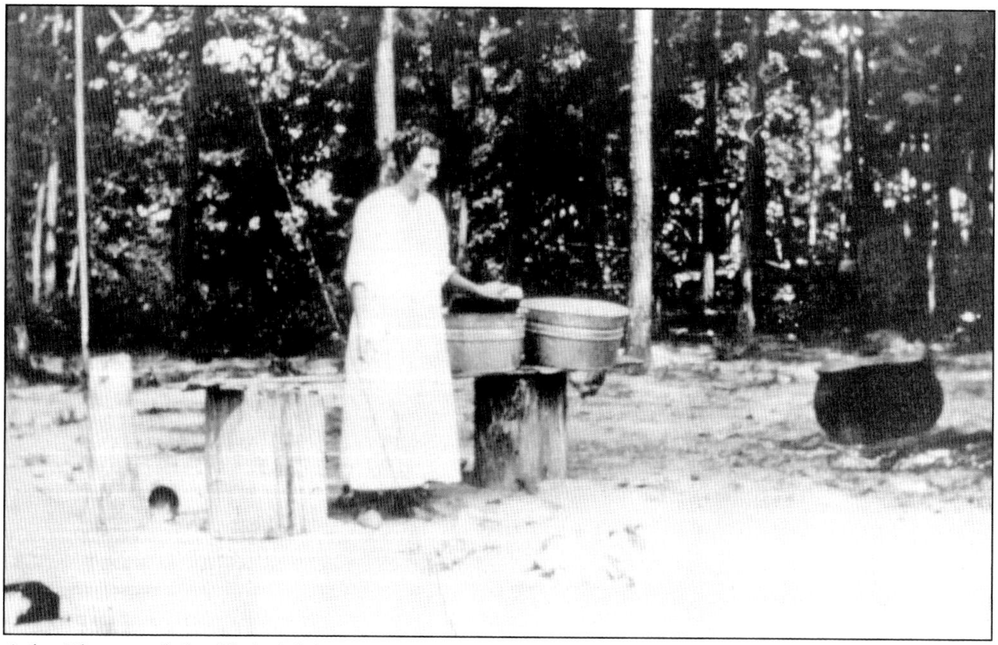

Athe Elmore of the Philadelphia community prepares for a long day of washing clothes. The most important part of the washing equipment was an old black pot, about 18 inches in diameter and rounded on the bottom. A fire was built under the black wash pot to provide hot water for washing the clothes, and lye soap was the typical cleaning agent. (Bill Elmore.)

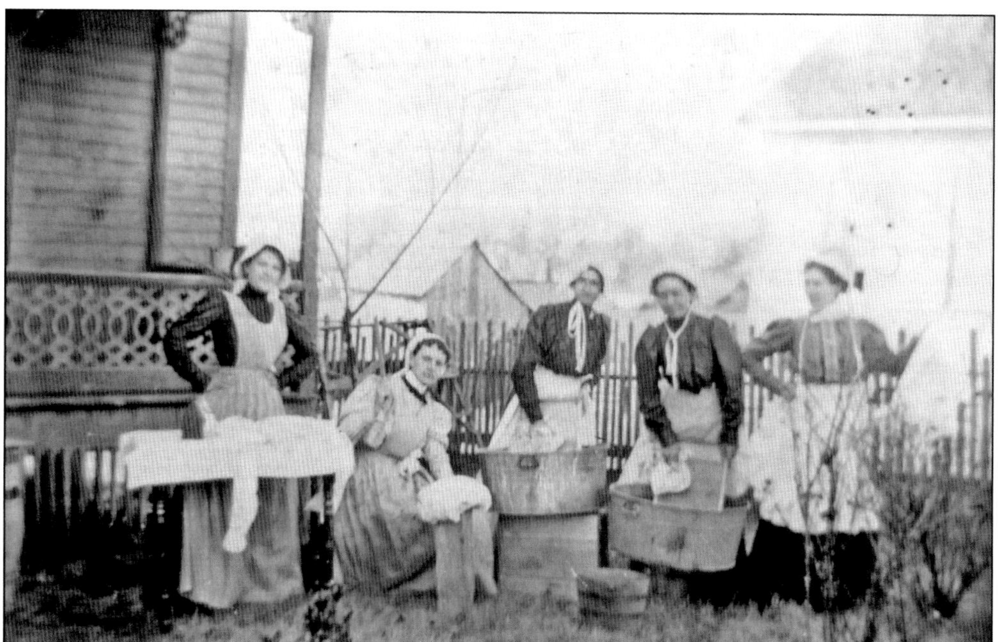

Around April 1899, a group of young women is doing the laundry at the Lyle home located on West McNeil Street in Magnolia. The ladies are named, but sadly, the correct order is unknown: Tillie Turrentine Lewis, Ruth Young Rogers, Tellina Lyle, Alice Couch Monroe, and Lulia Lyle. (Dr. Robert Walz.)

This amusing image of an unidentified woman and man was taken at Magnesia Springs during an 1896 outing. She is carrying a fan, wearing formal gloves, and smoking a cheroot. It is a beautiful day outside, and they are indulging in whimsy. (Dr. Robert Walz.)

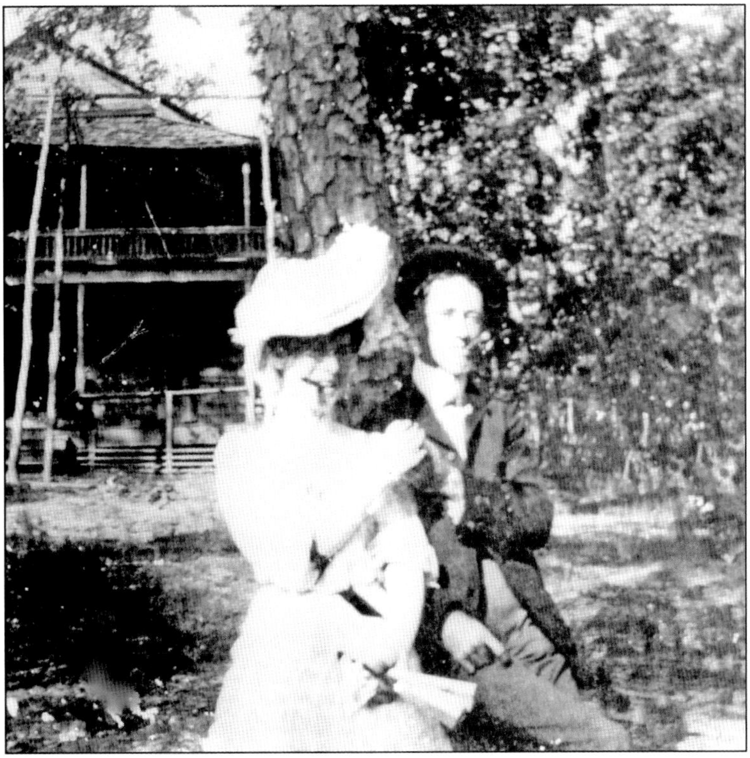

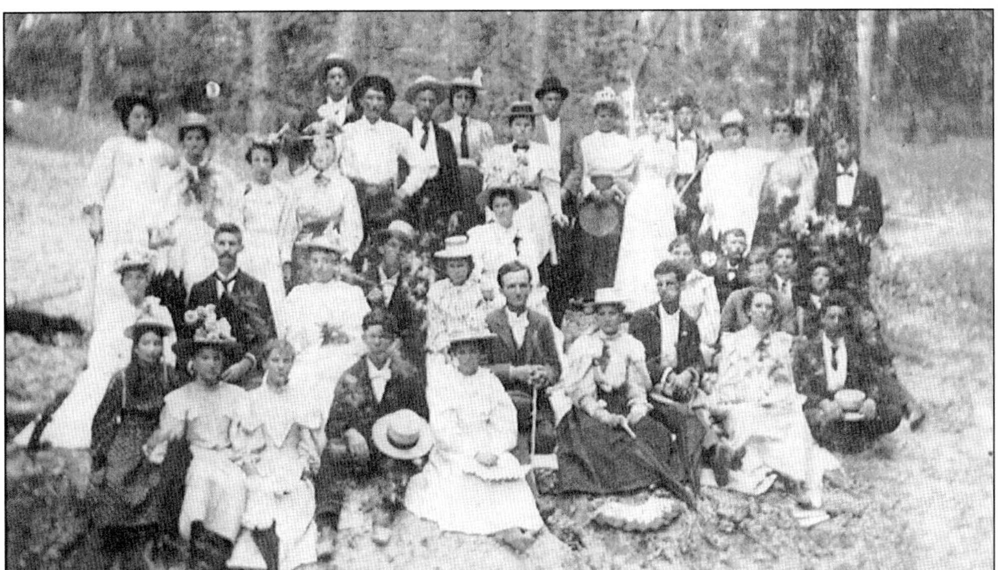

This is an unidentified group enjoying an outing during the 1860s. It is one of the earliest photographs offered in this book. The good health enjoyed by the participants and their attire indicates affluence. (Columbia County Library.)

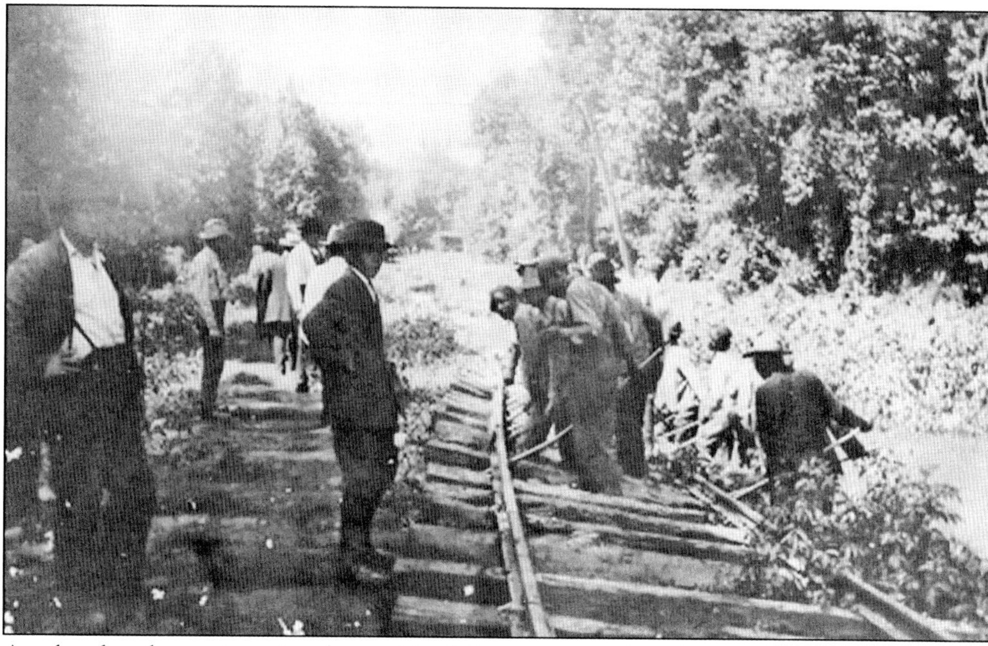

A railroad work crew is getting the track back in operating order after a washout on the Louisiana and North West Railroad line sometime in 1912. The line, "On the railroad, all the live long day!" seems to be fitting here. (Dr. Robert Walz.)

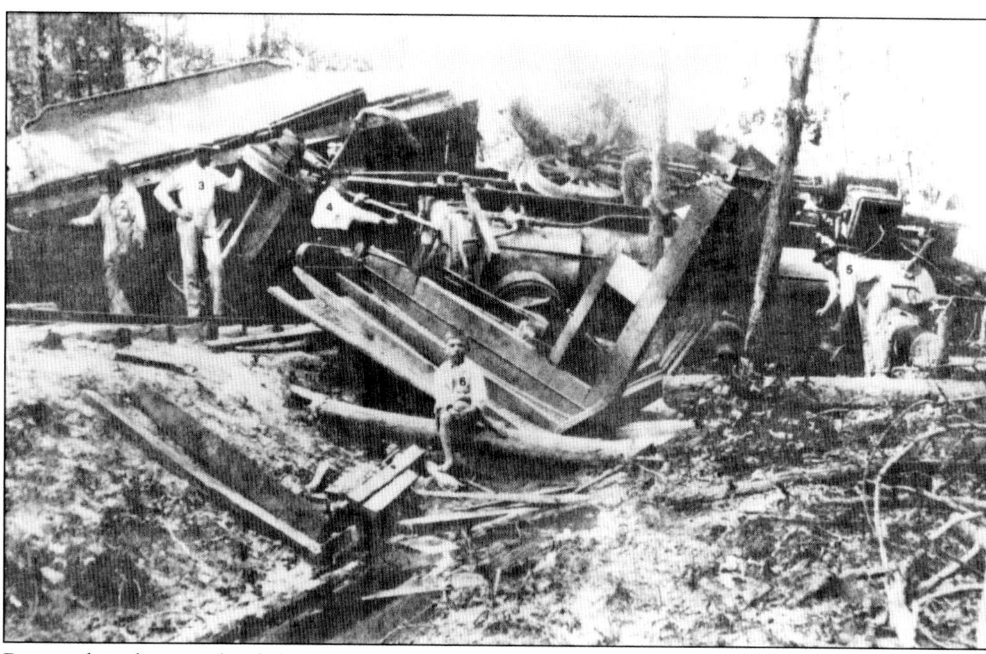

Pictured is the wreck of the Mohawk Lumber Company train, which occurred on June 12, 1912; the accident killed David Arthur Weldon. The Mohawk wreck occurred on a spur line extending southeast to haul logs to the mill. Examining the wreck are, from left to right, unidentified, J.B. Lee, W.D. Wingfield (manager of the Mohawk Mill), and two unidentified. (Dr. Robert Walz.)

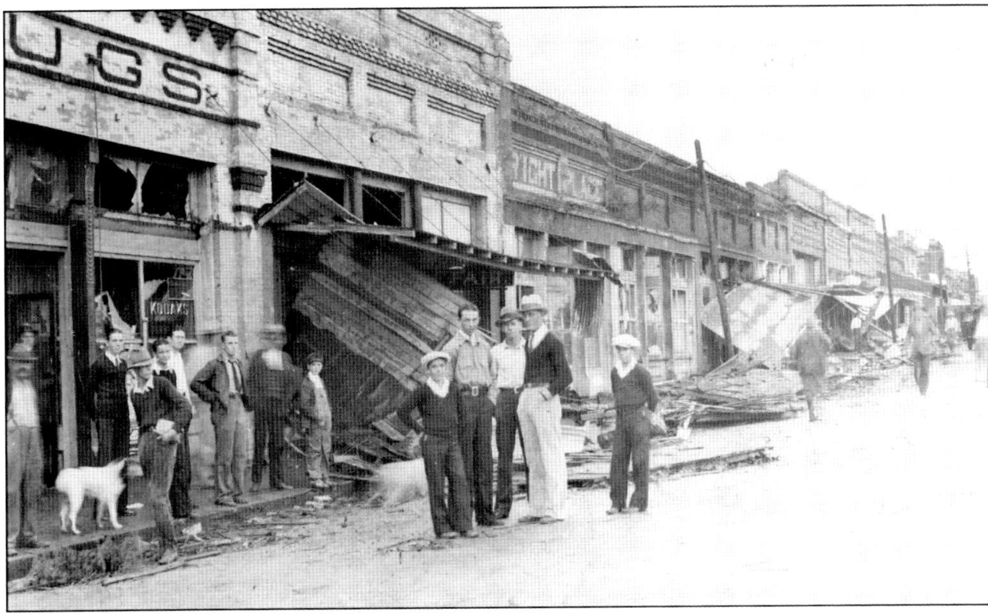

A tornado struck Waldo at 11:45 p.m. on Saturday night, December 12, 1931. Shown the next day are, from left to right, unidentified, Dr. Herschel Kitchens, Noel Ray Sr., James Crank, Donald Ray, unidentified, Woodrow Minor, unidentified, Snead Wynn Jr., ? Hayes (one twin), Clifton McMahen, ? Hayes, Clifton Sands, ? Hayes (the other twin), unidentified, and Bob Baird. (Peggy Goode Rudd.)

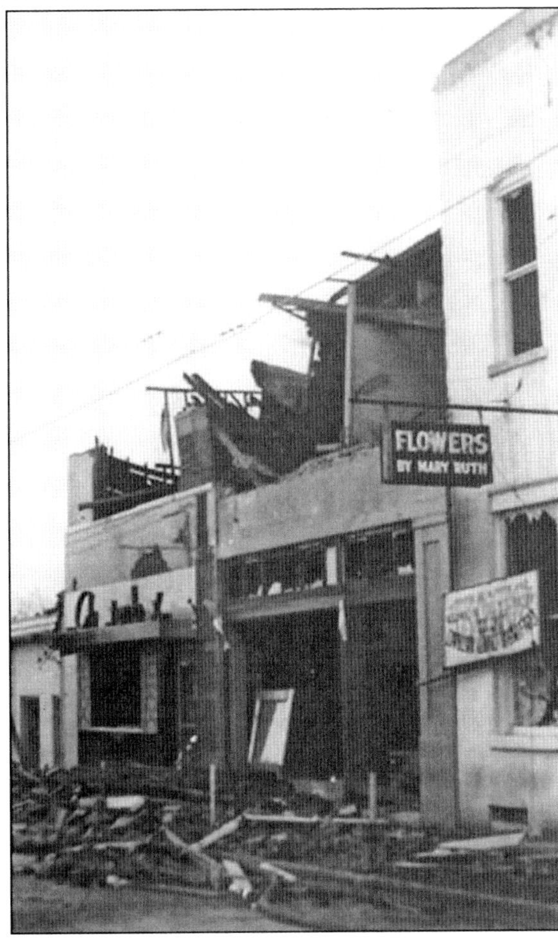

A later disaster in Magnolia occurred Christmas Day in 1950. A gas leak caused an explosion in the Chatterbox Restaurant and destroyed three businesses, which are, from left to right, a service station, the Chatterbox Restaurant, and Flowers by Mary Ruth. (Larry Taylor.)

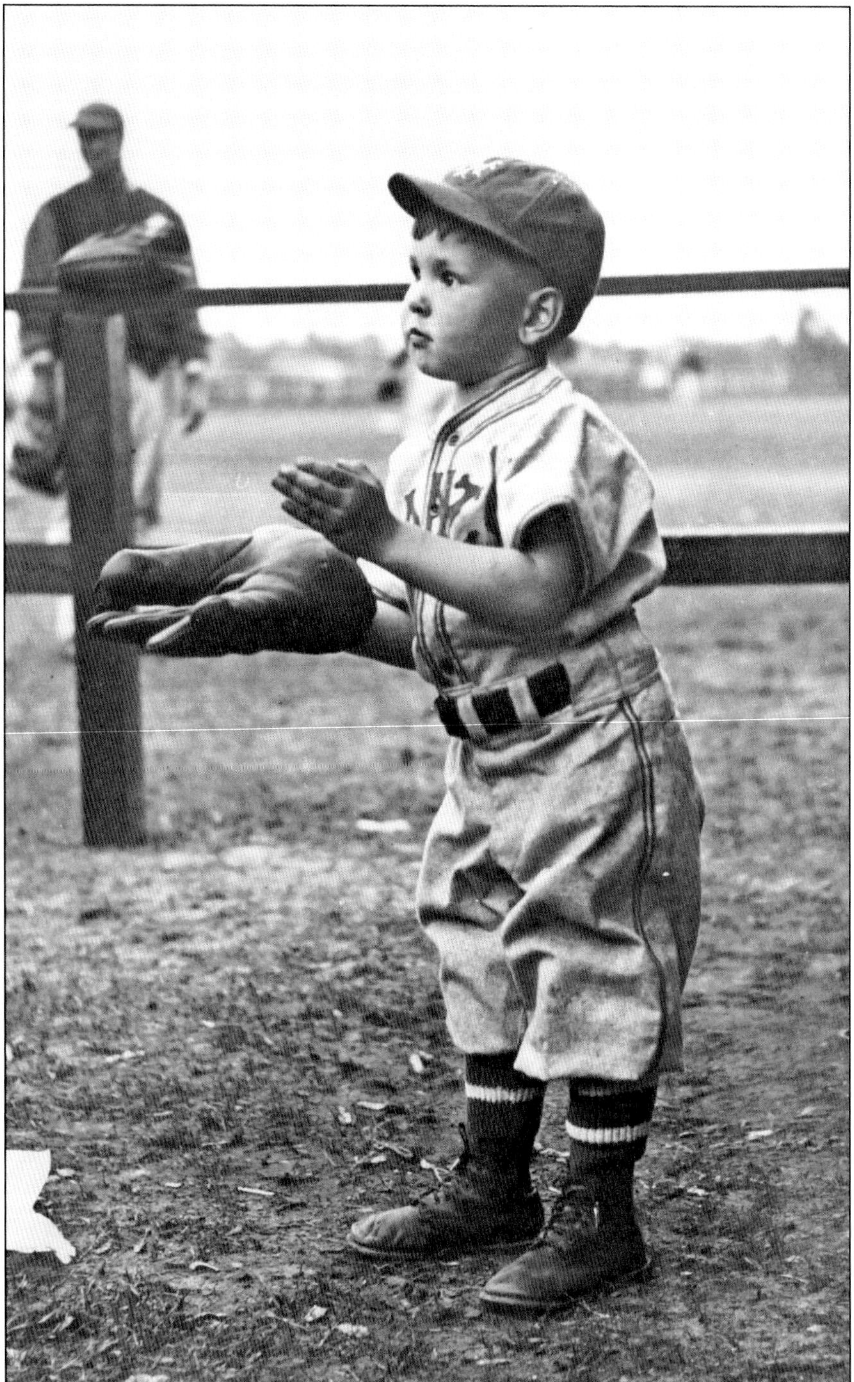

This is a photograph of William Travis Jackson, the son of Travis Calvin Jackson. Baseball was the chief sport of young Travis Calvin and his father, William Jackson. Travis Calvin's father bought the boy a hardball when he was only three years old, and William would sit in a rocker on the front porch while young Travis Calvin sat on the grass in the yard, and they would play catch for hours. (D.J. Fincher.)

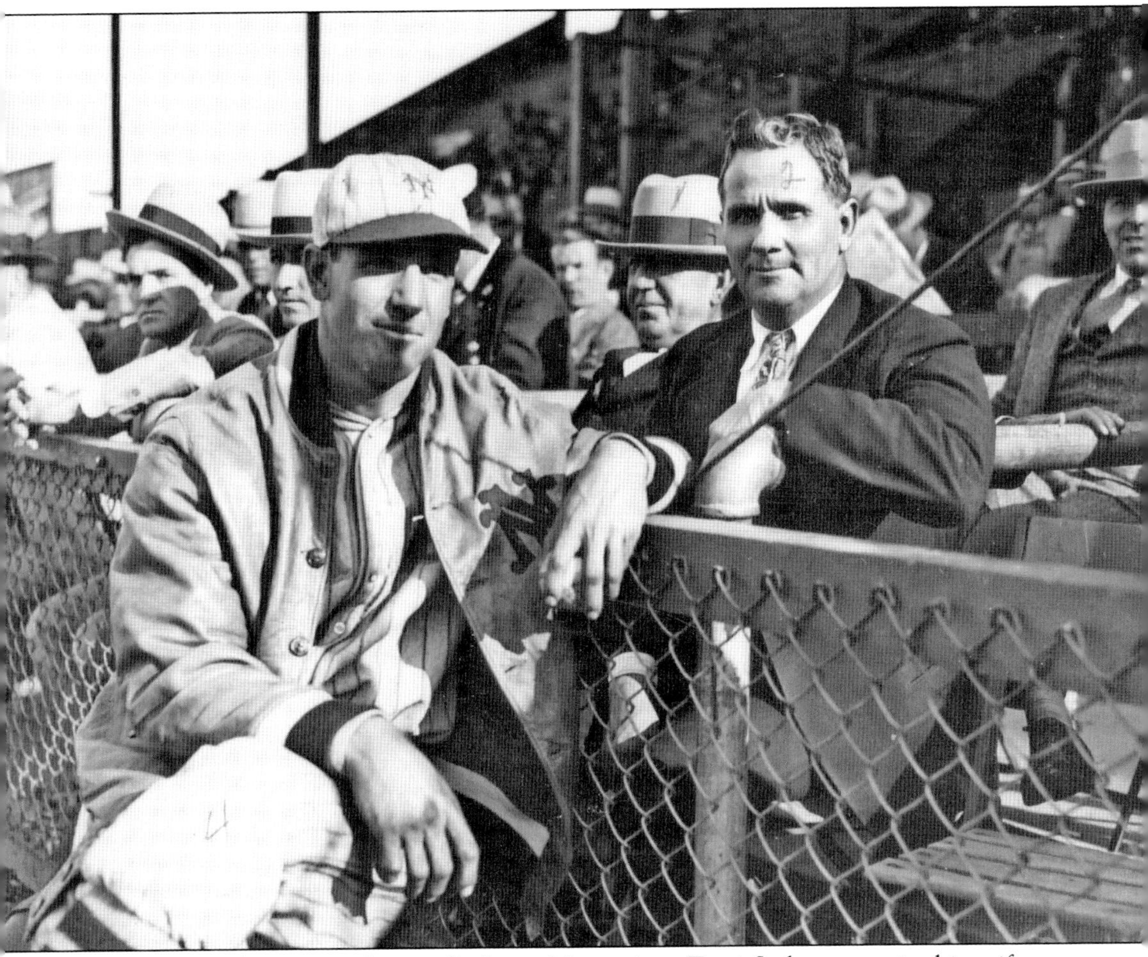

Pictured here in the 1940s in front in St. Louis, Missouri, are Travis Jackson, wearing his uniform in front; William Jackson, in the black suit; and Byron Jarnigan, on the far right; in profile, Archie Heath is seen over William Jackson's right shoulder. Travis was born in Waldo on November 2, 1903. He played shortstop for the New York Giants from 1922 through 1936 and won the 1933 World Series. The Veterans Committee inducted him into the National Baseball Hall of Fame in 1982. (D.J. Fincher.)

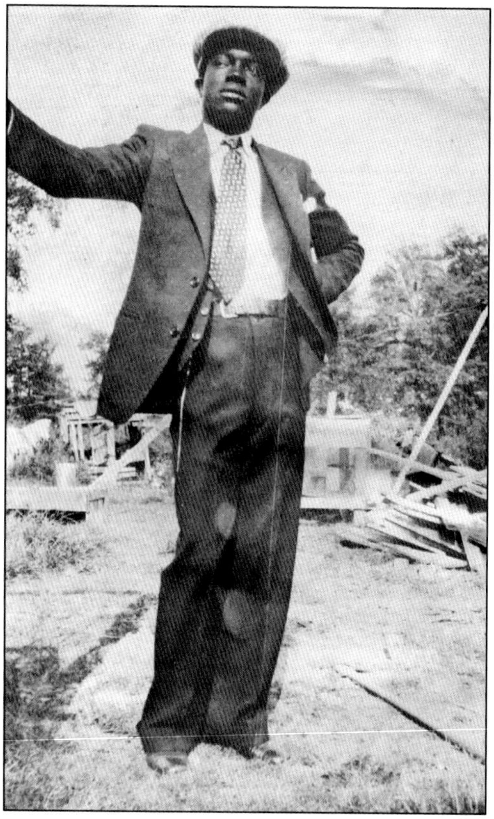

Artee Payne Sr. was the 1928 valedictorian of Columbia Baptist Academy and attended Agricultural, Mechanical & Normal (AM&N) College in Pine Bluff, Arkansas. He played baseball in the Negro "minor" Leagues with the West Black Socks. He was nicknamed "Jackrabbit" because of his speed and tenacity. After his baseball career, he was co-owner of a pressing shop and was employed at Sno-White Cleaners for 25 years until his retirement. He was a member of Bethlehem Baptist Church. (Peggy Goode Rudd.)

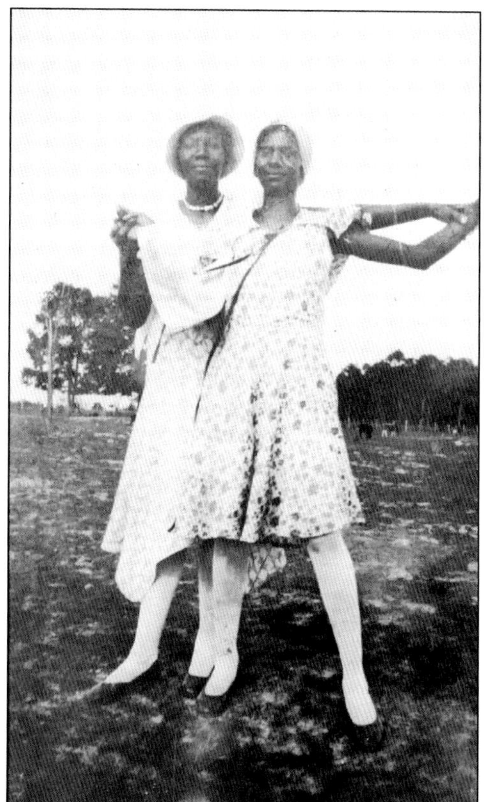

Two unidentified ladies are seen enjoying the outdoors. The asymmetrical hemline of the dress of the lady on the left was a popular fashion trend in the 1920s. Sadly, few African American families owned cameras during this time, and very few photographs survive. But this one is a dandy! (Peggy Goode Rudd.)

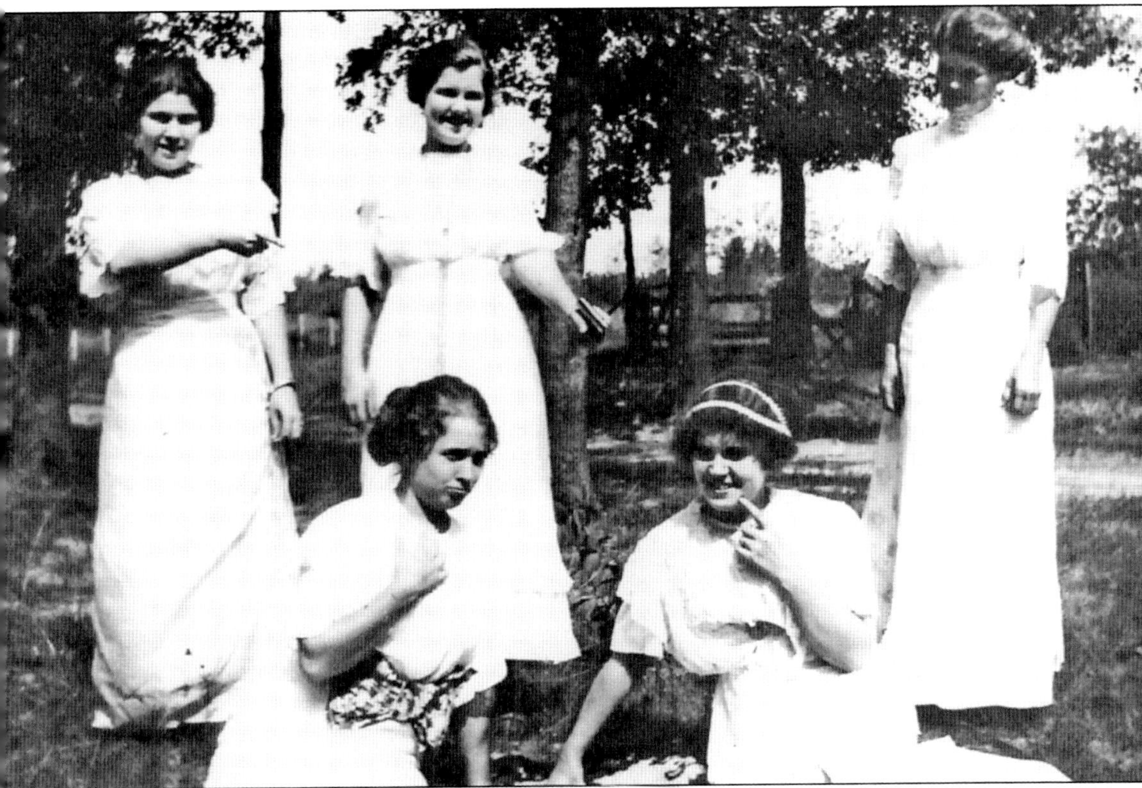

"The Cooper Girls" are posing for the camera wearing their beautiful, stylish white lawn dresses. From left to right are (first row) Annie and Etta; (second row) Eunice, Mary, and Cora. Several of these ladies were teachers, and Etta was Eileen Nall's mother. (Eileen Nall.)

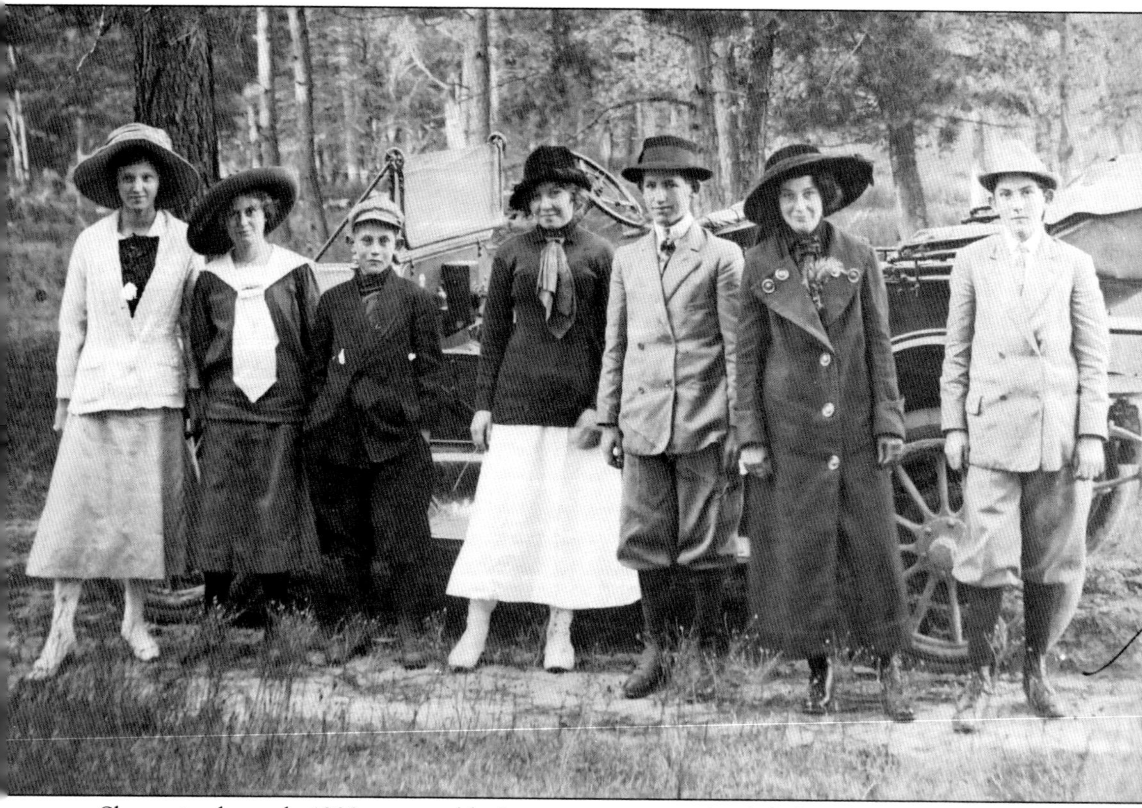

Shown in the early 1900s on a cold afternoon, a group of stylish friends enjoys a drive in the country. From left to right are Bernice Dickson, Levy Smith, Galen Davis, Faye ?, Thomas Dennis, Edna Clark, and Laurin Davis. Clark was Harold Herbert Fincher's mother. (D.J. Fincher.)

Nine

MAGNOLIA

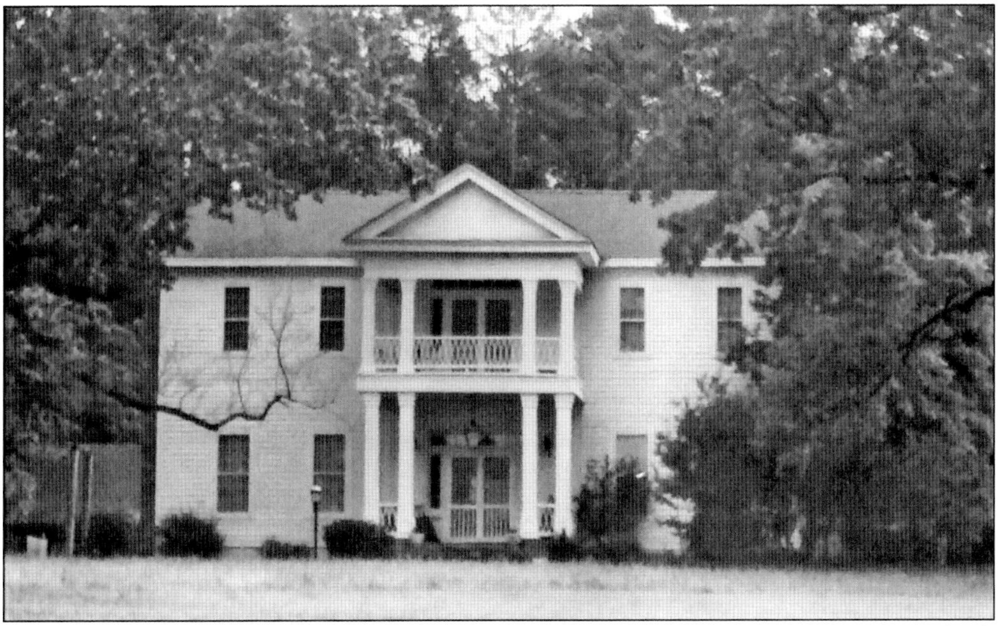

The oldest and most historic home in Columbia County is the Frazier Plantation, which was built in 1852 when the land was a part of Lafayette County. Columbia County was formed in December 1852, and at that time the Frazier land became a part of the new county. All the timber used to build the house was cut on the farm and carried by a two-wheel oxcart to Smithland, five miles away. Here, they were sawn into planks and returned to be hand-dressed by slaves at the farm. The first county court of the newly formed Columbia County was held at Ferguson-Morgan's store near Frazier Plantation. The name "Frog Level" was given to the house by young attorney B.F. Askew, who stated that he could not sleep because of all the noise made by the frogs. During the Civil War, a federal raiding party is said to have visited the plantation in search of gold. A wall safe is thought to have been torn from the wall—all jewelry and gold having been safely hidden elsewhere. No other damage was done, and no thefts were reported. Frog Level stands majestically today and is owned by the Joe Woodward family. (Authors.)

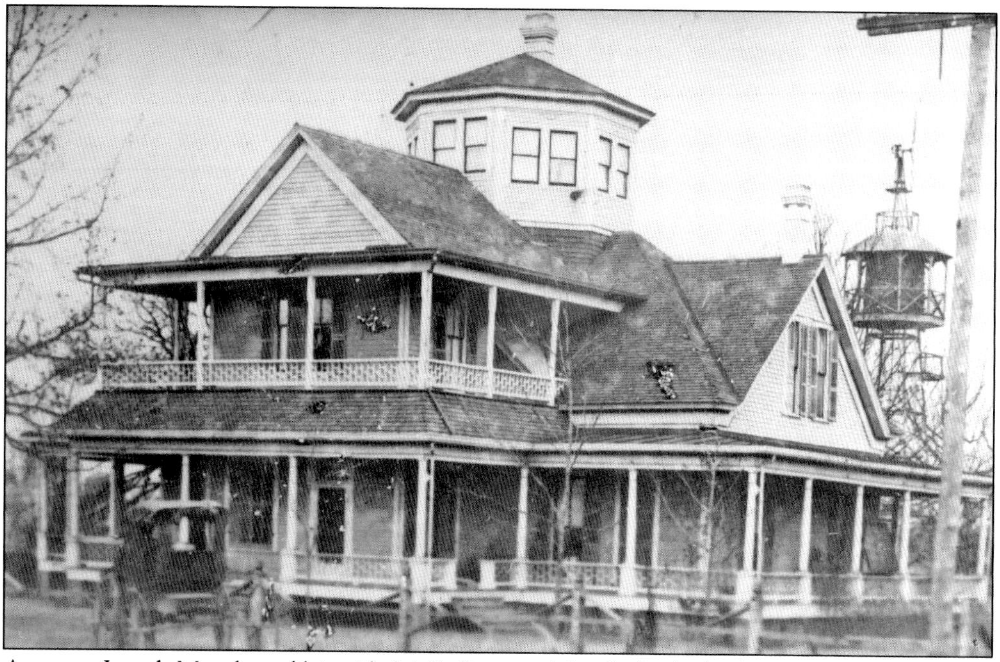

Attorney Joseph Magale and his wife, Molly Boreing Magale, built this house in 1893. They had two children, John Magale and Lillian Magale Stevenson. Joseph died in the early 1900s; however, Molly and their daughter, Lillian, lived in the home until they died in the early 1960s. The house was unoccupied until it was rented for a short period in 1971 and 1972. (Betty Epley.)

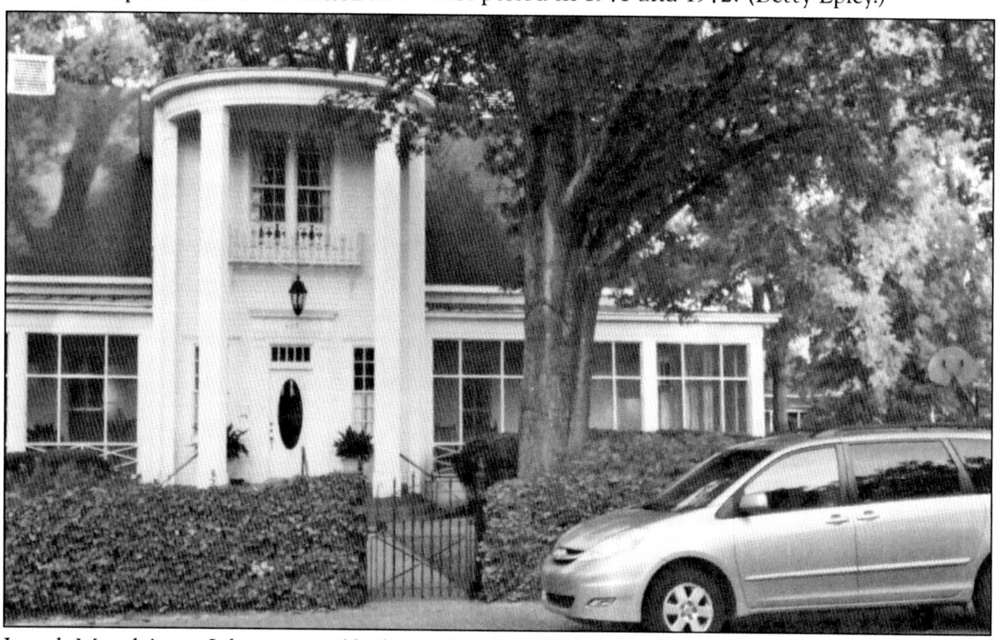

Joseph Magale's son John was a self-educated geologist who was instrumental in the development of the Magnolia Oilfield in the late 1930s. After he had become successful, he had the house extensively remodeled in 1939–1940, thus today the exterior appearance is very different from the original; however, it retains its antebellum splendor. The home is currently owned by Michael and Betty Epley. (Authors.)

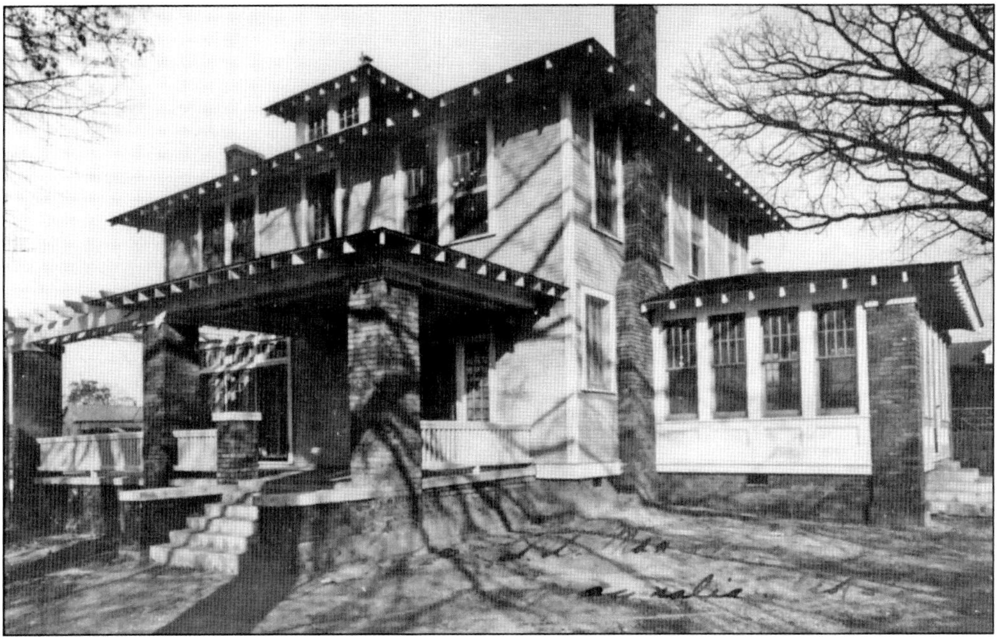

The T.A. Monroe home on North Washington Street in Magnolia is pictured just after completion in 1914. Columbia County's oldest citizen (at this writing), Archie Monroe, was raised in this home. (Albert Cooper.)

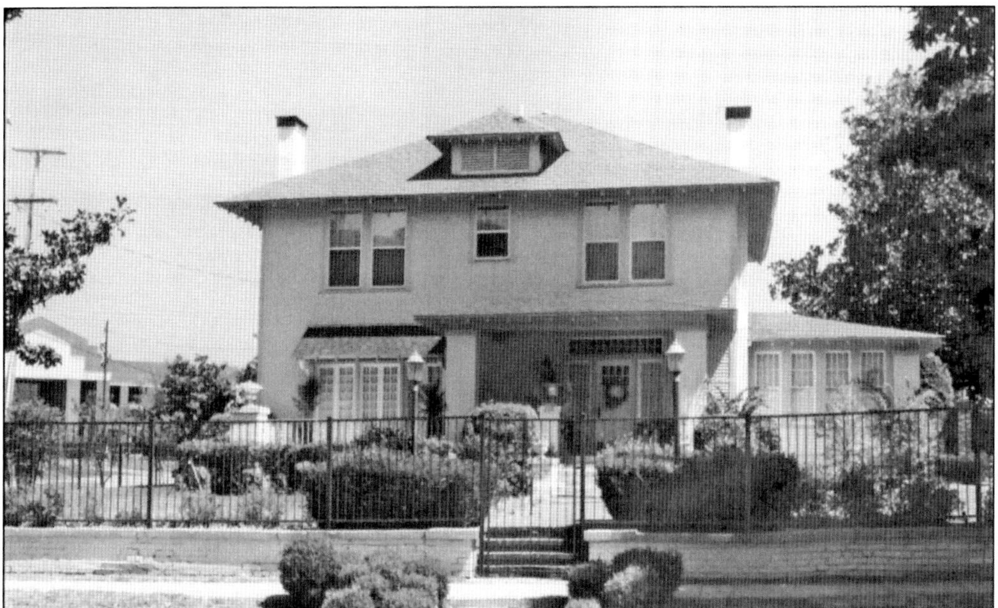

The Monroe home is now owned and cared for by Patty Bocan, and the beautifully landscaped lawn is enclosed by an attractive wrought-iron fence. It anchors the corner and continues to delight the eye of all who pass by. (Authors.)

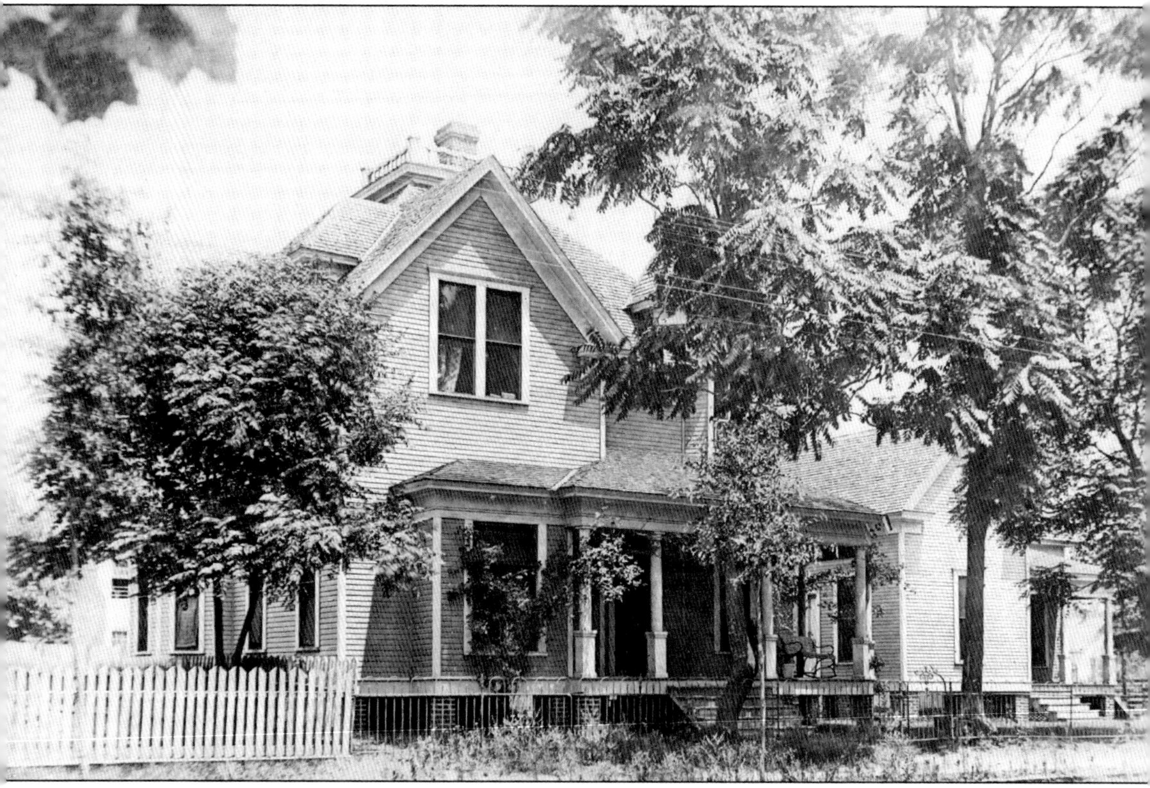

The Smith family home, located at 204 North Washington Street in Magnolia, was built in 1905 by Dr. G.E. Cannon. It was purchased by Dr. Parks Mathews Smith in 1909. When the street in front of the house was being built, Dr. Smith had the builders use the excess dirt from the roadbed to form the lovely elevated lawn seen today. For many years, Dr. P.M. Smith practiced medicine here. (Belva Smith.)

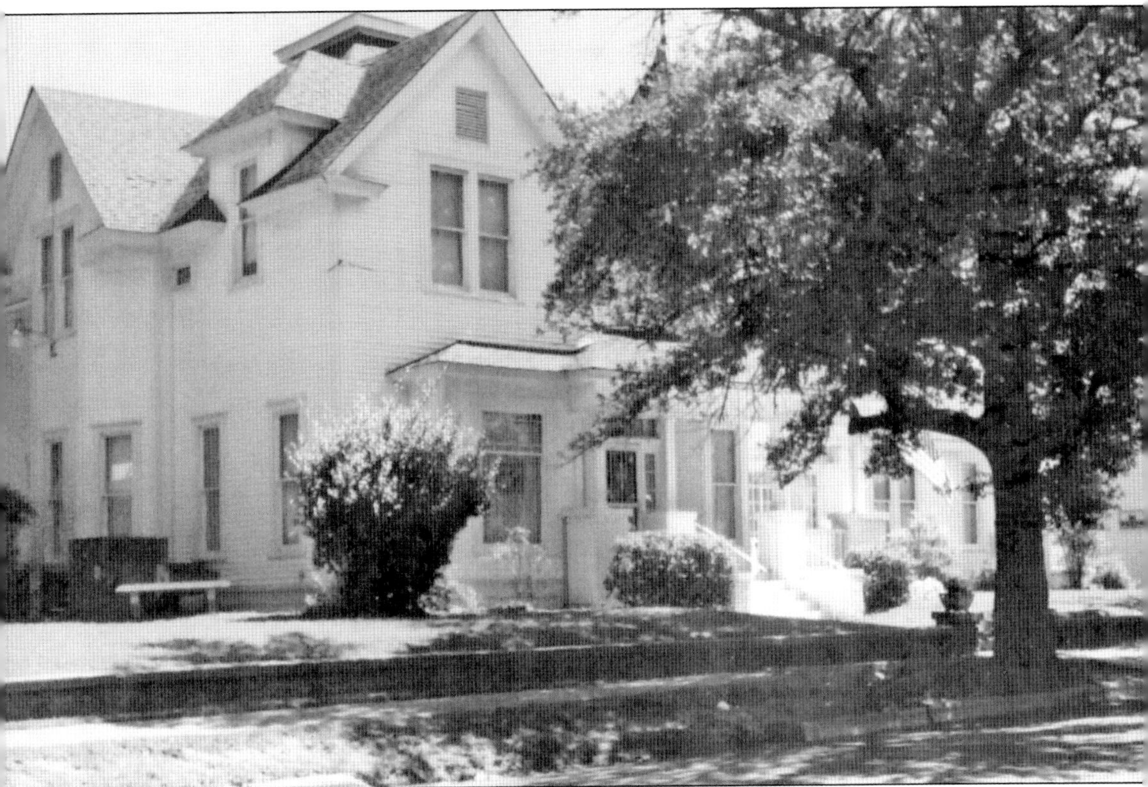

The Smith house is now called the Don Ross Smith home. Don Ross lived in the house along with his wife, Belva, and family for all of his life. Belva and their daughter Jane Waldow continue the tradition of this grand old dwelling, caring for the lawn and seeing that the property remains a showplace for the town of Magnolia. Although not shown in the photograph, a horse-and-buggy weather vane atop the house pays homage to the pioneer country doctor. (Authors.)

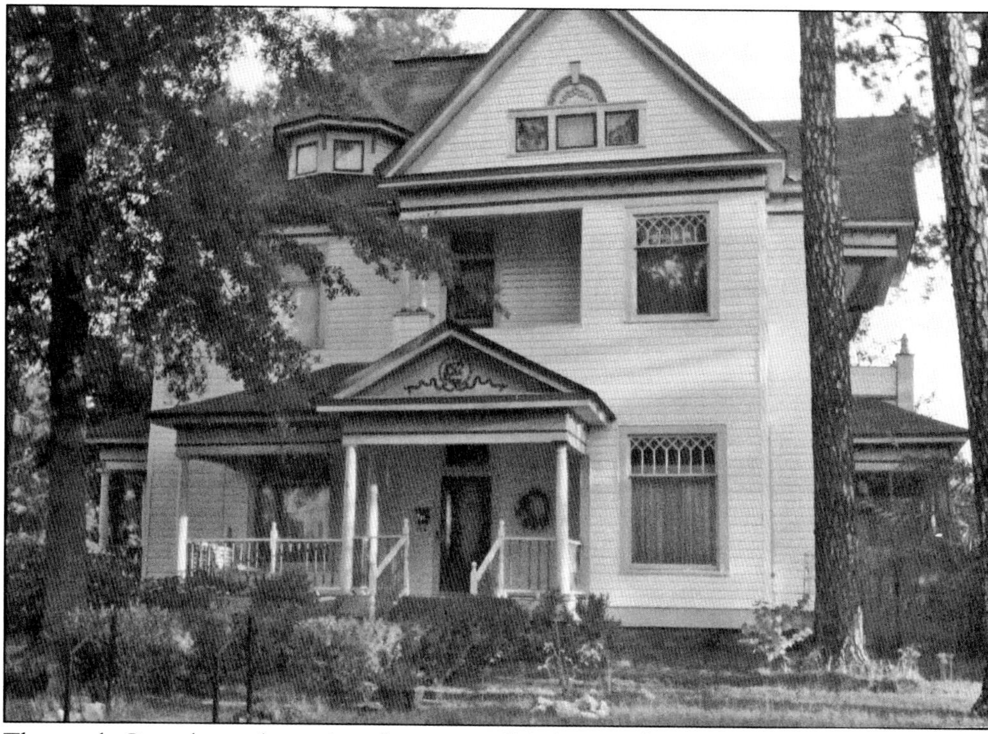

The stately Gantt home, located on the corner of Madison and McNeil Streets in Magnolia, was built by N.J. Gantt (1852–1931) and is still inhabited by family members. The house has been the centerpiece of many splendid social occasions and retains the dignity indigenous to the era in which it was built. (Authors.)

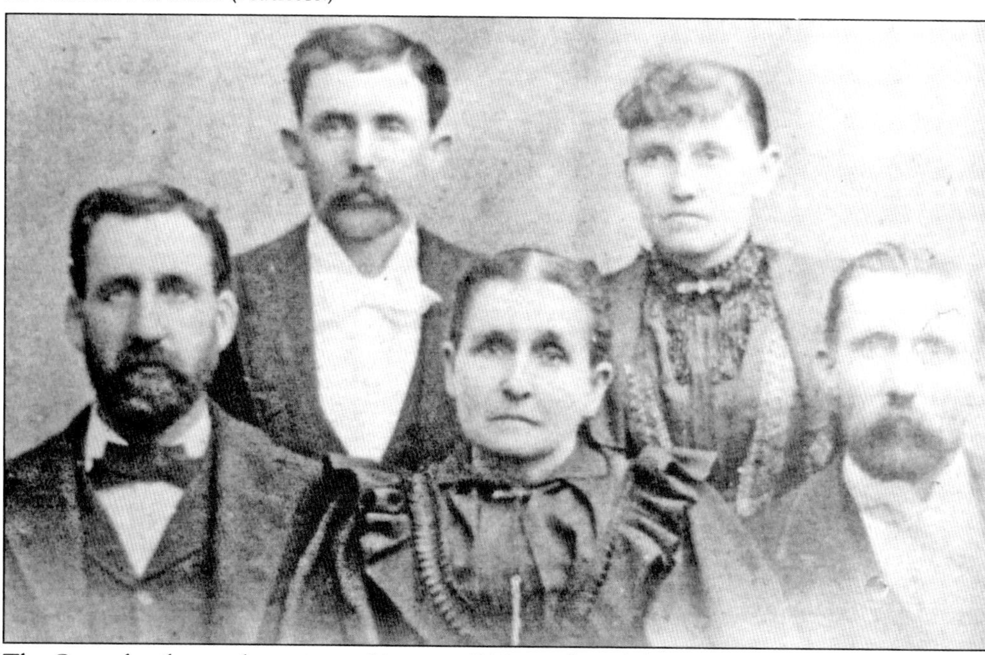

The Gantt family members pictured here in 1898 are, from left to right, (first row) N.J., Mattie, and Robert; (second row) T.P. and Mattie Couch. (Mary D. Woodward.)

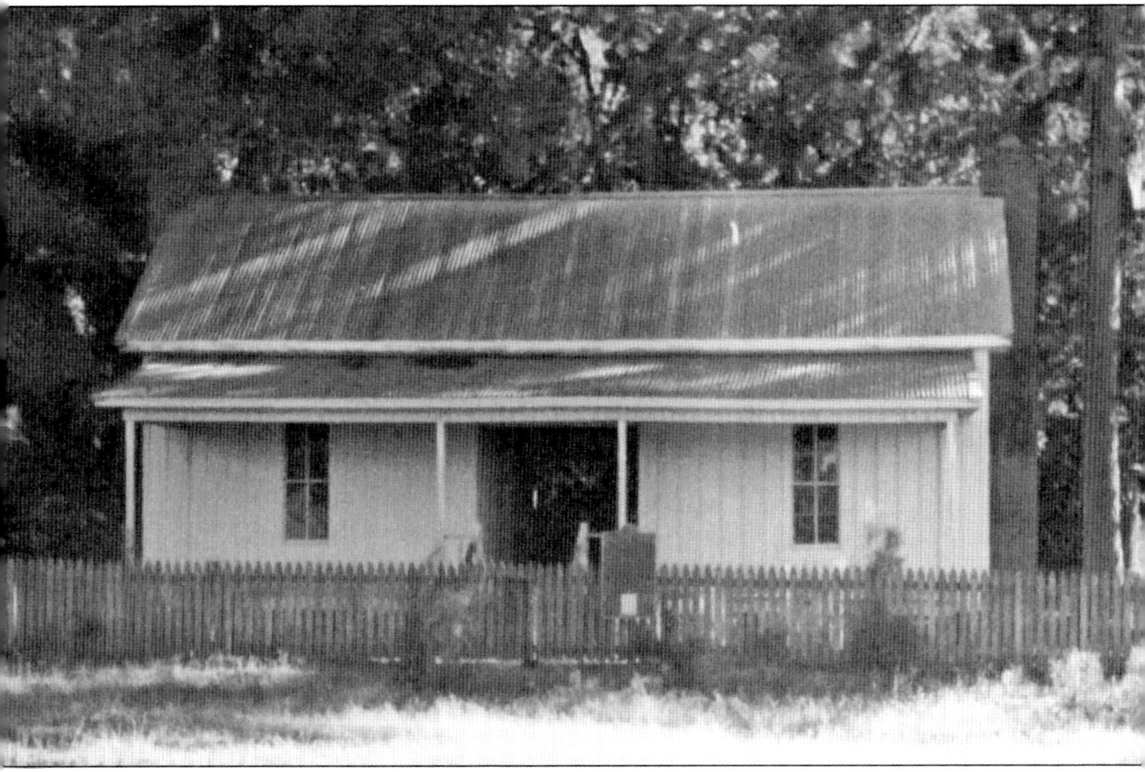

The Ozmers, a family of yeoman farmers, migrated to Columbia County in 1860 from Georgia by way of Alabama. Henry Ozmer, builder of the house, was born in Georgia. He married Virginia Faulk of Athens, Louisiana, in 1873. They lived in a log house close to where they would later build the board-and-batten structure pictured here. The Ozmer house is one of the few remaining unaltered structures of dogtrot style in Arkansas today. (Authors.)

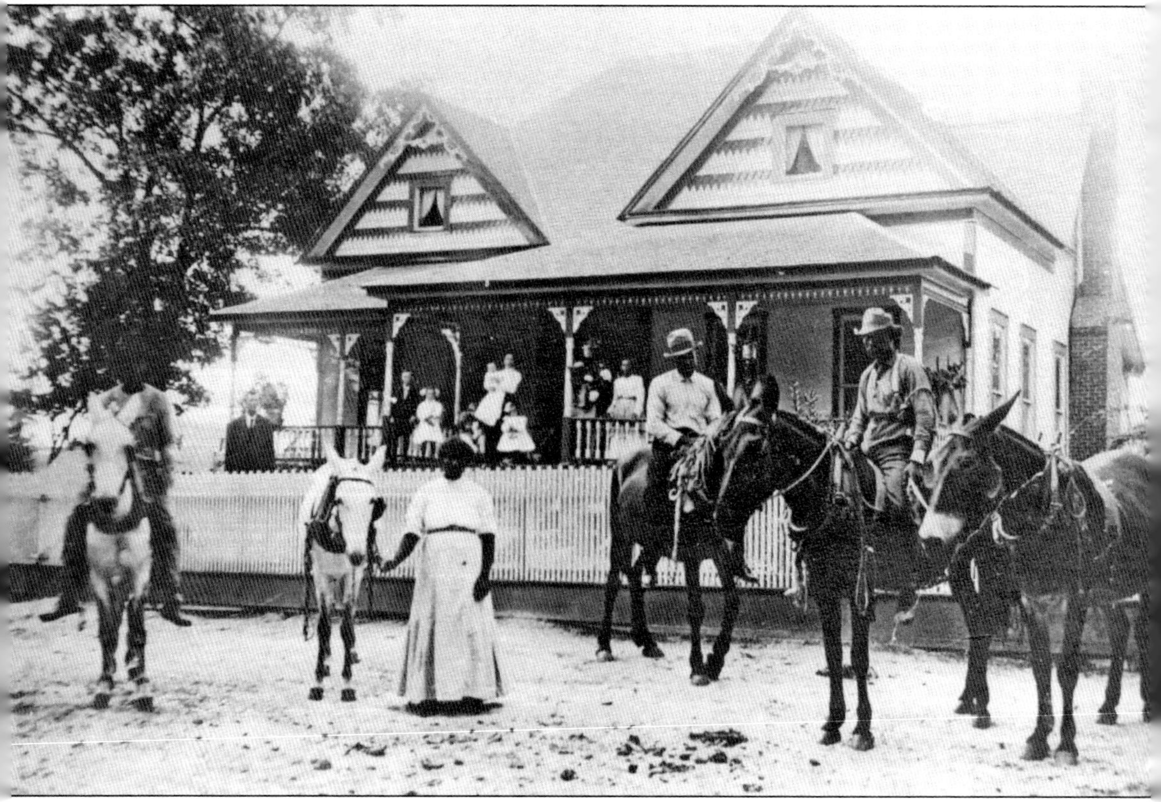

The W.H. Allen home was located in the Spotville community, which is south of Village and northeast of Atlanta. This image shows a group of working men and women with their mules. From left to right are (in front of the fence) Randal Easter, a former slave who traveled north and stopped at the Allen home to work at the request of the homeowner; "Sis Beck"; Floyd Johnson; and Cleve Johnson. W.H. Allen stands in the yard in front of the home. On the porch are, from left to right, Oswald, Gertrude, Hubert (the infant), Della Allen (wife of W.H.), Docia Allen Brasher, and "Aunt" Mary Easter, an African American woman. Later, one of the Allen daughters, Geraldine, married Homer D. Talley, and the home is now referred to as the Talley Ranch. (Authors.)

Bibliography

Atkinson, James Harris. "Memories of A University Student, 1906–1910." *Arkansas Historical Quarterly* (Autumn, 1971): 223.

Bradford's Map of Arkansas, 1838. Columbia County Library.

Colton, Arkansas, Road Map, 1854. Columbia County Library.

Encyclopediaofarkansas.net

Killgore, Nettie Hicks. *History of Columbia County*. Magnolia, AR: Southwest Arkansas Genealogical Society, 1976.

Lnwrr.com/RailFan.html

Martel, Glenn Gardner. *Early days in Columbia County, Arkansas*. Master's thesis.

———. "Origin of Columbia's Place Names Reviewed." *Arkansas Historical Quarterly* (Spring, 1952): 1–14.

Morse and Breese Arkansas Map, 1844. Columbia County Library.

Newell, Leslie and Frank Schambach. *Crossroads of the Past: 12,000 Years of Indian Life in Arkansas*. Little Rock: Arkansas Endowment for the Humanities, 1990.

Perry, Vernon Ray. *Columbia County Cemeteries*. Magnolia, AR: 2010.

Tanner's Arkansas Steamboat Routes, 1833. Columbia County Library.

Time, Major Marc. "Olden Days—Olden Customs." *Banner News*. Thursday, June 15, 1933.

Wilson, Rebecca. "Mary Ella Medlock Wilson." *The Arkansas Family Historian*. Volume 49, Number 1. March 2011, p. 54–55.

Youseemore.com/Columbia/readyref.asp

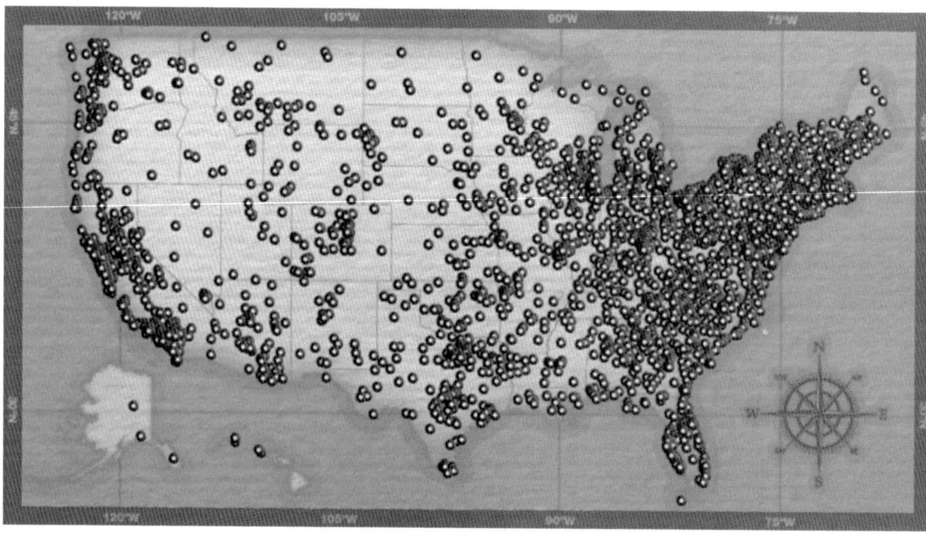

Consistent with our mission to preserve history on a local level, this book was printed in South Carolina on American-made paper and manufactured entirely in the United States. Products carrying the accredited Forest Stewardship Council (FSC) label are printed on 100 percent FSC-certified paper.

MADE IN THE USA